C000215166

In a
Unicorn's Garden

In a
Unicorn's Garden

Recreating the mystery and magic of medieval gardens

Judyth A. McLeod

MURDOCH BOOKS

Dedication:

For four wonderful friends who have supported the creation
of this book with constant enthusiasm, indulged many eccentricities,
and suffered uncomplainingly in its cause

Peter Stiles, David Ashton, Martin Wade
and Professor Laurent Legendre

and for

My 'parfit gentil Knight' … and photographer … Keith.

Contents

In detail

Prologue

One July day in 2005, I walked the Labyrinthe des Merveilles at the Château de Merville in the Haute-Garonne of France. Its design was developed from the popular secular labyrinths of the medieval period. The wooden palisaded path wound its way through natural forest and open sunny places. Here were druids' woods, a magic river, gardens filled with ingredients for love potions, strange whisperings in shaded forests and unexpected adventures.

For several years I had planned to write a book on medieval gardens. As a university landscape historian travelling annually to Europe, and particularly France, England and Italy, it was perhaps a predictable idea, and for several years my photographer husband had filed away a library of beautiful photographs of our travels. However, the book always floated beyond my grasp, refusing to take final form, and other books were written instead. That is, until the night after I walked the labyrinth. At one o'clock I literally sprang upright, wide awake, in our hotel room in Toulouse. The whole book had planned itself in my mind. It was not at all what I had expected, but instead a combination of my long-time searches through so many mythical, magical and mysterious aspects of Europe's past and my explorations of medieval gardens and plants. It was as if a dam had broken. Every half hour I woke again, turned on the bedside light and wrote down an outline of the content of another chapter. By dawn the

detailed outline of the book was complete. It just needed to be written. Otherwise it was all there, including a title that had been borne in on the soft night air. Also there was a yawning, sleep-deprived husband in dire need of hot coffee.

This is not a history of medieval times, but instead it opens nine casements on the medieval world. Kings and queens pass through, as they must, but this book is largely about the lives of ordinary people and their world, a world full of imagination and passion and prejudice, of valour and terror, a world that is often, by our twenty-first century standards, very small but deeply connected to the earth. Whether it tells of the strange and mythical animals and plants conjured by rich imaginations, or of monks or nuns, cooks or knights, fairies or pilgrims, sorcerers or alchemists, each story is connected to the others by the common thread of medieval plants and the beliefs that were woven around them, as well as the gardens in which they were grown.

Medieval gardens of quiet beauty and sweet simplicity, filled with the plants of the past, are being recreated throughout the world, particularly in France, England and Italy. Long deserted monastic buildings and castles are returning to life, orchards are being planted with ancient fruit cultivars, and enclosed gardens are filling with fragrant herbs, gentle colours and bees thrumming with industrious intent. Physic gardens flourish where there was only stone rubble, and ancient grain crops with their long forgotten nutty flavours ripple in the wind, again fashionable. Rare breeds of farm animals roam, rescued from extinction. Ancient medieval skills are being regenerated by artisans.

Flowering meadows filled with the old wildflowers that were once so common in the European landscape help sustain butterfly populations. Medieval fairs continue in many old towns and castles. Tournaments are enacted. Banquets are held, weddings celebrated, and the complex world of medieval cuisine is rediscovered. Exquisite costumes, accurate in every detail, are paraded. Guilds honour their ancient past with revived ceremony and celebration. Medieval music, from Gregorian chant to that of the troubadours, has become popular. A world barely remembered or greatly distorted by the intervening years is opening to us once more.

Each chapter in this book contains a design for a medieval garden that is easily adapted to most sites. The simplicity of design and gentle colours of these gardens are intended to create a private space where our modern world with its relentless pressures is excluded, a place to still the mind and calm the senses. Each is based on a theme within the book. There are also interviews with master gardeners who have recreated medieval gardens, and visits to superb examples of monastic and secular medieval-style gardens. To assist those inspired to create their own medieval gardens, there are also instructions on how to create devices such as wattle edgings and

fruit espaliers. Herbals describe plants from the medieval world and their uses and a rich and detailed list of resources has also been included.

A modern convention is widely accepted in which common names in current usage are written in lower case only, and this convention has been followed in the text of this book. However, many folk names of ancient usage have been included, names which have long been discarded or have become extremely rare. Many had religious or magical significance, and are to be found in texts from the medieval period and the Renaissance. The text of this book is largely historical, and respects the precedent set by a number of authoritative modern texts regarding ancient folk names, retaining the original capitals of the name. Such ancient and discarded folk names long preceded the modern discipline of botany.

The Middle Ages are considered to have begun with the progressive withdrawal of Rome from its colonised lands (although the Eastern Roman Empire, or Byzantine Empire, survived for another millennium until its conquest by the Ottomans in 1453), and to have ended with the Protestant Reformation, when powerful kings challenged the dominance of the Church and there was a rise in secularism. The Roman Empire, or *Imperium Romanum*, at its peak occupied almost six million square kilometres (two and a half million square miles) of territory, including Mediterranean Africa, and had a lasting influence on government, law, religion, military structures and campaigns, technology, architecture, and the arts and culture of Western civilisation.

Rome may have finally fallen in AD 476 but its control had been in gradual decline for two centuries in Western Europe. Successive waves of invasion, at first incremental rather than dramatic in nature, later increasingly violent, took place, particularly between the fifth and the eighth centuries. The invaders included Arabs, the displaced German kingdoms of the Goths and Visigoths and East German Vandals, displaced Slavic peoples and expansionist Norse who were encouraged by a warmer than normal climate and the absence of drift ice.

This period of low economic growth and major population movements is called rather deceptively the 'Dark Ages'. The German term *Volkerwanderung* (the wandering of the peoples) is far closer to the truth. Many of these 'wanderings' were movements of people driven from their traditional lands in a domino effect that began when the Huns, a Central Asian people highly skilled in war, conquered the Ostrogothic Kingdom that had stretched between the Black Sea and the Baltic Sea. The Ostrogoths were pushed back, displacing other kingdoms westwards and southwards. Despite these upheavals, the period saw the creation of literature, technologies, and organisational structures and governance.

The High Middle Ages commenced, at least in spirit, with the reign of Charlemagne the Great, but the mass migrations had not ceased. As an old man, Charlemagne was increasingly unable to deal with Viking raids along the northern coast of France and after his death the Carolingian Empire crumbled, with Vikings making incursions along the Loire and Seine Rivers and finally sacking Paris in 845. The High Middle Ages were marked by the growth of the feudal system and the seigneurial economic system, the increasing power of great lords, the building of defensive castles and walled towns, private armies, increasing trade and the overwhelmingly pervasive influence of Latin Christendom. It was also marked by great clearances, with settlements pushing into previously unpopulated areas as forests were felled and marshes drained.

The final part of the medieval period, the Late Middle Ages, saw the growth and consolidation of the power of kings, rapidly increasing commercial activities and wealth concentrated into the hands of the rich. Where all this might have led we will never know, because in the fourteenth century the Black Death killed one person in three, shook the Church to its foundations, and in the countryside much increased the value of peasant labour. Landowners held to old ways for some time, but popularly supported rebellions, such as the English Peasant's Revolt of 1381, resulted eventually in improved conditions for farm workers.

Just before the Black Death, France was one of the most highly populated countries in the world, with twenty million people. The population increase had been supported by the 'Medieval Warm Period', a time between approximately 800 and 1300 when increased mean temperatures had resulted in increased food production. The calamitous combined effects of a severe famine in 1315, the Black Death in 1348–50 and the deprivations of the Hundred Years' War resulted in the population remaining low until the sixteenth century.

Exactly when the medieval period ended and the Renaissance commenced is not clear and opinions vary depending on the area of Europe being discussed. The turning point was certainly determined in part by the great schism that occurred in the Christian Church in the sixteenth century. For this book, which ranges across Great Britain, Continental Europe and the Near East, the year 1500 has been used as an approximate date, so that the medieval period encompasses a thousand years in all.

Garden fashions and plants of the medieval period continued to be used well into the Renaissance by all but the rich and fashionable. They, of course, were the first to be able to include the exciting new plants introduced from the Near East, and to adopt the new designs. Much loved medieval flowers, herbs and fruits continued to be planted, although they were gradually supplemented with new species and varieties, and the comfortable, simple and practical designs based on the medieval past continued to please the eye in many country and town gardens. Garden books of the sixteenth and seventeenth centuries provided sound advice to housewives, farmers and jobbing gardeners, advice the authors based firmly on the knowledge of their forebears, and suggested designs that were often hybrids of the new and the old.

As to the title of this book, the *mille fleurs* unicorn tapestries described in the first chapter are indeed one of our important sources of information about the paradisiacal flowery meads of the medieval garden. The tapestry *The Hunt of the Unicorn*, now housed in the Cloisters Museum on Manhattan Island, has haunted me ever since I first saw an image of it, long before I finally saw the original. It said something intensely painful about beauty and purity and its betrayal in this world. The unicorn was not only the supreme mythical animal of medieval Europe, it also symbolised its highest aspirations. For many who lived in that era, life was truly a pilgrimage in search of redemption, and of purification of the soul through faith and good works. For them, the unicorn embodied the unattainable, the untainted soul, pure and incorruptible and uncompromising, gentle and loving and betrayed, a metaphor for the Christ who inspired their lives.

There is an increasingly uncomfortable parallel between our world and the medieval. In the medieval world fear and suspicion of the 'other' and conviction of superiority and of divine authority led to endless and ultimately fruitless invasions of other lands, destroying countless lives, creating lasting enmity, wasting opportunities for true advancement and destroying the wealth of nations. Fear created great wrongs and irrational beliefs. It bound whole societies in rigid conformity to ever tightening regulation, mental and physical. We are a mere five hundred years from the medieval mind. It would be wonderful if we could learn from that era the lesson of an open heart and the knowledge that we are truly all one.

Chapter 1

Unicorns and Other Magical Beasts

'Do you know, I always thought unicorns were fabulous monsters, too.
I never saw one alive before!'
'Well, now that we have seen each other,' said the unicorn, 'if you'll
believe in me, I'll believe in you.'
LEWIS CARROLL, *Through the Looking Glass* (1871)

The mystical unicorn

Dense, late morning mist thins under a pale December sun. Bare branches of black-budded ash and oak glitter with a million droplets. Trees of dark holly, studded with brilliant clusters of crimson berries, are filled with ancient green magic and prophesy the renewal of the world as it moves onwards from the winter solstice.

A soft luminescence glows in the lingering mist and a horse of purest silver white stands utterly still among brown bracken, its huge, gentle eyes seeing worlds unknown to mortals. From the centre of its forehead emerges an elegantly whorled, milk-white horn. Here stands the mystical unicorn in all its purity, its terrible beauty, its unshakeable virtue, and its gentle, radiant love.

The unicorn still haunts us today, as if we can almost remember a world that we once shared with it. Of all those fabulous beasts that lived so vividly in the medieval mind, it is the unicorn that most intrigues our modern world in endless stories of fantasy, a symbol of a lost world of innocence in which there was the possibility of absolute goodness. Some say that unicorns still live in wild and hidden places where only those of purest heart may ever hope to see them.

The unicorn was the symbol of chastity, of holiness, of Christianity, of uncompromising, incorruptible goodness, of moral courage and of sanctified marriage. It also became a symbol of knightly virtues and was widely used as a heraldic device. King Robert III of Scotland made the unicorn, the symbol of strength and goodness, part of the official seal of Scotland, and when James VI of Scotland became James I of England, he incorporated both the Scottish Unicorn and the traditional English Lion into the new royal coat of arms.

This was unfortunate and prophetic symbolism. As ancient stories from the Near East relate, the lion and the unicorn are great enemies, and conflict between England and Scotland was to continue after the Union. Salt was rubbed into Scotland's battle wounds by an English nursery rhyme (most recently used, in disguised form, in a Harry Potter book):

> The lion and the unicorn
> Were fighting for the crown.
> The lion chased the unicorn
> All around the town.

At the end of the fifteenth century two series of tapestries were created around the mystical unicorn, and they are among the world's greatest art treasures. One series, usually called *The Hunt of the Unicorn*, is now housed in the New York Metropolitan Museum collection at The Cloisters on Manhattan Island and consists of seven hangings. Woven c. 1495–1505, these hangings are believed to have been designed in Paris and then woven in Brussels, probably as a wedding gift. For centuries they were in the possession of the dukes of La Rochefoucauld and were displayed at the Château de Verteuil in the Charente region. They were purchased in the twentieth century by John D. Rockefeller II, who donated them to The Cloisters.

It was believed that the unicorn was a wild creature that could be tamed only by a true virgin. Coming under her dominion, the unicorn was vulnerable to the human world. The series depicts the heartbreaking betrayal of the unicorn by a young girl, the hunt for the unicorn within the forest by a group of richly dressed noblemen, accompanied by servants and hunting hounds, and the unicorn's tragic death at their hands.

Miraculously restored to life in the final tapestry of the series, the unicorn is confined within a tiny enclosure and bound by a gold chain, its milk-white coat splattered with what is thought by some to be the blood of its wounds, by others to be droplets of ruby-coloured juice from the paradisiacal pomegranates that hang from the symbolic tree of fertility above its head. The medieval world was filled with such multi-layered symbolism, and *The Hunt of the Unicorn* was understood to be both a representation of the ever-constant human capacity for cruelty and its

The unicorn is included on the official seal of Scotland as a symbol of strength and goodness.

betrayal of purity and goodness, and an allegory for the betrayal and sufferings of Christ.

The backgrounds in the tapestries are lush forests and flowery meads, ornamental meadows spangled with hundreds of tiny flowers in a style known as *mille fleurs*. There are thought to be 101 species of plants shown, all accurately depicted and in full bloom, regardless of season. The tiny flowers were woven in rich, subtle colours created from natural dyes, such as weld, madder and woad. Eighty-five have been identified by botanists, most of them having uses in medicine or magic, or of symbolic importance. In the final tapestry, near the unicorn grow two flowers symbolic of desire, the Early Purple Orchis (or Cuckoos), *Orchis mascula*, and Lords-and-Ladies, *Arum maculatum*, together with Bistort, a herb used medicinally for easy conception, for the prevention of miscarriages and for easy birthing, no doubt a wedding blessing. Other *mille fleurs* tapestries include that in the Abbey of Chaalis in France and the famous *Tausendblumenteppich* in Berne.

The second unicorn series, sometimes called *The Lady and the Unicorn* (*La Dame à la Licorne*), is altogether gentler. Five tapestries depict the five senses of hearing, sight, touch, smell and taste, while a sixth, called 'To My Sole Desire', depicts love. Every scene shows a gentle white unicorn with his lady, accompanied by whippet-like dogs, rabbits, a monkey and calm wild animals. Beneath their feet lies a rich, flowery mead. It is speculated that these tapestries too may have been intended as a marriage gift. Today they are located in the Cluny Museum in Paris, the

Musée National du Moyen-Âge. This series might so easily have been lost. They were found in 1841 in the Château de Boussac, apparently prey to rats and dampness. George Sand, the great nineteenth century French writer and friend of Frédéric Chopin, wrote about their discovery and ensured that the world would hear of the miraculous tapestries.

So real was the medieval belief in unicorns that even the well-educated intellectuals of the era, such as St Hildegard of Bingen, fully believed in the purifying medical properties of unicorns. Gruesomely, she advised grinding up a unicorn liver and mashing it with an egg to form an ointment for the treatment of every kind of leprosy, 'unless the patient is destined to die or God intends not to aid him'. This seems to cover all eventualities. For sufferers of the plague or of fever, she recommended that the patient wear a belt made from the pelt of a unicorn, and to ensure healthy feet and legs, she advocated wearing shoes made from unicorn's leather. Hildegard also shared a belief that the unicorn returned each year to Paradise to drink from its pure waters and eat its blessed food.

It is difficult to know where Hildegard obtained all her unicorn remedies. The horn of the male narwhal, which sailors called the unicorn of the sea, is thought to have been the unicorn's horn, or alicorn, of medieval commerce. It was very widely believed that alicorn could be used to detect poisons, and when ground and added to a potion would prevent poisoning. The powder was used in many cures for diseases such as gout, plague, leprosy and rabies. So popular

How to create a flowery mead

Flowery meads, planted with many different low growing flowers in lush turf, were part of a medieval version of Paradise.

The lush green meadow grass spangled with wild flowers depicted in the *mille fleurs* unicorn tapestries was a feature of the medieval pleasure garden. The flowers used included sweet violets, Heartsease, Lords-and-Ladies, wild strawberries, single-flowered stocks, cornflowers, carnations, white lilies, flag iris, campions, wild ground orchids, sweet rocket, cinquefoil, Lady's Mantle, cornflowers, pincushion flowers and poppies. The idea of a flowery meadow has again become very popular, partly in response to the ever-increasing need to provide habitats for butterflies and other wild creatures, and partly because when well made they can create a quite magical space.

Where every imperfection in turf displeases critical eyes, a flowery mead disguises unevenness, and meadow daisies, buttercups and dandelions are no longer outlawed with weedicide but are welcomed. The prairie garden fashionable in North America, with its mixture of native wild flowers and prairie grasses, is a variation on the theme, as are the wildflower meadows being created in Europe, particularly in England and France.

The easiest way to create a flowery mead in larger gardens is to mow a path as a boundary around a piece of turf and allow the seeds of wildflowers to have their way among the grasses. The mead can then be cut on the highest setting of a lawnmower, or scythed, twice a year to maintain its height and encourage dense growth. Alternatively, completely remove all turf from patches in the lawn, dig the soil over thoroughly, smooth it down and scatter with a mixture of meadow grass and wildflower seed, which is now available from a number of seed firms. Do not fertilise, as this encourages lank growth of grasses rather than of wildflowers.

In smaller gardens, an easily maintained solution is a raised and edged flowery mead. An ideal position would be in a sunny area that fails to grow a good turf lawn. Mark out a space for the flowery mead using pegs and string. An area of about 3.5–4.0 m (10–12 feet) square is ideal in a smaller garden. Strip off the turf, cutting it out in sods that include the shallow grass roots. Dig the area over thoroughly, removing any weeds and roots left in the soil. If the soil is heavy, incorporate horticultural sand to provide a free-draining soil with an improved texture.

Use treated boards to edge the flowery mead, pegging them into position with stout wooden stakes to create a medieval effect, or weave a low wattle fence, about 30 cm (12 in) high to surround the area (see Chapter 2). Rake the area over thoroughly in several directions to make sure that it is smooth. Scatter a suitable meadow grass and wildflower seed mixture over the site. You may like to make your own mixture of seeds, incorporating, for instance, red poppies, Meadow Cranesbill (*Geranium pratense*), Moon Daisies, wild larkspur, old-fashioned blue cornflowers, campions, double-flowered chamomile, marigolds (*Calendula*), wild columbines and soft meadow grasses for a summer-flowering mead, or sweet violets, wild strawberries, cinquefoils, cowslips, wild primroses, snowdrops, crocus, pulmonarias and small-flowered *Narcissus* for a spring-flowering medieval mead.

Many gardeners create their own mead mixture from soft, perennial native grasses and low-growing native wildflowers (other than those that are protected), so that they are contributing to the preservation of a local ecology while at the same time having plants well matched to local conditions. A valid argument, which is well supported in Europe, exists for using species that are not native but have been part of cultivated gardens and old estates for centuries. They are the adopted plants of the region and contribute to the unique qualities and beauty of landscapes created by gardeners over centuries.

As an alternative, raise grasses and wildflowers in pots and plant these directly into the prepared soil. The lawn should receive a light cut after flowering, and its second cut in late autumn.

Dedicated to both the Virgin Mary and St Peter in the medieval period, cowslips were favoured in flowery meads.

The Rose Campion (*Lychnis coronaria*) and its close relative Ragged Robin (*L. flos-cuculi*) were often depicted in *mille fleurs* tapestries.

The wild columbine (*Aquilegia vulgaris*) with its maiden hair foliage was planted in medieval meads.

Western Europe is not thought of as geologically unstable, but as the great earthquake of Lisbon in 1755 demonstrated it is not a region immune to earthquake activity. The Church of St Michael on Glastonbury Tor was ruined by earthquake, and a long-persistent story tells of the lost land of Lyonesse, which disappeared beneath the sea between Lands End and the Scilly Isles.

A second huge ley line discovered by Hamish Miller and Paul Broadhurst was named the Apollo–Athena ley line, running from the island monastery of Skellig Michael in Ireland, through England's St Michael's Mount, Mont St Michel in France, Sacra di San Michele, Assisi, Delphi, Athens, Rhodes and Mt Carmel in Israel. The Michael–Mary ley line and the Apollo–Athena ley line cross at St Michael's Mount.

The fireproof salamander

The salamander was another magical creature of fire in the medieval world. Bestiaries, medieval accounts of wondrous animals, differed in their stories of the salamander. In England the many-coloured, lizard-like creature, sometimes considered to be a miniature dragon, was thought to be able to extinguish the flames of a roaring furnace instantly. When it was placed in water, the water was said to turn ice cold. In France, however, the salamander was a kind of bird that lived on the energy of fire. It spun from its body a fireproof thread that could be woven into cloth.

Amphibians in general received bad press in the medieval period. Salamanders and newts inhabit moist places and, far from being fireproof, in reality have very delicate skins. In medieval times salamanders became symbolic of those who pass through the fires of earthly tests, and also came to symbolise chastity and courage. Christ, being filled with the purifying flame of the Holy Spirit, was also often associated with the salamander.

The griffin

The griffin had a body composed of the front end of a fierce eagle, with talons longer than ox horns, feathers strong as lances, and the hind end of a lion. It was a powerful creature far larger than a horse and it is, therefore, somewhat unfortunate that it was said to have had a predilection for mating with

Mont St Michel on the Brittany coast, a focus of medieval pilgrimages, lies on the Apollo–Athena ley line.

opposite
The Rollright Stones with their many stories associated with moving stones, witches and a mysterious ability to defy counting have been mapped for dragon lines.

horses, the resulting offspring being known as hippogriffs. Aesculus thought griffins came from Ethiopia, and Pliny located them in northern Russia. Marco Polo described the griffin as inhabiting Madagascar, while the peripatetic and endlessly creative Sir John Mandeville described griffins as inhabiting a land he identified as Bactria. He described their body as equal in size to that of eight lions and with sufficient strength to carry two yoked oxen up to their eyrie.

The reputation of griffins suffered a number of sea changes according to the place and era. They combined the powers and strengths of the eagle, lord of the air, with those of the lion, lord of the earth. At times during the medieval period such a noble chimera was seen as symbolic of the duality of Christ, King of both Heaven and Earth. But at other times the griffin, with its great strength, was seen as the personification

The winged griffin shares this medieval carving in Dubrovnik with a dragon and menacing apparitions.

of evil, as the Devil, as the Antichrist. The Crusaders in the Near East encountered the ancient Persian Zoroastrian symbolism of two griffins drinking from a flaming cup, and they made an association between this symbol and the Holy Grail. As a result, griffins were said to be the guardians of the Holy Grail and became the emblem of saints. They were sometimes depicted in medieval paintings eating from the fruit of the Tree of Knowledge.

No story of the griffin is complete without mention of the ambitious ascension of Alexander the Great. He is reputed to have succeeded in harnessing two griffins, tying them to his throne and ascending high into the heavens. For seven days he stayed there, until an angel chastised him for wishing to know of the things of Heaven when he still knew so little of the things of Earth. A contrite Alexander immediately descended to terra firma. This much-told story became a theme illustrated in French and Italian medieval churches. Both griffins and dragons were often carved in the facades of medieval cathedrals, such as that of Le Mans in the Loire Valley.

Fabulous sea creatures

If life on land required constant vigilance against these fearsome medieval creatures, the sea was no less dangerous. Sailors and fishermen brought home stories of incredible sea creatures. Lawrens Andrewe's book *The noble lyfe and nature of man, Of bestes, serpentys, fowles and fisshes y be most known*, published somewhere between the first half of the fifteenth century and the mid-sixteenth century, describes any number of fish one would

Strange plants

Mythical plant–animal hybrids were also a part of the medieval world. Probably the quaintest of these was the Barnacle Tree. Stalked goose barnacles are often washed ashore attached to driftwood. They live in colonies and are attached to their floating home by a flexible, rubbery stalk. In his 1597 herbal, John Gerard repeated an already long-established story, describing mussel-shaped shells that were produced by trees. He claimed that the shells grew and grew until they split open to reveal 'the legs of the Birde hanging out ... til at length it is all come foorth'. The bird was thought to remain in the shell until mature, when it would drop into the sea and 'gathereth feathers, and groweth to a foule, bigger than a Mallard, and lesser than a Goose'. The migration of birds was not understood then, and it seemed miraculous that full-grown barnacle geese (*Brantia bernicula*) appeared every winter but were never seen to nest. (The barnacle goose is now known to migrate in summer to the far north.) Goose barnacles feed underwater by sweeping plankton towards them with feather-like cirri. The everfertile medieval imagination simply filled in the rest of the story.

Gerard was far from being the only one to recount the story of the Barnacle Tree. The highly impressionable twelfth century Welsh monk Giraldus Cambrensis swore that he had actually witnessed the wonder of goose barnacles turning into geese. William Turner told the same story in his herbal, and the legend lingered until the mid-seventeenth century. However, two

An astonishingly athletic bifurcate-tailed mermaid cavorts on an ancient carving in medieval Dubrovnik.

rather not encounter, although many are recognisable and well observed, such as the filter-feeding baleen whale and the dolphin.

Fabulous half-human, half-fish creatures included Scylla, from the waters between Sicily and Italy. It was said to have the face and hands of a gentlewoman with the belly of a beast and a tail like a dolphin. It apparently appreciated music, but it was armed with fearful teeth and was immensely strong in the water. Syrene the Mermayd was another deadly beast. From the navel upwards Syrene resembled a woman, with a dreadful face and long, slimy hair. The body was fat, and the nether region resembled an eagle with feet and talons to tear at its prey and a scaly tail. Syrene suckled its young with exceptionally large nipples and was said to enchant mariners with sweet songs, ripping them apart once they fell asleep. The recommended procedure if a Syrene was encountered was to cover the ears and toss it an empty barrel as a plaything.

famed alchemists, Albertus Magnus and Roger Bacon, showed an admirably scientific approach and would have none of the story. Albertus Magnus even travelled to both Ireland and northern Scotland to search for any evidence of Barnacle Trees and was satisfied that they were entirely mythical.

This confusion of bird and sea creature proved very convenient for dodging the strict regimes of Lent and other religious fasting in the medieval period. The same Giraldis Cambrensis who swore he had seen goose barnacles hatching, and who seems in his various writings to have lost no opportunity for moralising, railed against this slippery evasion in 1187: 'Hence the bishops and clergy in some parts of Ireland are in the habit of partaking of these birds on fast days without apparent scruple'.

Despite his protests, it seems that many medieval fasts were relieved by this desirable goose, and such laxity was widespread. Pope Innocent III finally issued an edict against eating barnacle geese during Lent at the Lateran Council of 1215, and they were also forbidden to Jews in 1277 by Rabbi Izak on the basis that they were thought to be literally neither fish nor fowl.

Even so, the month-long fasting days of Advent were broken with a Christmas Eve feast that often included this goose among the officially permitted seafood dishes of oysters, crabs, winkles, clams, lobster and fish in various guises. Those selling geese in the market place were often remarkably and deliberately vague in identifying their poultry, and ordinary geese also appeared on many tables in place of the barnacle goose.

Another widely unquestioned animal–plant was the Vegetable Lamb. It was also known as the Scythian Lamb, Tartarian Lamb or the Barometz. The Vegetable Lamb certainly led an awkward life. It grew from a seed and was supposedly supported by a stalk in the ground attached under its middle. It was forced to eat only the very limited pasture it could reach and would die when it could reach no more. In some accounts, it was said to have golden fleece, flesh that tasted of fish, and blood that tasted like honey. It was also said that if an arrow severed its stalk, the lamb could be safely released.

Like the alicorn of the unicorn, the Vegetable Lamb was the subject of much deception. Lamb foetuses were passed off as Vegetable

The symbol of the lamb, possibly Scythian, appears on this carved fragment in the remains of the once powerful ancient Glastonbury Abbey.

Lambs, and in an inglorious moment the august Royal Society accepted a rhizome of a tree fern (*Cibotium barometz*) from China as the Vegetable Lamb of Tartary. The appearance of the rhizome had been judiciously enhanced to improve the resemblance. This took place sometime in the early eighteenth century, so the belief died hard. The tree fern itself was not introduced into cultivation in England until 1824.

There is a possibility that the story of the Vegetable Lamb was embroidered from early travellers' observations of cotton. A species of cotton (*Gossypium herbaceum*) does grow in the region where the Vegetable Lamb supposedly lived. A specimen of a Vegetable Lamb is also in the collection of the Museum of Garden History on Lambeth Palace Road in London.

Legendary trees

The Apple of Sodom was believed to be a giant tree found only in the area that once housed the ill-fated cities of Sodom and Gomorrah. If even half an apple were picked from the tree it would burst into fire and turn to ashes, a sure sign that God would rebuke anyone who succumbed to the temptation of this fruit in the place that had earned such terrible retribution.

The Tree of Knowledge described in the Old Testament was portrayed as an apple tree in most medieval paintings, but quince, Sycamore fig, pear, grapes, etrog (citron), dates and banana have also been depicted. The Sycamore fig (*Ficus sycamorus*) is a large tree with heart-shaped leaves that has been grown for thousands of years in Egypt and Syria for its dense shade and sweet fruits. One such tree was said to have opened its branches to enclose the Virgin Mary and the infant Jesus hiding from Herod's soldiers, and a large Sycamore fig called the Pharaoh's Fig was long shown to travellers as the blessed tree.

Others said that the Tree of Knowledge had grown from the spilled blood of a dragon. However, in a thirteenth century cathedral in Indres in France a fresco showing the Tree of Knowledge was intended as a strong warning to all. The tree emerges out of the hallucinogenic and poisonous fly agaric or spotted toadstool (*Amanita muscaria*). A serpent writhes up the tree and its face, emerging from among the fruit, is that of a temptingly pretty and exceptionally well-endowed maiden. Thirteenth century France was well aware of the visionary power of the poisonous fly agaric, its gifts of sexual endurance, prophetic insight and remarkable erotic capacity, as well its great dangers.

What wonderful mythical and mystical creatures the medieval mind conjured up. They papered the spaces between known facts about the natural world with their imagination. Their world was rich with wonders, a place where dragons breathed fire and threatened to toast damsels in distress, griffins roamed, salamanders emerged unscathed from flames and geese grew on trees. The human talent for spinning fantasies was never more potent.

The medieval gardens of Salagon

This simple medieval style fountain is the focal point of the gardens at Salagon, a grotto surrounded by flowers and fruits.

In Haute Provence in southern France, not far from the Durance River and the town of Manosque, lies the medieval priory of Salagon. It is one of the most important historical monuments in Haute Provence. The land was first used as a farm, then towards the end of the first century AD it was the site of a Gallo-Roman villa. A basilica was later built on the site, together with a Christian cemetery. Towards the end of the eleventh century, Salagon came into the possession of the Benedictine abbey of Saint-André de Villeneuve-lès-Avignon and the new priory of Notre Dame de Salagon was built on the foundations of the old basilica. A small monastic building was added in the thirteenth century and enlarged in the Renaissance. Built on a slight mound and facing west, Salagon retains that purity, simplicity and elegance of facade that often typifies medieval French priories.

In 1981, Salagon was taken over by the regional government of the Alpes-de-Haute-Provence, and the buildings restored. The Alpes de Lumière Society has added an ethnobotanical centre and museum, which has gained wide recognition. The gardens that surround Salagon today represent the plant knowledge of the people of Haute Provence. Laid out around the ancient priory are a Medieval Garden; a Garden of Simples; the White Oak Garden; the Salicetum, with its collection of willows so valuable in the medieval period for basketry (and favoured for magic wands); the Noria Garden, inspired by medieval court gardens; the Fragrance Garden; the Contemporary Garden; and the Centre for Ethnological Research.

right
The Medieval Garden of Simples and useful plants, based on Charlemagne's *Capitulare de villis*.

far right
The extensive Fragrance Garden is a herbal sampler filled with the fragrant herbs of Provence.

The Ethnological Botanical Garden is laid out in a manner reminiscent of Persian gardens, complete with water canal.

The Garden of Simples was the first to be developed and occupies the site of an old vegetable garden, still marked by a pear tree, a lilac, iris and peonies. A 'simple' was any remedy based on a single plant, as opposed to the complex formulas of alchemists and physicians. In time the plants used in these remedies became known as simples. The garden contains, among many species, the Greater Celandine (*Chelidonium majus*), Pellitory-of-the-Wall (*Parietaria*), nettle (*Urtica dioica*), wormwood (*Artemisia absinthum*), horehound (*Marrubium vulgare*, known locally as Mont Blanc) and the very unusual Plantain Badasson (*Plantago sempervirens*), with thread-like foliage unlike any other plantain. It has always been regarded as a local panacea, used for inflammation, sprains, bruises and festering wounds. Knowledge of this plant's healing ability appears to have been purely local.

The clock tower gable with bells surmounts a simple yet strong and elegant medieval priory building.

The Medieval Garden, with its tiny grotto, is a wonderful place. Numerous small wattle-edged gardens house more than four hundred plants used in medieval times, including fibre crops, dye plants, plants for sorcery and magic, grains, culinary herbs and medieval vegetables. The plantings are based on the famous late eighth century *Capitulare de villis*, drawn up on the command of Charlemagne the Great to list all the plants grown in Carolingian gardens, orchards and fields.

The Garden of Fragrance is a delightful place to linger, filled with sweetly scented flowers such as the Rose of Provins, anise, curry plant (*Helichrysum italicum*), and various artemisias and lavenders. The Contemporary Garden is modern in design, yet with hints of Persian gardens, and is devoted to economic plants of many kinds, both Old World and New World.

A herbal of medieval dye plants

Until the 1850s, when brilliant aniline dyes were discovered, fabrics were coloured with the subtle dyes of nature. Fabrics and embroidery threads were dyed with plants, including lichens (for instance, the purple dye Orchil is derived from a lichen), weld, woad, the bark of oak, madder, Dyer's Chamomile, cinquefoils such as Silverweed, broom, St John's Wort, bracken, Bedstraw, tansy, yarrow, parsley, walnuts, rue, heather, iris, Sweet Cicely, alkanet and elderberry. Textile dyes in the Near East during the medieval period included safflower, indigo plants, madder and saffron. England became famous for its rich red madder dyes in the fourteenth century.

Dyes also came from the animal world, such as the Phoenician 'Tyrian Purple' or 'Imperial Purple', an intense red-purple used for the robes of emperors and high church dignitaries. It was derived from a species of sea mollusc, the spiny dye murex, *Murex brandaris*. A second mollusc, the

dye murex *M. trunculus*, was the source of another Phoenician dye, indigo or 'Royal Blue', a rich blue-purple colour. Both murex dyes were colourfast and very expensive.

Indigo dye was also derived from several plants. To make the dye, plant material was shredded and boiled in water to obtain a concentrated solution.

From early times, fibres were pre-soaked in substances called mordants, which help the colour adhere to the fibre. Mordants included the tannins from bark, nuts and wood, as well as solutions of mineral salts of metals such as iron, tin and copper.

While all mordants act as fixatives, some also have the ability to alter the final colour of the dye. The commonest mordant used was colour-neutral alum. In northern Europe, clubfoot moss, which is an active absorber of aluminium from the soil, was used for the same purpose. Salts of iron, such as iron sulphate, were used to deepen and enrich colours,

and salts of tin, such as stannous chloride, to brighten colours. Dyes could also be altered by turning a solution acid with vinegar, or alkaline with lye or washing soda. Gervase Markham in *The English Housewife* suggested that cloth be taken to the local dyer, for one of the charms, but also frustrations, of natural dyeing is that two batches are almost never the same. Guilds of professional dyers emerged in the medieval period to specialise in the art of using natural dyes.

ALKANET or DYER'S BUGLOSS (*Alkanna tinctoria*): This relative of forget-me-not yields purple and grey dyes.

BOX (*Buxus sempervirens*): While fabric dyes were important in medieval time, so too was the use of hair dyes. The leaves and wood of box were also used to colour hair auburn.

BRAMBLE or BLACKBERRY (*Rubus fruticosus*): These fruits were used in monasteries and by country people as a dye, yielding a blue-grey colour, while the roots gave an orange dye. Brambles were gathered wild from the hedgerows.

CALENDULA or POT MARIGOLD (*Calendula officinalis*): The petals were used as a dye for wool, yielding a yellow colour with alum as a mordant. It has also been used from the medieval period onwards as a food colourant, particularly for cheese and butter, and as a pleasantly spicy substitute for very expensive saffron. It is still used for these purposes in the cooking of the Netherlands.

CHICORY (*Cichorum intybus*): Chicory was in cultivation in Egypt five millennia ago. It found use as a food, as a cattle fodder and as a medicine, but was also used in the medieval period as a dye for wool,

producing either a blue or orange colour depending on the mordant.

DYER'S CHAMOMILE (*Anthemis tinctoria*): The bright yellow petals of this species were used to create a rich gold dye using chrome as a mordant, and a yellow dye that used alum as the mordant.

DYER'S GREENWEED or DYER'S BROOM (*Genista tinctoria*): This golden-flowered broom yields a yellow dye when alum is used as a mordant.

MADDER (*Rubia tinctorum*): Madder was native to the Near East but was grown in England from the Anglo-Saxon period onwards. The roots yield a very colourfast dye in shades of rich red and England was famed for this dye. 'Turkey Red' was also derived from madder.

SAFFLOWER or FALSE SAFFRON (*Carthamnus tinctorius*): The petals were used extensively as a textile dye in the Near East and in Spain during the medieval period. The flower can yield a red or yellow dye,

and a number of attractive colours in between, depending on the mordant. It was commonly used in Egypt, less so in Europe, particularly for wool and silk.

WELD or DYER'S ROCKET (*Reseda luteola*): The famous 'Lincoln Green' colour worn by Robin Hood's band of merry men was achieved with a combination of weld and woad. Weld yields a yellow dye when using alum, and orange using a combination of alum and tin.

WOAD (*Isatis tinctoria*): The leaves of woad were used to produce a renowned medieval colourfast indigo cloth dye. The process involved cold fermentation. The last remaining woad mills in the world, located in Lincolnshire, were closed in the 1930s.

Garden Design: The Unicorn's Garden

This is a magical woodland garden well suited to the reputed preferences of unicorns, and is entered via the flagstone 'Fiddlehead Path' which echoes one of nature's mathematical patterns, seen in the shells of molluscs such as snails and winkles and in the whorled horns of some land and sea creatures.

The path curls upon itself to reach its secret heart, 'The Spring of Eternity'. This low, glittering pool with a small fountain might also be interpreted as a small bubbler fountain emerging from a bed of smooth dark river rocks surrounded by filmy ferns, or as a large ceramic glazed ball in deep blue or or moss green with a low bubbler fountain emerging from the top.

The garden is surrounded by trees associated with deep magic, forming 'The Sacred Glade'. The trees include golden ash, hawthorn, a weeping silver pear, elder and rowan. Two stone benches have been positioned to view 'The Spring of Eternity' from different viewpoints. A flowery mead (see instructions for making this feature, along with many additional plant suggestions within this chapter) is planted with flowers found in the medieval French tapestry series 'The Hunt of the Unicorn' including the snake's head fritillary (*Fritillaria meleagris*), requiring moist light shade, primrose, wild strawberry, clove pink, columbine, carnation, daffodil, periwinkle, bluebell, field daisy and sweet violet, and in the shadowy depths of the glade clumps of male fern (*Dryopteris filix-mas*).

In keeping with the woodland feeling of this garden, it is enclosed with a rustic clipped hazel hedge supported internally by a pole fence. A clipped blackthorn hedge would also be also be in keeping with the style. In an urban setting, it might be considered preferable to use an ornamental diamond pattered pole fence.

 Legend

1 ROWAN
2 GOLDEN ASH
3 ROWAN
4 ELDER
5 RECTANGULAR TURF OR STONE SEAT
6 CLIPPED HAZEL HEDGE SUPPORTED BY POLE FENCE, 1.8 M (6 FT) HIGH OR DIAMOND PATTERNED POLE FENCE
7 APPLE
8 CRAB APPLE
9 ELDER
10 HAWTHORN
11 'THE SACRED GLADE'
12 WEEPING SILVER PEAR
13 ELDER
14 'THE SPRING OF ETERNITY'
15 THE FLOWERY MEAD
16 FLAGSTONE PATH, 'THE FIDDLEHEAD PATH'

Chapter 2

The Monastery Garden

Talke of perfect happiness or pleasure, and what place
was so fit for that as the garden place where Adam was set
to be the Herbalist.

JOHN GERARD, *The Herbal* (1633)

St Benedict's Rule

From the second century onwards, Christianity in Western Europe was based on the hermitic or anchorite tradition of a life withdrawn from the distractions of the world in order to refine the soul and be more closely attuned with the will of God.

That this gradually developed into a monastic tradition based on self-sufficient communities of Christians was largely due to the teachings of just one man, St Benedict.

St Benedict was born into a noble Roman family in AD 481, one of twins (his sister was St Scholastica). After studying in Rome, he spent his early life as a hermit in a cave in the Simbruinian Mountains, but he ended his days in the great abbey of Monte Cassino near Naples, dying there in 547. Benedict preached a gospel of redemption through work. He considered that work, joyfully and humbly carried out to the glory of God, was of equal importance to prayer in leading an individual to salvation. He founded thirteen monasteries, as well as various schools, and gradually formulated what was to be known as the Rule, a way of living in a self-sufficient community that emphasised hospitality and care of the sick, hard work, and a life of simplicity and prayer.

Those who followed St Benedict were admonished never to accept charity but to earn their food and lodging through honest labour. Gardening became one of their central activities. The Rule was based on Christ's statement: 'For I was hungry and you gave me food, I was thirsty and you gave me something to drink, I was a stranger and you welcomed me, I was naked and you gave me clothing, I was sick and you took care of me, I was in prison and you visited me.'

In its final form, St Benedict's Rule consisted of seventy-three chapters that prescribed in great detail the life to be led, the administration of the monastery and the maintenance of all religious activities, along with very practical issues such as meals, the care of sick brethren and the aged, the reception of guests, work, clothing and footwear, tools and handling the possessions of the monastery. Despite the severity of the Rule in modern eyes, it was tempered by a real concern for the welfare of all members of the community.

Many copies of the Rule were made at the abbey of Monte Cassino, and when it was sacked in the seventh century the monks spread out to other monasteries, taking the copies with them. St Augustine, a fellow Roman, took a copy of the Rule to England. The majority of monasteries in the centuries that followed would belong to the Benedictine Order, or the Black Monks as they were called, and the monks, with their keen interest in agriculture and horticulture, would continued to develop the knowledge they had inherited from the crumbling Roman Empire.

However, far more than agricultural and horticultural activities were pursued by those who lived in the Benedictine monasteries. The intellectual life of many monasteries was a rich one. Libraries of precious manuscripts were maintained, manuscripts were copied and richly illustrated, theological concepts were debated and refined, conferences were held, meticulous records were kept, and botanical and herbal knowledge increased. Monasteries were at the forefront of medical knowledge and practice.

Monks were also involved in the brewing of ales, cider and wine, the excess adding to the income of the monastery, and more than a few monks created secret formulas for herbal medicinal liqueurs. Others tended to the needs of elderly monks, or to the feeding and housing of visitors and pilgrims. Monks taught in the schools, milled grains, baked the monastery's bread, cooked for large numbers or held administrative positions. None were idle.

The garden of St Gall

The garden of St Gall never existed, and yet it lives in our imagination as the perfect monastery garden of the Carolingian period. The plan presented on five parchments was drawn in the scriptorium of Reichenau Abbey, near Lake Constance, for Abbot Gotzbert of the St Gall monastery in Switzerland. St Gall, or St Gallus,

was one of a number of early medieval monks who found their way to Europe from Ireland. He was a disciple of St Columbanus, who in turn had been instructed by St Columbus. In a long life (he died in 615 at the age of eighty-five) Columbanus travelled widely in Europe, and in 590 reached the court of the Merovingian King

A segment of the plans drawn
for the monastery of St Gall in
Switzerland, with a square
central cloister garth, paradise
and physic garden.
Stiftsbibliothek St Gallen

Guntrum of Burgundy and established several monasteries in the area, as well as one at Bobbio in Italy. Not surprisingly, St Gall followed his teacher's example, travelling through both France and Italy before, in 613, founding the hermitage in Switzerland that was destined to become the monastery of St Gall. The saint never entirely broke his ties with Ireland and, like his teacher, lived a long life that spanned the entire second half of the sixth century and almost the whole first half of the seventh century.

St Gall later housed a famous school, founded by Othmar in the eighth century to instruct in the sciences, arts and literature, and a very significant library, containing valuable manuscripts that attracted monks from Ireland and England as copyists. A copy of the Plan of St Gall was discovered in this library, which still exists. The abbey lies some 70 kilometres (40 miles) east of Zurich. It was for centuries one of the most significant Benedictine abbeys in Europe but it no longer holds much of the

manuscript collection. Threats to the abbey by the Huns in the tenth century led to the contents of the library being moved to Reichenau, on an island in Lake Constance, for safe keeping. These manuscripts were, for the most part, returned, but in 1712 the abbey was pillaged by the Swiss, who removed most of the library's contents to Berne and Zurich. Books seem always to be a victim of war.

The garden plans for St Gall are practical in concept, as could be expected of a designer who followed St Benedict's Rule, yet they are at the same time charming. It is impossible to study the design without visualising the simple beauty that these gardens would have possessed.

The overall plan was for a self-sufficient community in keeping with the Rule. The buildings include a grand church, the monastery and a range of separate buildings such as the refectory, abbot's house, kitchens, bakery, brew house, mill, kiln, grain store, barn, stabling, enclosures for animals (including geese and fowl), hospital, school, and housing for travellers, guests and pilgrims (an itinerant population that often outnumbered the resident population). All are arranged around a central square cloister garth with columns and arcades reminiscent of the Roman peristyle.

Cloister garths were always placed so that one side ran along the wall of the church. At St Gall, the garth is simply turfed and cut by two intersecting paths forming a cross. Such simplicity was common at that time. In large cloister garths, the cross created by intersecting paths might be repeated within each of the original quarters. The cloistered walk around the edge allowed protection from inclement weather and heat, and provided a thoroughfare. It also created a contemplative space, the simple repetitive columns easing the mind and the expanse of green grass refreshing and soothing eyes tired from studying, copying manuscripts or illustrating. A well or a fountain was usually placed within.

At the rear of the church the plan shows a semicircular space designated a 'paradise', a design element reflecting the Church's encounter with the glories of Eastern architecture in Constantinople. Jews, Christians and Muslims all share the belief that God created the first garden, and the very word 'paradise' comes from the ancient Persian word *pairidaeza*, which described an enclosed space containing a garden or park. Just where the Garden of Eden was located has always been a matter for speculation, but the Book of Genesis offers clues and it is thought to have lain between the Tigris and Euphrates rivers, in what is now Iraq.

The gardeners of Constantinople had adopted the Persian 'paradise' and from there it spread to the West. By the eighth century a paradise in Rome was a garden created in the Byzantine spirit, an ornamental garden filled with flowers and beautiful trees. Early interpretations of a paradise in Western Europe were generally very simple, but an example of a true paradise garden was created in the eleventh century in the newly restored Monte Cassino. In the same period Romsey Abbey in England possessed a well-documented rose garden that would have contained the intensely fragrant, ancient, summer-flowering Gallica, Damask and Alba roses. It is recorded that in 1093 William Rufus, anxious to foster an acquaintance with a pretty young woman in the care of the Abbess of Romsey Abbey, entered the cloister and offered the rather unlikely excuse that he come to inspect the famous rose garden.

The medicinal herbal garden

The physician's house on the St Gall plan is placed adjacent to the infirmary (hospital), which is provided with a *herbularius*, or physic garden. This garden devoted to healing herbs was a square area containing sixteen straight-sided and raised beds. The plants listed to

The delightful reconstructed medieval garden at Tusson Abbey in the Charente region of France, with authentic plantings of physic plants.

opposite
The cloister garth of Fontfroide Abbey in southern France reflects the later more ornamental style, with flowers and a water feature.

be grown in the physic garden included roses and lilies, as well as aromatic herbs such as rue, lovage, cumin, fennel, tansy, pennyroyal, sage, flag iris, fenugreek, mint, savory, horsemint and beans.

Herbal cures of all kinds, from teas to electuaries and salves, were prepared from the herb garden, and the physician monk would be expected to care not only for the needs of the cloistered monks but also for the needs of wandering friars, local artisans and the peasants who worked for the monastery, local villagers, and visitors and pilgrims. Only in the event of a serious illness would a doctor be brought in from a nearby town.

In larger monasteries, the infirmary was sometimes virtually autonomous, arranged around its own cloister garth, with independent amenities for water and cooking, a *herbularius* or garden of simples, vegetable gardens and a pleasant, fragrant garden with an orchard to stroll in gently while recuperating. The semi-autonomy of the infirmary may have been in part a means of quarantining those who were ill in times of plague or other epidemics. Very poisonous medicinal plants, including mandrake and Opium Poppy, seem to have been secured safely behind fencing. Others of a poisonous nature, such as henbane, bryony and hemlock, were often gathered wild from the countryside.

Herbal knowledge was very extensive in medieval times. In England, the tenth century *Leechdom* provided a compilation of herbs used in human and veterinary medicine. The Welsh physicians of Myddfai were perhaps the most

significant medical school of their era in Western Europe. The *Meddegon Myddfai*, containing their knowledge of medicine and herbal plants, was copied and distributed from the thirteenth century. It contained extensive Celtic and Druidic plant knowledge in combination with Hippocratic sources. Another Welsh text, *Hafod*, written c. 1400, contains additional information on herbal remedies.

One of the least pleasant preventative measures taken to maintain the health of monastery residents was blood letting with the use of leeches, and monks were subject to this from twice to as many as six times a year. After blood letting, they were allowed to convalesce for up to a week in the infirmary and were fed nourishing herb broths. The triangular wounds were covered with a poultice, commonly of mallow, but it was not unusual for an allergic reaction and an episode of weakening fever to occur. The convalescents were allowed to relax with fresh air and exercise, strolling through the orchard and contemplating nature. The monks of Clairvaux Abbey in north-eastern France had a very pleasant scene to soothe them. A fourteenth century source describes how the infirm looked from a green bank into a huge basin filled with fish. Similar basins are described elsewhere.

Brother Cadfael is perhaps the most famous fictional herbalist monk, but Brother Odo is well known to many who have read the delightfully humorous poetry of Tom Stewart, written over many years and published in a series of books to celebrate the life and deeds of a humble, gentle, guileless, but by no means clueless, medieval garden monk. Odo is a Benedictine, a sturdy Black Monk intent on salvation through work and prayer. This quote from the poem 'The Monastery Garden' is true to the times:

A lay brother of the Cistercian order tends a garden in his religious robes, c. 1200. Getty Images

'Brother Odo, how did you spend your day?'
'I rose in the dark and went to pray,
And after a meagre breakfast I
To the garden went with the reddening sky.
And there till noon I planted true Coriander, dill and rue.
Pennyroyal, mint and yarrow,
Marjoram, thyme and sage
And a bed of lovage.'
'Brother Odo you have done well
A glass of cider drink in your cell.'
'In the afternoon I too was busy:
I planted a bed with rosemary.
I weeded the iris, cumin and leek
And sowed some seeds of fenugreek.
Horehound, wormwood, camomile,
I tended them all with a patient smile.
The Madonna Lilies I cut with love,
On altar placed of Our Lady above.'
'Brother Odo, the Lord will repay
All the work you did this day.'
'Oh yes, when the day was getting late
I planted near our kitchen gate
Some betony and parsley,

Agrimony and savory,
Poppies red and lavender blue,
Soon cook might make a decent stew!
And as I heard the evening bell
I scattered far, seeds of fennel.
My Lord I want our garden to be
Even better than Glastonbury.'
'Brother Odo how pleased I would be
If all the monks worked like thee.
Come change with me, take my habit.
A jewel like you should be the Abbot.'

The vegetable garden

The cook in a monastery had almost as large a number to care for as the physician monk. The monastic diet was largely vegetarian, and practical vegetable gardens were a necessity. The Church was an absolute in the lives of everyone in medieval Europe, and neither the Faith nor Church rulings appear to have been questioned for many centuries. Fasting was a part of that unquestioned regulation by the Church, and the laity as well as the religious were bound by very strict rules that were progressively relaxed during the thirteenth, fourteenth and fifteenth centuries. Every week, Wednesday, Friday and Saturday were set aside for fasting and all 'four footed' meat was forbidden. The diet of the monks in the great French Abbey of Cluny in Burgundy, for instance, consisted of two meals a day based on cheese, fish, dried beans and seasonal vegetables. While monks continued this weekly observance, by the fifteenth century it appears to have been reduced to 'Friday fysshe day' observance among the laity.

A number of additional fasting periods were observed during the year, including six weeks for Lent (which imposed additional bans on eggs and dairy foods), and four weeks for Advent. The boredom of the monastic diet must have been very great, and during fasting days most monks could expect no more than servings of salted fish such as herring. The only supplement to the diet at such times would have been vegetables from the gardens, often reduced during the winter months to stored dried field beans and frost-resistant vegetables such as coleworts (early cabbages) and leeks, simmered together into a pottage and served with rough bread. So common was the leek in the monastic diet that in England the monastery vegetable garden was often called the 'leac garth'.

It is an irresistible temptation at this point to quote a second poem of Tom Stewart's, 'Lady Godiva', which describes a delightfully devious plan to overcome monkish boredom:

As Brother Odo dug (or delved) a thought ran through his brain:
Each day is the same. I'm in a rut, maybe a drain.
Arising in the dark to pray then working dawn to night

How nice a long sleep-in would be (a heavenly delight)
But alas, there's not a feast day in sight.

Then inspiration! To a brother in whispers did he speak:
'I think I can arrange sleep-in for all this coming week.'
He had some words in Abbot's ear who later spoke to all:
'On Monday next I declare a SLEEP-IN DAY will fall.
I do not want you rising until mid-day at least.
As well
In fact, I insist, lunch will be eaten in your cell.'

The brothers were amazed how Odo's promise had come true
(And at the glass of wine served them for elevenses too).
With toes delightfully warm, with blankets pulled up to each chin
The brethren let the luxury soak in.

When Odo was asked how he managed such a feat;
'I merely said to Abbot that Monday would give our eyes a treat
With Lady Godiva due to come riding down our street.'

The practical vegetable garden used to feed the monks of St Gall was typical of the time, planned in eighteen long, narrow raised beds arranged in double file. Each bed was easily accessible from all sides and was planted to vegetables such as onions, leeks, shallots and garlic, together with smallage (or celery), coriander, parsley, dill, chervil, open-headed lettuce, radish, parsnips, carrots, coleworts, beets, black cumin (*Nigella sativa*) and poppy. The poultry houses were arranged conveniently next to the vegetable garden to provide manure for fertiliser. Field grown crops are not shown in the St Gall plan but these would have been grown on surrounding land. Water was an obvious necessity and watering cans would have been carried from holding ponds or wells, but miniature canal systems were also employed in a number of monasteries. At Clairvaux Abbey, for instance, in the early twelfth century small canals flowed around the vegetable garden and were also used for raising fish. Complex irrigation schemes were employed in some larger medieval abbeys. A famous example is described in a document from 1165. It was drawn up for the Priory of Christ Church and shows provision of water to several gardens.

Medieval plant lists

The plants chosen for the monastery gardens at St Gall were all selected from the *Capitulare de villis*, a decree issued in 800 as a praiseworthy opening to a new century by Charlemagne the Great after he was crowned King of the Franks and Emperor of the Holy Roman Empire by Pope Leo III. Charlemagne's early reign as a king was a bloody one. After a series of eighteen battles, he conquered Saxony and forced conversion to Christianity by the sword, slaughtering those who refused to accept baptism. He also attempted to take Spain. However, the later stages of his life, particularly after he was crowned emperor, were marked by his attempts to create peace and stability throughout Europe. He saw the work of gardening as being as useful in creating peace as the Benedictines had seen it as useful for aiding the salvation of the soul.

It is true that gardens can only survive where there is relative peace and security, but Charlemagne argued that the reverse also holds true: that peace comes when the hoe and spade replace the sword. He divided his empire into 350 counties, each overseen by an administrator holding the rank of count and entrusted with considerable powers. To prevent any disloyalty he set up a system known as the *Missi Dominici*, under which every county was inspected annually by two representatives, one of the Church and one of the emperor. His *Capitulare de villis* ordered that a garden be created in every town in 'all crown lands' throughout the empire, and that it be stocked with useful plants from the extensive list he included in the *Capitulare*, a list that was almost certainly compiled by Benedict of Aniane near Montpellier.

In Britain, the Glastonbury *Herbal*, which was in the care of the very powerful Glastonbury Abbey, listed similar useful fruit trees and plants, although like Charlemagne's listings not all were suited to cool, cloudy regions. The Glastonbury list included sweet cherries, peaches, dates, and various plums and pears. The *Herbal* also revealed a sophisticated knowledge of horticulture comparable to that on the Continent at the time.

Other monastery gardens

The plan for St Gall appears to represent a general consensus on the appropriate design of monastic gardens and the pattern changed little over a number of centuries, although it was often augmented in later times. Abbots and senior monastery officials, or obedientiaries, in important monasteries frequently required a separate garden for quiet contemplation, and there is no provision for this in the quite modest St Gall design. While the primary role of the abbots in some of the most powerful and well-endowed abbeys remained a religious one, they were often in charge of vast estates and empowered by wealth. As a result, many were on intimate terms with royalty and were themselves not infrequently drawn from the ranks of nobility. The standard of their accommodation and their table, and their access to a private garden of some elegance, were in keeping with their status and their need to act as intermediaries with the secular world. Their social status in England was the equivalent of a baron.

One such abbot's garden, a quite simple twelfth century one that must nevertheless have given much pleasure to its owner, was that of Alexander Neckham, Abbot of Cirencester. He concluded in his *De Naturis Rerum* that the garden should be ornamented with violets, daffodils, roses, lilies, the vanilla-scented heliotrope and acanthus, plus culinary and physic herbs, including mandrake, and vegetables.

Walahfrid Strabo, who was not only a brilliant abbot but also an able botanist and herbalist, also possessed a private garden, and he listed a total of twenty-three flowers growing there, most of them useful as well as fragrant. A ninth century garden may have been primarily for sustenance, but personal gardens designed to give pleasure existed, even for the hard-working Black Monks. It was Strabo who first wrote the often repeated advice, 'Get a garden! What kind you get matters not ...'

In later centuries and particularly on the Continent, the cloister garth often lost its simple severity and became more ornamental. It could be planted with trees for coolness or with flowers, and it could be supplied with a water feature and

opposite
An orchard of ancient apple varieties flanks the ruins of Melrose Abbey, founded by King David I in 1136, the first Cistercian abbey in Scotland.

perhaps a cross or statue. Many of the more affluent monasteries allocated a separate garden for cut flowers used to ornament the church, particularly on feast days. This garden was cared for by the sacrist, and the flowers were also used to create the chaplets (wreaths to crown the head) worn on such days as Corpus Christi. These garlands are an almost lost but delightful tradition worthy of revival. The cutting garden might have a special gardener, as was intended at St Gall where a monk gardener's house is shown on the plan. The sacrist was required to supply far more than flowers to the church. He was also required to supply herbs and osiers for strewing, and the evergreens of Christmas, such as holly and bay. Winchester Cathedral possessed a sacristan's garden at much the same time as the plans for St Gall were drawn, and it seems to have been quite a common feature of English monasteries.

Beyond the cloister walls many monasteries grew extensive field crops, such as field peas, beans and cereals, together with the blue-flowered flax and hemp for fibre. There were also vineyards and additional orchards. Provision was often made for a stewpond, where freshwater fish such as roach, carp, pike and tench caught elsewhere were kept alive until needed by the cook. Ponds and canal systems might also be devoted to fish breeding, an important activity in some monasteries, where such an inclusion was called a piscina. Richer monasteries might own additional coppiced woods to supply fuel and branches for weaving wattle fences, any number of manor houses and farms with a peasant labour force, and perhaps also osier beds.

While the Benedictine Order was dominant in the story of gardens, it was not by any means the only monastic Order involved in agriculture and

Gardens for use and delight

Around the year 1440, a not necessarily coincidentally named Mayster Jon Gardener wrote a book in verse called *The Feate of Gardening*. It was to become the first practical manual for English gardeners, and contained information on plant cultivation, the growing of herbs, and skills such as grafting. It is worth noting that John Harvey considers the text to have been copied from an original manuscript that was at least fifty years older. As a result of the research carried out by A. G. Rigg, the manuscript written c. 1440 is now thought to have been in the possession of a monk in Glastonbury Abbey.

Some ninety-four plants were included, some with names that have undergone the usual changes with time, but others quaint and unusual. Examples include Floscampi (Ragged Robin, *Lychnis flos-cuculi*), Langbefe (Viper's Bugloss, *Echium vulgaris*), Lavyndull (lavender, *Lavandula angustifolia*), Wyldresyl (Common Teasel, *Dipsacus sylvestris*), Wodertofe (Sweet Woodruff, *Asperula odorata*), Warmot (wormwood, *Artemisia absinthum*) and Bigold (Corn Marigold, *Chrysanthemum segetum*). Among the culinary plants were saffron, fennel, thyme, coriander, parsley, sage, garlic, lettuce, turnip, leek, spinach and strawberry.

The orchard

To the north of the infirmary on the St Gall plan lay an orchard containing trees of apple, pear, peach, fig, plum, mulberry, medlar, quince, service berry, sweet bay, hazelnut, chestnut, almond and walnut. The orchard also served as a cemetery garden. Perhaps it was practical to bury monks beneath the soft green turf of the orchard, but lushly beautiful orchards were deeply intertwined with the concept of Paradise in the medieval mind, and it seems a gentle and loving gesture towards those who had served their God and fellow men to the best of their ability. Even in death, the monks were kept within the life of the monastery, and perhaps in its most beautiful space. Here they were showered with the petals of fruit trees on spring days, shaded by cool, green foliage in summer and were a part of the glowing harvest days of autumn.

The monastery's orchard was generally planted in the ornamental, but also practical, quincunx pattern, which consists of four trees planted at the corners of a square with a fifth tree in the centre, an arrangement that allowed for maximum sunlight exposure and air movement. This pattern could be repeated indefinitely in larger orchards. The fruit and nut trees chosen for St Gall were typical of those grown in cool climate gardens, but in southern Europe, with its mild and sunny climate, the orchard garden included pomegranates, oranges, lemons, almonds and apricots.

The orchard served yet another purpose for the monastery. A description of the Abbey of Clairvaux, at the time when St Bernard was the abbot, spoke of an orchard that resembled a small artificial wood within the abbey walls. Created on level ground near the infirmary, it was a space where monks might stroll comfortably or take their ease. William of Malmesbury provided a description of a similar woodland orchard in England.

Orchards seem to have had an important aesthetic role in many monasteries. Walahfrid Strabo, a brilliant German abbot of the Benedictine Abbey of Reichenau during the first half of the ninth century, described a delightful orchard he remembered from the days of his novitiate at Reichenau in the dedication of his famous poem *De Cultura Hortulorum*. The poem honoured his teacher Grimaldus, who had by then been appointed as abbot of nearby St Gall Abbey. Strabo was just thirty-four when elevated to Abbot of Reichenau, having already gained fame for his elegant Latin and poetry. In a short period (he died at forty), he made Reichenau famous for its manuscript acquisitions and scriptorium.

Echoing a Biblical Paradise, fruit orchards provided food and fermented beverages, peaceful places for meditation and healing, and a final resting place for monks.

This small gift … is offered to you Father Grimald …
I can picture you sitting there in the green enclosure of your garden
Under apples which hang in the shade of lofty foliage,
Where the peach-tree turns its leaves this way and that
In and out of the sun, and the boys at play
Your happy band of pupils, gather for you
Fruits white with tender down and stretch
Their hands to grasp the huge apples …

WALAHFRID STRABO, *De Cultura Hortulorum*, trans. Raef Payne, Pittsburg, Pennsylvania, 1966 gardening. The cloistered Order of Chartreuse, the Carthusians, was founded by St Bruno in 1084 and has celebrated the nine hundredth anniversary of its uninterrupted existence. The pattern for Carthusian life has remained largely unchanged since the days of St Bruno. It consists of a life devoted to prayer and meditation and to humble work, some of it solitary, but with shared communal activities. Gardens and gardening are a part of that life. Each monk within the community has a small, separate cell that extends into a secluded individual garden in which to cultivate flowers, herbs and vegetables. A simple workroom is a part of the cell.

Those in the Order of the Cistercians, known as the White Monks or Reformed Benedictines, made considerable contributions to agricultural management and were considered the leading agricultural technologists of their day. Melrose Abbey was a typical example. Old Melrose was a monastic settlement founded in the seventh century by St Aidan of Iona, who also founded nearby Lindisfarne. A new Melrose Abbey, built a short distance from the original and founded in 1136 by King David I, became the first Cistercian abbey in Scotland and was renowned for its sheep production.

The Capuchin monks of Belgium are noted for developing two vegetable varieties, both of which are still quite readily available: the purple-podded 'Blue Pod Capucijner', which is excellent in soups and for making 'mushy peas', and a form of endive known as 'Belgian' in English-speaking countries but as 'Barbe de Capuchin' in France.

Monasteries under Viking attack

What many monasteries lacked in their early development were defences. Charlemagne was right to maintain that gardens arose where peace prevailed. While the monastic gardens of southern England, France, Switzerland and parts of Italy thrived, the monasteries along the coasts of Britain were subjected to raids from the sea by Scandinavian pirates. Many monasteries in the north were destroyed, including the beautiful monastery of Lindisfarne on Holy Island, a tidal island connected by a causeway to the Northumberland coast.

Lindisfarne was founded by the Irish-born St Aidan, who had been sent from Iona c. 635 at the request of King Oswald. Other monks from Iona joined him, and St Cuthbert was at first a member of the brotherhood at Lindisfarne, later becoming the abbot, before his death in 687. He was famous for his miracles, which were recorded in detail by the Venerable Bede. Lindisfarne became a focus of pilgrimages to the relics of St Cuthbert, who had become the patron saint of Northumbria. Somewhere in the early eighth century, the famous, superbly designed illuminated manuscript of the *Lindisfarne Gospels* was created. It is believed to be the work of a single artist-monk, said to have been Eadfrith, who became the abbot when Cuthbert died. The manuscript survived against all odds and is today housed in the British Library in London.

The year 793 is generally said to mark the beginning of the Viking raids, and terrible portents were apparently seen before the raids began. The *Anglo-Saxon Chronicle* recorded that: 'In this year fierce, foreboding omens came over the land of Northumbria. There were excessive whirlwinds, lightning storms, and fiery dragons were seen flying in the skies. These signs were followed by great famine, and on January 8th of the same year, the ravaging of heathen men destroyed God's church at Lindisfarne.'

The attack on the monastery was reported by Alcuin of York, a great scholar of the Church and member of the royal court of Charlemagne, to both the Bishop of Lindisfarne and Ethelred, King of Northumbria. With a predictably medieval mindset, Alcuin recommended a strict moral reform in the monastery to prevent further attacks, rather than suggesting the more obvious

The ruins of medieval Lindisfarne Abbey on Holy Island, connected by causeway to the Northumberland coast, destroyed in the terrible Viking raids of 793.

approach of strengthening the monastery's defences. Lindisfarne survived the attack of 793 but fell to a later raid. Those monks who survived finally found a home for the relic of St Cuthbert at Durham Cathedral and the bishopric was transferred to Durham in 1000. The great circle of time has once again seen the rise of Lindisfarne, and today the Holy Island is a focus of the re-emerging Celtic Christian Church, which in 664 had been effectively suppressed at the Synod of Whitby.

Just how many monasteries were destroyed in the Viking raids will never be known as many records were lost, but the number was very substantial, particularly in Scotland. Blessed Iona was sacked and burned in 802, and then in a raid in 806 sixty-two monks were killed. Those who survived the attack fled to Ireland, to Kells in County Meath, and it has been suggested that the exquisitely illustrated *Book of Kells* may have been taken to Ireland with them. There was, in any case, considerable communication between the monasteries of Scotland and Ireland. Many of the most precious possessions of the monasteries in the north found their way to

How to create wattle fences

The wattle fences and garden edges illustrated in this book were widely used in medieval times. A revival in interest in this ancient technique has occurred in parts of Europe, including the United Kingdom, and wattle hurdles for fencing, screens and edgings can be purchased from specialist suppliers or directly from craftspeople. The wattle fence is usually constructed from woven hurdles that are then firmly attached to stout poles sunk well into the ground. Wattle fences are commonly 1.8 m

(6 ft) high, and treated posts of 2.2 m (8 ft) are used, with the bottom 60 cm (24 in) sunk into the earth and often cemented in place. Low wattle garden edges can be simply attached to short, stout wooden posts or, for a truly authentic look, lengths of straight tree branches can be hammered into soft ground.

The materials most often used for creating this basketwork on a grand scale are the long, flexible branches of hazel (*Corylus avellana*), although willow is also widely employed. Hazel and willow

have the additional advantage of growing quickly. However, any thin, flexible, straight branches can be used for this purpose. To produce the long, supple branches that are required for wattle fencing, trees are coppiced by cutting them back severely, an ancient art long predating the medieval period.

If you have access to lengths of freshly cut, flexible branches, you may want to create your own wattle fences. The process itself is quite simple, but it is advisable to begin with an easy project such as a low garden edge about 30 cm (1 ft) high. Gather a bundle of freshly cut, thin, straight branches, each at least 1.5 m (5 ft) long. Draw a line in the earth where the fence is required. Taking straight branches cut into 50 cm (20 in) pieces for stakes,

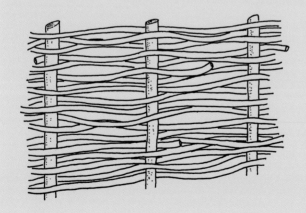

Wattle fences, based on a simple basket weave design, were popular ornamental edgings in medieval gardens.

roughly sharpen one end of each with a small axe. Mark out intervals of 30 cm (12 in) along the fence line and use a sledgehammer or heavy mallet to embed each stake. In exceptionally dry soil you may want to dig the holes for the stakes with a crowbar. Take the branches for weaving, trim them of any side branches and leaves with a small pruning saw and secateurs, and weave them in and out between the stakes, in the same manner as basket weaving. Ideally all the branches should be approximately the same diameter but, if not, weave the thicker branches first and then weave the thinner branches through to fill in any gaps. Trim the ends off neatly.

The elegant gardens at Ferme de Bois Richeux are among the finest medieval reconstructions and feature wattle garden retaining walls.

The garden saints

Working with nature, gardeners have always been aware of their own limitations when faced with droughts, clouds of insects, out of season frosts and diseases, A very special group of saints have been called on to assist with the efforts of the 'grubby ones' who dream of beautiful flowers, rich harvests and the song of birds while up to their elbows in dirt and manure. Such trials were shared by many holy men and women throughout the medieval period. For many centuries the lives of religious hermits and monks were inseparable from hard daily toil in the earth.

St Fiacre is generally accepted as the patron saint of gardeners, particularly in France, and of herb and vegetable gardens. Fiacre was born in Donegal, where he lived for the early part of his life. He left his native Ireland for France, and c. 628 arrived in the diocese of Meaux, where the bishop offered him as much land as he could surround with a furrow in one full day. It is said that Fiacre walked in prayer throughout that day, until he located land suitable for his needs.

A lateral thinker, Fiacre then used the tip of his crozier to dig the furrow, rather than, as the bishop had expected, a plough. Wherever the crozier touched, a great furrow miraculously appeared, boulders rolled out of the way and bushes uprooted themselves. He managed to acquire in twenty-four hours enough land to hold a very large monastery. A peasant woman, believing that she was witnessing the work of the devil, asked the bishop to come and see what was happening. The bishop, later to become St Faro, found Fiacre kneeling in prayer and remained true to his promise, giving him the land.

Fiacre cleared the land of brambles by more conventional means and built an oratory and a hospice that gave refuge, in particular, to the many impoverished Irish pilgrims who travelled to France. He surrounded the buildings with beautiful gardens and spent the rest of his life tending them. He was reputed to be very knowledgeable in the ways of herbs and their cultivation and was said to have performed many miraculous cures before he died in 670. He was particularly sought out for the cure of haemorrhoids, and it was said that a stone on which he had been in the habit of sitting brought relief and healing to those who sat on it.

Another saint honoured by the tillers of the earth is the gentle St Francis of Assisi, founder of the Franciscan Order and patron saint of the birds and animals that are part of garden life. It was said that wild birds would come to him completely unafraid. His favourite bird was the lark, 'for Sister Lark has a cowl like a religious'.

The patron saint of farmers and all toilers of the soil is St Isidore the Labourer, also known as St Isidore the Farmer. St Isidore (San Ysidro in Spanish) was born into poverty in Spain in 1070 and lived throughout his life near Madrid. He began work as a farm labourer but, being very devout, began each morning by attending Mass. As a result, he often arrived late at work and his fellow labourers finally complained to their master, Juan de Vargas, saying that Isidore was not shouldering his fair share of the work.

So the story goes, de Vargas hid in the woods one morning to watch. Isidore, as always, was late and de Vargas was about to reprove him when he saw an angel on either side of Isidore, ploughing the land with him so that his work

Giotto di Bondone,
St Francis Preaching to the Birds, 1296–97.
Getty Images

was that of more than three men. Not surprisingly, de Vargas did not dismiss him. Isidore worked several miracles for the de Vargas family, including raising their daughter from the dead, and was responsible for several miraculous cures. He died in 1130 and was canonised by Pope Gregory XV. St Isidore's feast day is the fifteenth of May and he is the patron saint of Madrid.

St Phocas was a Christian and a gardener who maintained a hospice at Sinope, beside the Black Sea, some time in the third or fourth century. Soldiers were sent from Rome with orders to kill him and, arriving at the hospice and not realising who their host was, they begged Phocas for food and overnight lodging. Phocas gave them food and water, and a bed for the night. On rising in the morning, they found Phocas, who identified himself. While they slept, he had dug his own grave and prayed throughout the night. With that devotion to duty rather than conscience that has been displayed too often throughout history, the soldiers slew him. The martyred St Phocas is honoured as a patron saint of gardeners, particularly those who create beautiful flower gardens, and of mariners. His feast day is the fourteenth of July. In the 1990s the remains of a fourth century church, thought to be the site of St Phocas's death, were discovered by English archaeologist Dr Stephen Hill. It is thought that the site was an early place of pilgrimage.

Other saints connected with gardeners are St Urban, the patron saint of vineyards and those who grow grapes; St Elizabeth of Hungary, patron saint of rose gardens; St Adelard, a patron saint of gardeners; St Dorothy, patron saint of orchards and fruit trees; and St Patrick, who has now been adopted as the patron saint of organic gardening. St Bernardo Abad is the patron saint of beekeepers.

Weather is all important to gardeners, and the weather saints are certainly significant in any garden saints' calendar. St Swithun is regarded as a weather saint in England. He was born in Wessex and became the Bishop of Winchester, honoured for his charity to the poor and for his deep humility. When he died in 862 he was buried at his own request where rain might fall on his grave. There is a belief in England that if it rains on St Swithun's Day, it will continue to rain for forty days. Similar beliefs are held for St Cewydd in Wales, and St Prostase and St Menard in France. If all else fails gardeners, perhaps they should turn to St Jude, patron saint of lost causes.

monasteries in the south of England, which were safer but by no means immune from these piratical attacks.

Many medieval monastic gardens are being recreated with great care for authenticity and it is possible to see how such gardens would have looked in the context of the original monastery. In England, the Reformation was responsible for the destruction of many monasteries and, apart from some cloister garths, no original gardens have fully survived. The restored gardens in Britain have often been constructed against a background of damaged facades, eyeless windows and tumbled stone. Examples include Melrose Abbey with Priorwood orchard in the Borders, Michelham Priory in Sussex, Peterborough Cathedral in Cambridgeshire, Stanbrook Abbey in Worcester, the physic garden of Burnham Abbey in Buckinghamshire, the exquisite orchard in a flowery meadow of Tymawr Convent in Gwent, Wales, and the cloister garden of haunted Beaulieu Abbey in Hampshire. However, the magnificent Glastonbury Abbey in Somerset has been laid down to a simple green sward and its once famous orchards, vineyards and herb and vegetable gardens must be imagined. The

abbey was sacked during the Reformation and the last abbot, heroic Richard Whiting, who defied the edict of Henry VIII, was dragged from the abbey and hung for treason on sacred Glastonbury Tor.

In France, many monasteries were destroyed or damaged during the Protestant Reformation. Others, such as the Cathar churches, were destroyed by instruments of the Church itself and still further damage was done during the French Revolution. Despite this, a remarkable number remain, in ruins or restored, and beautiful monastery gardens have been recreated, including the very fine gardens of the Priory of Notre-Dame d'Orsan with their superb design and authentic materials matched by impeccable taste, the Abbaye Royale de Fontevraud, the Abbaye de Vauclair, the Abbaye Royale de Chaalis, the Priory of Salagon, Rodemack in the Moselle, the charming little Abbaye de Valsaintes Boulinette near Simiane La Rotonde in the Alpes-de-Haute-Provence, the magnificent Abbey of Fontfroide near the Franco-Spanish border, Milly-la-Forêt, the monastery garden of Tusson and the medicinal herb garden of the Abbaye de Dignac, both of which are in the Charente.

Garden Design: The Sacrist's Garden

The Sacrist's garden was expected to supply the flowers for decorating the church and for religious festivals, as well as provide some of the fragrant herbs for the aisle of the church. Clove pinks were woven into coronets to be worn by priests during special feast days.

Lilies and roses were the first choice for ornamenting the altar and were rarely omitted from such gardens. A number of flowers dedicated to the Virgin Mary were also commonly included.

This design is both practical and ornamental with three rectangular circuits of brick pathway, each one metre wide to allow the gardens to be easily tended and for two people to walk abreast while conversing. The circuit paths are linked to each other by short paths that alternate their exit positions, inducing the user to move more slowly and to experience the entire garden. The use of recycled bricks in runner bond design emphasises the patterning of the design.

The entrance to the garden is through a clipped hedge of fragrant upright growing rosemary (varieties such as 'Portuguese Pink' with palest pink flowers and reaching 1.8 m (6 ft), 'Herb Cottage' with very rich deep blue flowers and compact form, and 'Salem' with its equally compact growth habit, reaching a height of 1.5 m (5 ft) with prolific pale blue flowers are ideal). Add lime or dolomite to the soil when planting, unless your soil is already alkaline. In areas with cold winters where rosemary may be affected, a hedge of flowering quince would be suitable, and it flowers well despite regular trimming. The exit to the garden is through a hedge of Alba roses, a mixture of the White Rose of York *R. alba* 'Semiplena' and the Jacobite Rose *R. alba* 'Maxima'.

The sides of the garden might be edged in various ways. A square patterned pole fence would be suitable, or alternatively in a more rustic fashion a wattle fence. A diamond patterned live willow fence would provide another authentic alternative, and one with considerable elegance.

The plants included in the metre wide beds include china blue flowered chicory, deep blue flowered borage, Florentine iris, and English lavender (in mild to warm climate areas substitute with *Lavendula* x *intermedia* (lavandin) varieties such a 'Grosso', 'Seal', 'Super, or 'Provence', or if preferred the white lavender *L.* x *intermedia* 'Alba' or 'Dutch White' with their high sweet fragrance notes. Other plantings include Mary's Gold or Pot Marigold used for ornamental, medicinal, and culinary purposes, fennel, tansy, milfoil yarrow, clove pinks, sage, hyssop, spearmint, garden thyme (used here as a clipped garden edging), Madonna lilies, and *Rosa gallica* 'Officinalis' (Red Rose of Lancaster).

Medieval medicine

The care of the sick often fell upon the shoulders of the abbess, and Hildegard was not unusual in her care of both religious and laity. During the medieval period, medicine relied heavily on the medical texts of the classical world. The writings of Hippocrates of Kos (c. 460–370 BC) offered endearingly sane, holistically based advice on healthy lifestyles that would win considerable approval today. His wisdom and ethical principles were handed down through the centuries to another Greek, Galen (AD 129–c. 216), who included many of Hippocrates' ideas in his own books, which were to be the standard medical texts of Europe until the Renaissance.

Galen synthesised knowledge from several sources, and enlarged his knowledge considerably when he practised in the famous medical school at Alexandria in Egypt. There he adopted a system that included astrology and numerology. This led him to link the prevailing theory of four bodily humours (blood, phlegm, yellow bile and black bile) to the four elemental forces of the alchemists (fire, air, earth and water) and the effects of the four seasons. Fortunately Hippocrates' sound advice was also evident in the emphasis placed by medieval doctors on preventative medicine, such as a balanced and restrained diet, regular exercise, moderation and a healthy environment.

Galen's astrologically influenced medicine was slow to fall into disuse. Even in the seventeenth century, the herbalist Nicholas Culpepper placed great reliance on astrological prognostications in his famous books *The Complete Herbal* and *English Physician*, although in fairness many of his more eccentric ideas were greeted with widespread scepticism by the majority of the medical fraternity of his day.

One of the most authoritative herbal texts for medieval physicians was *De Materia Medica* written in AD 64 by Dioscorides. A Sicilian of Greek extraction, Dioscorides is believed to have been a doctor in the army of the Emperor Nero. His book contains descriptions and uses for over five hundred plants and was considered an essential reference for over fifteen hundred years. It was Dioscorides who was responsible for the long upheld Doctrine of Signatures, a belief that the form of a plant or plant part mimics the part of the body it will cure. Another important reference for medieval doctors was the botanical work of Theophrastus (c. 372–287 BC).

Medieval texts on aspects of medicine were written in Latin. This was no barrier for a well-educated abbess, but it did exclude the great majority of women who would have had no access to a Latin education. From the fifteenth century onwards English translations of medical treatises became increasingly available, and there are a number of records of women who became adept at preparing healing waters, salves, plasters (poultices) and other medicines found in the classical texts for their households and neighbours, and even for the royal household.

The healing system employed by Abbess Hildegard was derived from visionary messages. It stands outside the Galen school in many ways. She speaks of harmonising the four states of hot, cold, moist and dry, a belief reminiscent of the Chinese medical school, and placed her reliance on the plant world and the 'subtleties', or healing powers, of different plant species. Hildegard often used the term *viriditas* with respect to foods. The word literally translates as 'greenness' but anyone versed in New Age thinking would recognise her meaning to be 'life force'.

Hildegard undoubtedly had some beliefs that we would find strange today, but harmonisation of foods in the diet, the concept of foods that are mood altering and the idea of consuming foods with high levels of life force (raw foods) have some remarkably modern resonances and are backed by current research. Should you be tempted to try some of Hildegard's foods to promote a positive outlook, they included spelt wheat, oats, almonds, chestnuts, fennel, mint and parsley.

The Glastonbury Thorn

Many medieval abbeys housed sacred relics such as the bones or garments of saints, not all of impeccable authenticity. These became a focus of veneration by pilgrims, and the nobility not infrequently endowed the abbeys that held them with wealth and additional lands. However, very few abbeys have claimed a herbal plant as a sacred relic. The 'Glastonbury Thorn', or 'Holy Thorn of Glastonbury' held at Glastonbury Abbey in Somerset, England, has a fascinating story. Botanically it is a species of hawthorn (*Crataegus monogyna* 'Biflora'), but unlike the common hawthorn, which flowers around May Day, the Glastonbury Thorn flowers twice, once at Christmas and the second time in May. Every Christmas, sprays of flowers are cut from the Glastonbury Thorn and sent to Queen Elizabeth as an adornment for the royal table.

According to a story that has persisted for a very long time, after Christ's resurrection a group of His followers, led by Joseph of Arimathaea, fled from the Near East. This story is supported by accounts in early, but not contemporary, manuscripts such as that of Rabanus Maurus, Archbishop of Mayence, who lived from 766 to 856, as well as those of later chroniclers such as John Hardyng, in the late fourteenth and early fifteenth centuries.

The story also appears in the account prepared by the careful twelfth century historian William of Malmesbury, who stated that he based it on manuscripts he found preserved at Glastonbury. These were later destroyed, together with the original abbey buildings, in the fire of 1184. Glastonbury Abbey was rebuilt by King Henry II and was finally destroyed by fire

The Holy Thorn of Glastonbury flowers twice yearly, at Christmas and in May. The tree photographed here in the garden of Chalice Well is said to be a descendant of a miraculous thorn tree which grew from the staff of Joseph of Arimathaea, planted in the ground of Wearyall Hill.

The herbal rose

The Gallica Rose grows wild from central southern Europe through to the Caucasus and Turkey and usually has large, single, pink, fragrant flowers with golden stamens. It was described by Pliny in Italy in AD 79 under the name of Rose of Miletus, and it is thought to have reached Italy on Ionian vessels from the west coast of Turkey. In France, it acquired the names of *Rosa rubra* and the French Rose.

In the Minoan palace of Knossos in Crete, a rose painted in a frieze dating to approximately 2000 BC has long fascinated plant historians. This Minoan Rose, frozen in time, strongly resembles the rose that is now known as the Abyssinian Rose or St John's Rose, with exquisitely formed single, pale pink flowers. It was classified as *Rosa sancta* in the past, but botanists have renamed it *R. x richardii*, realising that it was not a separate species but a natural hybrid of the wild Gallica Rose.

There is a story that the ancient Abyssinian Rose, or Holy Rose, acquired its name when it was taken from Phoenicia to Abyssinia by St Frumentius in the fourth century AD. Phoenicia, occupying more or less the area of modern Lebanon, was home to one of the greatest seafaring and trading cultures, and the Phoenicians established colonial outposts along their shipping routes, which extended as far as the British Isles, a source of tin. The name 'Phoenician' means 'dealer in purple' and refers to the extremely profitable trade in the purple dye sourced from the *Murex* sea snail.

St Frumentius built monasteries and churches in the Phoenician outposts within Abyssinia, and the Holy Rose was extensively planted throughout his diocese.

Dried rose flowers closely resembling those of the Holy Rose have also been discovered in Egypt, twisted into chaplets placed on the heads of mummies.

The Gallica Rose 'Officinalis' is almost certainly the oldest horticultural variety of the Gallica Rose still in cultivation. Thibaut de Champagne is said to have taken it from Damascus to France in the thirteenth century, and it was for him that the rose gained another name, the Champagne Rose. The famous altarpiece created for Ghent Cathedral c. 1430 clearly depicts this rose.

'Officinalis' (the name refers to its officially sanctioned use in medicine) is also known as the Apothecary's Rose. It has petals that retain their fragrance long after drying, and which are astringent, antiseptic and contain Vitamin C. The town of Provins, south-east of Paris, was famous for almost 600 years from the thirteenth century onwards for its vast fields of fragrant red 'Officinalis' roses, and as the exceedingly busy centre for

The beautiful Gallica Rose 'Officinalis' was taken to France from Damascus in the thirteenth century.

present from the people of Provins, France, in 1967. John of Gaunt was the last member of the dynasty to live at Bolingbroke and his son, the future Henry IV, was born in the castle in 1366.

'Officinalis' was the rose planted in virtually every monastic herbal garden on the Continent and in England, as much for its fragrance and beauty as for its considerable usefulness in herbal medicine. John Gerard listed seventeen separate uses for 'Officinalis', including staunching blood in any part of the body. Avicenna used daily doses of a conserve of the red rose petals to treat the 'spitting disease', tuberculosis, and recorded successful cures.

This red rose was also dedicated to the Virgin Mary and was used to decorate the church in summer.

trade in a remarkable range of medicinal, fragrance and beauty products made from the petals. One of the most famous customers of Provins was a young Marie-Antoinette, who requested an overnight stay in Nancy, near Provins, on her way to marry the Dauphin, later Louis XVI. In addition to her many purchases, the town of Provins gave the couple a marriage bed made entirely of rose petals.

In England this ancient rose was to gain another name. It was adopted by Edmund, Earl of Lancaster, as his emblem in 1280 and was then incorporated into the arms of the Duchy of Lancaster, thus becoming. As a result, the rose also became known as the Red Rose of Lancaster. A current planting near the remains of Bolingbroke Castle, which passed to the House of Lancaster in 1311, was a in 1539, on the command of King Henry VIII.

The story of those who embarked with Joseph and settled in Provence, including Mary Magdalene, is told in Chapter 5. However, in AD 63 Joseph is said to have travelled on, at the bidding of St Philip, to Britain. Joseph had been a merchant trading in tin from Cornwall and would have been familiar with the south-west of England. It is said that he took with him twelve disciples and they made landfall in Somerset. Sea walls, canals and pumps have progressively reclaimed the rich land of the Somerset levels, or 'summer country', from the sea during the last fifteen hundred years, but at that time it was tidal marshland. A small area of higher land, joined to four hills, rose above the marshes and made up an island known as Avalon, or the Isle of Apples, an island of enchantment in Celtic lore. This mystical place had become a prominent Celtic centre and well-known trading site. The highest of the hills is Glastonbury Tor, today crowned with the ruins of a church dedicated to the Archangel Michael.

The River Brue provided a deepwater passage through the marsh to Avalon, and Joseph made landfall on Wearyall Hill, a ridge projecting towards the Bristol Channel. He stuck his staff, cut from a hawthorn, into the soil before gratefully lying down to rest. When the travellers rose the next morning, the staff had taken root and blossomed. Joseph left his flowering staff there on Wearyall Hill and over many centuries it grew into a massive shrub.

The company lived good and sober lives as a community of hermits and when they approached the local king, Arviragus (or Caractacus), asking for a grant of twelve hides of land free of tax on the border of his kingdom at Yniswitrin (Glastonbury), their request was granted. The land was a considerable grant despite the marshy conditions. It was here that they built their first church, from osiers wattled together. It is said that the remains of the wattle church still lie beneath the foundations of the great Glastonbury Abbey. The gift of the land, tax-free, was later recorded in the Domesday Book. According to the story, King Arviragus was eventually converted to Christianity.

The Holy Thorn on Wearyall Hill was again mentioned in 1535 in

The remains of a church dedicated to Archangel Michael and largely destroyed by earthquake stand on Glastonbury Tor.

The healing waters of Chalice Well emerge from the lion's head fountain at the foot of Glastonbury Tor.

a letter written by Thomas Cromwell, Earl of Essex. In 1653 during the Civil War the tree was reputedly cut down by a fanatical Parliamentarian soldier, and some variations of the story relate that a retaliatory chip of wood hit him in the eye. Fortunately, by that time the tree had been frequently propagated from cuttings. A number of these plants survive. One grows again on Wearyall Hill, one is in the magical gardens of Chalice Well and one is in the gardens of the parish church of St John the Baptist. Each continues to bloom at Christmas and in May.

It has long been said that there were two Christian missions to Britain, one by pre-Roman Christians, the other by Romano-Christians. The earliest surviving manuscript reference, by Tertullian (AD 155–222), states that Britain had already received and accepted the gospel at the time in which he wrote, and Jacob Sabellus wrote c. AD 250 that the first nation to proclaim itself Christian was Britain. This would argue, even if conversion to the faith had been very rapid, for the introduction of Christianity into Britain in the era associated with Joseph of Arimathaea.

There have been theological arguments from time to time as to the seniority of the national Christian churches, with claims coming from France and Spain, yet many ancient manuscripts yield that honour to Britain. Eusebius, Bishop of Caesarea, who lived from 300 to 376, wrote that 'the Apostles passed beyond the ocean to the isles called the Britannic Isles'. St John Chrysostom of Constantinople and St Hilary of Poitiers (300–376) both recorded similar accounts, and the Councils of Pisa (1409),

Constance (1417), Siena (1424) and Basle (1434) all led to the declaration that the Church was founded in Britain immediately after the Passion of Christ.

The majority of historians today dismiss the entire story of Joseph in Britain and maintain that the first conversion of the Celts was by Columba, who travelled from Ireland to Iona. Priests trained at Iona then Christianised ancient Northumbria and Mercia. There is undoubted evidence to confirm Columba's role, but it does not necessarily negate the story of Joseph on the then coast of south-western Britain. In the next stage of the Christianisation of Britain St Augustine was sent from Rome and in 597 landed in Kent. Interestingly, he wrote of a Christian church that already existed in western Britain, on a royal island surrounded by water. Was he writing of Glastonbury, a royal island then surrounded by water?

At the very least, the story of Joseph and the twice-flowering Holy Thorn adds a wonderful dimension to the already magical qualities of the landscape of Avalon, its associations with King Arthur and his queen, Guinevere, and the magnificent medieval ruins of the famed Glastonbury Abbey. If you choose to believe, you are in very good company.

As for the famous Thorn, twice-flowering forms of *Crataegus monogyna* are known to occur in the Near East in places such as Lebanon. This Eastern form of the common hawthorn differs from the native hawthorn of England in leafing out very early and flowering twice yearly, in December and in early spring.

A herbal of medieval physic plants

The main duties of the herbalist in a monastery consisted of planting and managing medicinal crops, as well as supervising the harvesting of herbs and their processing.

Other ingredients for the infirmary were gathered from the countryside. Herbs gathered wild often contain concentrated active principles because of the tough conditions under which they grow and they often come from less contaminated environments. Sage, lavender, fennel, mallow, thyme, wild strawberry, savory,

melissa, hyssop, lichens, hawthorn, White Willow, Blessed Thistle, Greater Plantain, bramble, meadowsweet, soapwort, agrimony and yarrow were among the herbs that might be gathered wild, together with narcotics such as henbane, mandrake and hemlock to be used as painkillers.

Many medicinal herbs have quiet charms in their fragrance and flowers, and the physic garden was not only practical but offered simple, orderly beauty and a place to rest the

spirit and breathe the beneficial air. Such a garden was sometimes called a *cordon sanitaire*, and there was a widespread belief in medieval times that the scents of sweet-smelling herbs and flowers were health preserving. John Malvern, Bishop Physician to Henry VI, for instance, advised filling the house with sweet herbs such as mint, fennel and bay, as well as violets and roses, to ward off plague. The essential oils in some of these plants do indeed have antibacterial properties, and the immune system would have been enhanced by the pleasure and tranquillity of fragrant herbs and gardens.

AGRIMONY, CHURCH STEEPLES or STICKLEWORT (*Agrimonia eupatoria*): Agrimony was used by the Anglo-Saxons for treating wounds, but in Chaucer's time it was used to treat bubonic plague. Pliny used it steeped in wine for dysentery, and it was also used to stimulate liver activity.

A pharmacy in the cloister of the Franciscan monastery, Dubrovnik, in use since 1317.

Agrimony tea, with its astringent action, was used to treat sore throats. The plant has compound leaves and long spikes of tiny yellow flowers, and the whole plant smells faintly of apricots.

ALEXANDERS (*Smyrnium olusatum*): This herb supposedly originated in Alexandria and was introduced to Western Europe during the Roman period. It has been referred to as the 'rock parsley of Alexandria', and all parts were boiled to promote the appetite of the ill and elderly.

ALOE or ALOE VERA (*Aloe barbadensis*): Aristotle is said to have requested Alexander the Great to conquer the island of Socotra and install Greeks on it, in order to access the precious aloe plants that grew there. The fresh juice has long been used to help heal burns

and regenerate skin tissue. The gel that oozes from the broken leaf contains the active substance allantoin. The plant is a succulent that forms rosettes of thick, spiky, pale green leaves with paler spots.

ANGELICA or ROOT OF THE HOLY GHOST (*Angelica archangelica*): This tall, dramatic herb has bright green, ferny leaves and huge umbellate inflorescences of tiny lemon to white flowers. Every part of the plant has a clean, sweet scent, and candied angelica is made from the petioles of the leaves. John Parkinson, writing in 1629, rated angelica as the most valuable of all herbs. Its reputation came from its use as an anti-plague medicine, a use supposedly revealed by the Archangel Gabriel to a monk in Niort, which was being ravaged by plague at the time. Angelica was also used for

gastrointestinal tract problems and loss of appetite, and it was included in many medieval liqueurs. It has been in cultivation since the twelfth century. Angelica has also been used to soothe aches and pains, including those of rheumatism, influenza and migraine, and in the treatment of colds and coughs.

APPLE (*Malus domesticus*): Apples had a reputation as something of a cure-all in the medieval period. The fruit was used, cooked or raw, to aid digestion, reduce stomach acidity and treat constipation. A decoction of the bark was used to treat fevers. Rotten apples were applied as a poultice bound onto sore eyes. A similar country remedy is still used today, although it is now stewed fruit that is used for a poultice. According to John Gerard, in his herbal of

1633, pomatum was a popular, commercially available facial treatment designed to soften the skin and fade freckles. It was compounded from rosewater, apple pulp and swine's grease. The crab apple (*M. sylvestris*) was used in much the same way as apple.

BALM, BEE BALM or LEMON BALM (*Melissa officinalis*): This plant, native to southern Europe, was recognised by the ancient Greeks for its calming effects and was usually administered as an infusion in wine. It was used to counter depression. Culpepper, in his seventeenth century herbal, echoed this use, saying that it 'causeth the mind and heart to be Merry ... and driveth away all troublesome cares'. It is still used in modern aromatherapy for that purpose. The plant resembles mint, but with a fresh, strong, lemon scent. It is

both antibacterial and antiviral in activity, and it improves digestion when used as a tea made from the fresh or dried leaves. It is one of the most important bee plants. Bee-keepers knew in the medieval period that rubbing a new hive with balm would calm bees down so that a newly captured swarm would settle there.

BETONY, WOUNDWORT or BISHOPWORT (*Stachys officinalis*): Betony was one of the 'magic bullets' of medieval medicine. One Italian proverb optimistically advised, 'Sell your coat and buy betony'. Antonius Musa, the physician to Emperor Augustus, claimed that it cured forty-seven different disorders, but it is difficult to know why its reputation grew to such a degree. It is regarded today as an astringent bitter, and the tea is used to treat sore throats and urinary tract infections. In the medieval period it was used to calm patients with nervous complaints, and as a remedy for those with hives and eczema. Betony was commonly planted in monastery gardens.

BIRTHWORT or COBRA'S PLANT (*Aristolochia clematitis*): This plant is endemic in the Mediterranean, and the juice from the stems was used both as an abortifacient and as a birthing herb. It was introduced into England (where it is now rare) during the medieval period by the monastic community. It is a tall, rhizomatous herb with smooth-edged, heart-shaped leaves and clusters of small, yellow, pipe-shaped flowers borne in the leaf axils. It favours moist soil and can still be found on some monastic sites in England, including Godstowe Nunnery near Oxford, founded in 1130. The herb also had a reputation for relieving flatulence, as a cure for skin infections and animal bites, including those of snakes (it is known as *le serpentaire* in France), as a treatment for rheumatism, gout and tumours, as a poison antidote, and even as a means of repelling demons.

BISTORT, SNAKE ROOT, ADDERWORT or GOOSE-GRASS (*Polygonum bistorta*): The snake-like rhizomes of this knotweed led to some of its common names and, by sympathetic magic, its use against snake bite. A number of its old country names, such as Easter Ledges and Passion Dock, refer to its use in a special pudding during the last two weeks of Easter, which is known as Passion-tide. The young shoots were also boiled as a vegetable. Bistort was believed to aid both in conceiving and in giving birth.

BLACKTHORN or SLOE (*Prunus spinosa*): Sloes were common in Europe and Britain and were employed to make cattle-proof hedges. The dark blue, small, round fruits are very astringent when raw but were used to make wine, verjuice, jams and jellies. The wine is a gentle diuretic, while the jam is useful for dyspepsia, and for mild infections of the mouth and throat. A tea made from the flowers was used as a gentle herbal laxative, to stimulate the appetite and for mild bladder infections. The bark has sedative properties. Both the leaves and the fruit preserves were used as blood purifiers in spring.

BORAGE (*Borago officinalis*): The beautiful, star-shaped, rich blue (or rarely pure white) flowers of borage were associated from the time of Pliny with a happy outlook and were used as a cure for melancholia, often by adding it to wine. Gerard wrote of it, 'The leaves and floures of Borage put into wine make men and women glad and merry, driving away all sadness, dulness, and melancholy', and a very old proverb said, 'I Borage bring alwaies courage'. The flowers are very attractive to bees, and the borage flower, together with a bee, was one of the motifs often embroidered on scarves by the wives and sweethearts of knights. It was also used as a diuretic tea and to increase the flow of milk for nursing mothers. The young leaves smell and taste of cucumber and in medieval times were used in salads.

BRAMBLE or BLACKBERRY (*Rubus fruticosus*): The leaves of blackberry were used as a gentle astringent tea to treat diarrhoea and dysentery. The leaves were also used to staunch bleeding, as a poultice on burns and ulcers, as a gargle for sore throats, and as a remedy for bleeding gums. A tea made from the roots was used for dropsy. The fruits were eaten both fresh and cooked, in pies and tarts, jams and jellies, and were fermented for wine.

BUGLE or CARPENTER'S HERB (*Ajuga reptans*): Bugle found particular use in staunching cuts, hence its association with carpenters. The apothecaries knew this herb as *bugula*. The plant contains tannins, is astringent in action and was also used for the treatment of coughs. With its many dense spikes of rich blue-lipped flowers, it is a popular ground covering plant for lightly shaded areas.

BURDOCK, GREATER BURDOCK or BEGGARS BUTTONS (*Arctium lappa*): Burdock roots were used in the medieval period for breaking stubborn fevers, treating leprosy, boils and eczema, as a blood purifier and

to improve resistance to colds. Culpepper, echoing older beliefs, recommended wine in which the seed had been soaked for the treatment of sciatica. The leaves were applied externally as a poultice for the treatment of bruises and ulcerated skin. The roots were cooked as a vegetable or used in making ale, and the young stems were cooked or candied like angelica. Modern research has confirmed that burdock has antibiotic properties, strengthens the immune system and has value in treating skin diseases, including eczema and psoriasis.

CHAMOMILE (*Chamaemelum nobile*): Chamomile was used by the Greeks and has been in continuous use as a medicinal herb ever since. All parts of this ground-hugging perennial plant with finely divided, fresh green leaves and daisy-like white flowers smell of green

apples. The double flowered form is also grown for herbal use. Tea made from the flowers is used to relieve dyspepsia, as a mild sedative and to treat nausea and vomiting.

CHASTE TREE, MONKS' PEPPER or CLOISTER PEPPER (*Vitex agnus-castus*): This beautiful tall shrub is indigenous to the Mediterranean region and Central Asia. It flowers in summer, when the plant is smothered in multiple-headed spikes of lavender (very rarely white) flowers that are very attractive to bees. In cold areas it will often die down to the ground each winter. The Greeks believed the plant calmed sexual passions, and the peppery fruits were nibbled by monks to still dangerously wandering minds. Both Hippocrates and later Dioscorides recommended sitz baths of *Vitex* for problems associated with the uterus and this use was continued through the medieval period. Scientific research in the twentieth century demonstrated that *Vitex* has a regulatory effect on oestrogen and progesterone. The closely related and even more floriferous *V. negundo* is also used in herbal medicine for coughs, fevers and as an expectorant.

CHICKWEED or HEN'S BITE (*Stellaria media*): Chickweed is a very modest member of the carnation family and was an ingredient in spring salads to clean the blood. It was known to medieval apothecaries as *morsus gallinae*. It was then, and remains, a favourite treat for domestic poultry, especially in winter when it continues to flourish. Gerard added that 'Little birds in cadges (especially Linnets) are refreshed with the Lesser Chickweed when they loath their meet whereupon it was called of some "Passerinæ"'. Pigs and rabbits share this same passion. Chickweed was applied as a poultice and in salves for painful rheumatic

joints and was particularly useful for itchy rashes, festering insect bites and sores. It has recently been shown to have antihistamine effects. Taken internally, it has been used for chest infections, to relieve constipation and for some kidney problems. It should not be taken internally during pregnancy. Hairy, Mouse-ear or Star Chickweed (*Cerastium vulgatum*) is remotely related botanically and has been used in skin salves.

CHICORY, SUCCORY or WILD SUCCORY (*Cichorum intybus*): This is a deep-rooted perennial with a profusion of exquisite china-blue daisy flowers in late summer to late autumn. From the Roman period onwards, the blanched leaves have been used as a popular salad addition, their slight bitterness being considered good for promoting the appetite and digestion. It was said that they had 'vertue to coole the hot burning of the liver ... and helpe the yellow jaundice'. The root was also boiled to yield a broth to aid digestion.

CINQUEFOIL (*Potentilla* spp.): A number of species of *Potentilla* were used in medieval medicine. Silverweed (*P. anserina*) has soft, silvery leaves and single, golden-yellow flowers on a ground-hugging plant. It was used to treat cuts and wounds, to relieve mouth ulcers and sore throats, and for indigestion. Common Tormentil (*P. erecta*) is powerfully astringent and was considered an effective remedy for severe diarrhoea, staunching cuts and abrasions, healing burns and sunburn, and as a gargle in relieving sore throats. Creeping Tormentil (*P. reptans*) found comparable uses.

CLARY SAGE, CLEAR EYE or SEE BRIGHT (*Salvia sclarea*): This plant is native to southern France and Italy, forming a large rough-leafed rosette of leaves from which emerge spectacular spikes of flowers with showy pink bracts. The plant, now grown for its essential oil for perfumery and aromatherapy, smells of muscatel and grapefruit. The Germans called it *Muskateller Salbei*, or muscatel sage. It was used for painful wind and disordered digestion, and in the form of a ground mucilaginous paste of the seeds was applied as a poultice to draw out embedded thorns and splinters. The seeds, which are very high in mucilage, were also used to clear the eyes of gritty dust. To bring boils to a head, Culpepper recommended a salve made by boiling leaves in vinegar and then adding sufficient honey to make a paste. A wine was also prepared from the whole plant. It had a muscatel-like scent, but clary ale apparently caused remarkable inebriation. Vervain Sage or wild English Clary (*S. verbenacea*), also known as Christ's Eye and Oculus Christi, is less spectacular, with long spikes of purple-blue flowers. Culpepper advised using a decoction of its leaves for the digestion, and its distilled water to strengthen the

eyesight, particularly of the elderly, saying it 'cleaneth the eyes of redness waterishness and heat'.

CLOVE PINKS or GILLIFLOWERS (*Dianthus plumarius*): The clove pink, with its delicious clove spice fragrance and profusion of small carnation-like flowers, was grown as much for pleasure as for practical reasons, but it was used to reduce both fevers and the raging thirst that accompanies them. These plants were also used to add clove flavouring to mulled ales and spices.

COLUMBINE, CULVERWORT or HERBA LIONIS (*Aquilegia vulgaris*): Columbines, particularly their seeds, are poisonous if ingested. This was one of the herbs prescribed during the medieval period for curing the plague, probably because of its association with

the Holy Spirit, as the flowers resemble doves around a bowl. It was also used in cures for sore mouths and throats, in retrospect not at all advisable, and externally for skin diseases. Columbine is no longer used at all internally. The roots are still occasionally used to treat skin ulcers.

COMFREY, KNITBONE or SARACEN'S ROOT (*Symphytum officinale*): Comfrey was a very important herb used in treating broken bones. It contains a compound, allantoin, that encourages rapid healing by accelerating cell proliferation. This was probably the *symphyton* discussed by Dioscorides. Its medieval name was *consolidae maioris*. Gerard wrote of it: 'A salve concocted from the fresh herb will certainly tend to promote healing of bruised and broken parts.' It was also used to promote healing of burns, wounds that healed slowly and ulcers. Comfrey was also an important animal feed, high in protein.

COMMON MALLOW (*Malva sylvestris*): Mallow has much the same properties as Marshmallow. The young leaves, seed cases (cheeses) and petals were used in salads. Romans cultivated mallow in their gardens where the beautiful, purple-striped, lilac-pink flowers would have added beauty. The leaves, flowers and sometimes the roots were used for their emollient properties in soothing lotions and salves for the skin, to relieve irritating coughs and as a mild laxative.

CORNFLOWER or BACHELOR'S BUTTONS (*Centaurea cyanus*): In medieval times, cornflowers were common in the cornfields, along with scarlet poppies, but mechanisation and weedicides have taken their toll. A decoction of the flowers is mildly astringent and was used to relieve eye strain. It was one of many herbs used against the plague, as an antidote to poisons, to reduce fever, as a diuretic, and was also used to treat inflammation.

COSTMARY, ALECOST, MACE, BIBLE-LEAF or BALSAM HERB (*Chrysanthemum balsamita*): Costmary is an ancient herb with a very pleasant, sweet mint and balsam scent. In the medieval period it was popular as a flavouring agent in the making of ales, but it was also cultivated in gardens for its medicinal value in settling upset stomachs and was incorporated into salves for insect bites and burns.

DILL or DILLWEED (*Anethum graveolens*): Apart from its culinary uses in flavouring fish, soup, cakes and pickles, particularly in Scandinavia, dill has for many centuries had widespread use as dill water, which gently relieves wind in children. The deep green, thread-like leaves (dillweed) were added to salads and sauces (particularly to accompany fish), and the seeds were popular for pickling.

ELECAMPANE, SCABWORT or ENULA (*Inula helenium*): Elecampane is a tall, attractive perennial that in summer has plentiful, large, golden flowers, bearing a resemblance to ragged-petalled sunflowers. It was used, usually in candied form, for treating coughs and bronchitis, as an appetite stimulant after illness and as a treatment for skin diseases, including 'scabbiness'. It was one of the Anglo-Saxon herbs of magic.

FENNEL (*Foeniculum vulgare*): In the monastic diet, rich in beans and pulses, fennel was a blessing for treating stomach aches and flatulence, and the seeds were nibbled to relieve the pangs of hunger on fasting days. If regularly eaten, it was also reputed to increase both longevity and strength, as well as improve memory. It was added to gripe water for babies, the seeds were added to liqueurs and an eye-wash of fennel was used to strengthen the eyes. Culpepper recommended it for treating the bite of serpents, and also for poisoning from toadstools and toxic plants. Its aniseed flavour was added to soups, sauces (particularly for fish), stuffing and stews, as well as salads, bread and pies. Fennel broth, made from the whole plant, was used for slimming, and a fennel and honey facial was recommended in the medieval period to soften wrinkles.

FEVERFEW (*Tanacetum parthenium* syn. *Chrysanthemun parthenium*): Feverfew is native to south-eastern Europe and it appears to have been used there to break fevers. Its flattish clusters of simple daisy-like white flowers have all the freshness and innocence of a gingham fabric. The dark green, ferny leaves are very bitter but interest has been revived in this old herb as a treatment for migraine, and to relieve facial neuralgia. Gerard said it was 'good for such as be melancholike, sad, pensive and without speech'.

It has also been gathering interest for normalising menstrual cycles and should not be used during pregnancy.

FIELD POPPY, CORN POPPY or FLANDERS POPPY (*Papaver rhoeas*): This red-flowered poppy is widely distributed across Europe and the Near East, as well as Asia. The flowers have a sedative effect and were used to calm anxiety and treat colic. The closely related *P. dubium* found similar uses. The seed was sprinkled over breads and cakes.

FLORENTINE IRIS or ORRIS (*Iris germanica* var. *florentina*): The beautiful Florentine iris grows prolifically over the hillsides of Tuscany, the white-flowered form being associated with the medieval city of Florence. The flowers often figured in medieval manuscripts and tapestries. The rhizomes are

dug, dried and stored for a period of time before crushing to a violet-scented powder used since ancient times in perfumery. Orris is a term also applied to *I. pallida* and *I. germanica*. Florentine iris was used to treat bronchitis and asthma, and it was an ingredient in various recipes for eau de vie. The fresh juice of the rhizome was used as a quite violent purgative.

GOOSE GRASS or CLEAVERS (*Galium aparine*): This plant was popularly used in salves to staunch and heal wounds and grazes, sores, burns, ulcers and skin inflammation. It was also one of the spring herbs for purifying the blood, usually served in soup.

GREATER CELANDINE (*Chelidonium majus*): This is one of those plants regularly encountered in the wasteland around ancient monasteries, where it was once grown in physic gardens. It has soft, fern-like foliage and small flowers resembling golden poppies. It was used medicinally for inflammations of the biliary duct and gall bladder. When broken, the stem exudes an acrid, yellow latex, which was mixed with vinegar to cure warts.

GREATER PLANTAIN, HEALING BLADE, JOHNSMAS FLOWERS or WAYBREAD (*Plantago major*): Plantain was one of the herbs mentioned in the Anglo-Saxon 'Charm of the Nine Herbs'. It is a herb of mixed magical and medicinal use, a herb of divination and one of the herbs of St John's Eve. With its powerful associations in pre-Christian magic, not surprisingly it was renamed for St Patrick in Ireland (Patrick's Leaf) and became Christ's Heel in Wales. It was used in salves and poultices for bruises, bites, ulcers and skin infections. It was also used as an eye-wash, particularly for conjunctivitis. Internally, the leaves were used in the treatment of diarrhoea, to control bleeding and for coughs.

Plantain has been found to have bacteriostatic activity, to stimulate healing of the skin, and to be astringent. The spring leaves were used as a potherb. While the Greater Plantain is a common weed, the Rose Plantain is an ancient and quaintly beautiful form of the species with inflorescences resembling green roses and having similar herbal properties.

HAWTHORN, MAY BUSH or QUICKTHORN (*Crataegus monogyna, C. oxycantha*): Hawthorn has long found service in medicine. The ripe haws were used as an effective tonic for the heart and circulatory system. The haws and flowers are astringent and have been used in a decoction as a gargle for sore throats. They were also used as a diuretic for dropsy and kidney problems. Culpepper recommended that the seeds in the berries be ground to a powder and administered in wine for kidney stones and dropsy. Pliny advised women to take the flowers in wine to assist conception 'within forty days'.

HEARTSEASE or HERBA TRINITATIS (*Viola tricolor*): This pretty annual found uses in purifying the blood, in treating fevers and for indigestion. A lotion made with Heartsease was used to heal sores and ulcers, and according to Gerard it was 'good for such as are sick of the ague, especially children and infants'. It contains salicylates and rutins, which account for its uses.

HEATHER (*Calluna vulgaris*): This beautiful, honey-rich, lilac-pink subshrub is found on the high moorlands in Britain. In the medieval period it was used as a herbal medicine for urinary tract and kidney infections, and as a mild sedative. The honey from heather, a plant very attractive to bees, was thought to contain some of the same valuable properties. Heather found additional use in thatching.

HELLEBORE or CHRISTMAS ROSE (*Helleborus niger*): Also known as Melampode and Christe Herbe, the beautiful hellebores find very little use other than in homeopathy now, but in the medieval period the dried rootstock was used as a purgative and also to treat various skin problems. In powdered form it was incorporated into snuff. Parkinson said that 'purgation of black hellebor is good for mad and furious men'. Certainly it would have kept them otherwise occupied. All parts are very poisonous and the plants contain cardiac glycosides. Closely related species, such as Green Hellebore (*H. viridis*) and Stinking Hellebore (*H. foetidus*) were used in the same way.

HEMP (*Cannabis sativa*): In the medieval period, long before the modern demonisation of marijuana, hemp was extensively grown, not only as an excellent fibre crop for everything from rope to paper, sailcloth and 'hempen homespun', a very hardwearing clothing fabric, but also for its extensive medicinal uses. It was widely cultivated in monastic gardens for use in melancholia, pain relief (particularly in gout, arthritis and rheumatism), as a sedative and to relieve facial tics and other muscle spasms.

HONEYSUCKLE or WOODBINE (*Lonicera periclymenum*): This is the wild pink- and cream-flowered honeysuckle of English hedgerows and has a glorious rich fragrance that intensifies and becomes more ethereal at night. In the medieval period it was a favourite climbing plant to train over arbours and covered alleys and was named for the fact that children enjoy sucking nectar from the blossoms. The stems contain salicylic acid and were used to treat aching muscles, inflammation, infections and fevers. Gerard recommended that 'the flowers, steeped in oil and set in the sun, are good to anoint the body that is benumbed'. The fresh flowers are harmless and were used to decorate salads and to make a fragrant tisane, but the berries are poisonous.

HYSSOP (*Hyssopus officinalis*): This beautiful perennial herb, native to the Mediterranean, bears spikes of rich blue (rarely white or pink) flowers, which are very attractive to bees, and has small leaves with a bitter mint flavour. It was used sparingly to flavour soups and stews, and the flowers were used to decorate salads. Hyssop was used to treat bronchitis and, as a warm tea gargle, to treat sore throats and externally to bathe wounds. A hot hyssop tea sweetened with honey was administered for chest infections. Large quantities were sometimes consumed to bring about an abortion but it is dangerous for that purpose.

JASMINE, POET'S JASMINE, CATALONIAN JASMINE or SPANISH JASMINE (*Jasminum officinale*): This very fragrant, white-flowered jasmine is grown in France, the Near East and India for the perfumery industry, in particular. It flowers over a very long period in warm climates. The Crusaders would have encountered this plant, as well as the non-climbing, intensely fragrant Sambac, or Arabian, Jasmine (*J. sambac*). These were carried back to southern European gardens but did not reach England until the sixteenth century. The flowers were primarily used for perfumery but both the flowers and the oil were used as an aphrodisiac (particularly for women), and to treat melancholia, stress disorders, including nervous exhaustion, and respiratory infections.

LAVENDER (*Lavandula angustifolia*): Lavender was valued for its calming and sedative properties, particularly in treating hysteria and nervous stress, melancholia and

exhaustion. It was used widely as an effective antiseptic on burns and abrasions, and for treating giddiness. According to John Gerard, 'The distilled water of Lavender smelt into ... is refreshing to them that hath the catalepsie, a light migrain, and to them that have the falling sicknesse and that use to swoune much'. It was also used in southern France as an antitoxin for snake bites and poisons. Lavender found popular use as a culinary herb and has become popular again for that purpose. In France it is the vital ingredient in *herbes de Provence* mixtures. Lavender was also a favourite strewing and toiletry herb.

LILY-OF-THE-VALLEY (*Convallaria majalis*): This exquisite plant, with its racemes of nodding, white bell flowers and lovely perfume, inhabits moist woodland areas and is native to Europe, Asia and North America. To the apothecary it was known as *Lilium convallarium*, and it contains cardiac glycosides with a heart strengthening action similar to that of

foxglove. It is again considered a significant medicinal plant and is listed in a number of pharmacopoeias. It should never be used other than under medical supervision as the plant is poisonous.

LOVE-IN-A-MIST (*Nigella damascena*): This beautiful annual with its misty, fine foliage and exquisite blue flowers is native to the Mediterranean. It was grown, together with Black Cumin (*N. sativa*), in medieval gardens. Medicinally, it was used to clear phlegm from the lungs. The seeds of both species were used as a spice in medieval stews and baked goods.

MARSHMALLOW (*Althaea officinalis*): This is an erect, tall-growing, hardy perennial, bearing five-petalled pink or white flowers in clusters along the flower spike, and it is indigenous to most of Europe. The Romans considered it an excellent vegetable: the young tops were eaten in spring and the roots boiled, then gently fried. Marshmallow has been widely used for its soothing properties. Gerard mentions a number of medicinal uses, including skin-soothing poultices and the use of the roots boiled in wine for the treatment of sciatica. The closely related hollyhock (*A. rosea*), which is said to have reached Europe from the Near East in the 1500s, found similar uses as an emollient, and a tisane made from the flowers was used to soothe chest and throat infections. It is naturalised in and around many medieval towns and ruins in southern Europe and on the Dalmatian coast.

MEADOWSWEET, BRIDEWORT or QUEEN-OF-THE-MEADOW (*Filipendula ulmaria*): This was one of the most popular strewing herbs in the medieval period. The plants occur in moist meadows and have large, somewhat irregular, fern-like foliage. The flowering stems can reach 1.2 metres (4 feet) in height with spectacular dense, fluffy racemes of small almond-scented, creamy white flowers in summer. The leaves contain salicylic acid (first cousin to modern aspirin, and with the same effect when administered as a decoction). Culpepper described it somewhat vaguely as being useful 'for a merrie heart'. A tea made from the dried plant harvested in full flower was used for its antacid properties and it was made into salves that, like modern ointments based on salicylic acid, were useful as anti-inflammatories for arthritic joints and muscle aches.

MISTLETOE, DRUID'S HERB or KISS-AND-GO (*Viscum album*): While mistletoe was better known for its association with Christmas and as a plant of ancient magic, it also found use in medieval medicine. The white berries are poisonous but were widely employed in the medieval period in treating blood pressure, heart disease, gout, epilepsy, palsy (Parkinson's disease) and tumours.

MONKSHOOD or WOLFSBANE (*Aconitum napellus*): The intense blue flowers of this beautiful plant each resemble the cowl of a prayerful monk, but the other common name reveals the highly poisonous nature of the plant, which should never be within reach of small children. The Chinese used it as a poison to tip arrows. It was used as a sedative and painkiller by the greatest medical school of the thirteenth century, the Welsh physicians of Myddfai, but does not appear to have been more generally used in Western Europe for another four centuries. The plant was used as a sedative, for fevers and, incorporated in a salve, as a painkiller for sciatica. Monkshood is no longer used by herbalists as all parts are very poisonous.

MUGWORT (*Artemisia vulgaris*): The name 'mugwort' is thought by some to derive from the plant's old Saxon name of 'muggin wort', meaning midge plant. This refers to its insect repellent properties. 'Mugwort' may also derive from 'moughty', meaning a moth, as it was used as a moth repellent from ancient times, but it may simply derive from the word 'mug', referring to its use as a brewing herb. The bitter principle in mugwort, absinthum, is an appetite stimulant, and the herb has also been used as a tea in southern England and as a stuffing for roast goose and duck, as well as other fatty roasted meats. Like its relative wormwood, it found medicinal use in the treatment of hysteria and epilepsy.

ORPINE or LIVELONG (*Sedum telephium*): This is a succulent, forming a rosette from which arise the flowering stems. It is found in the wild in Europe and is very common on the lower slopes of Mont Ventoux in Provence, a site once much visited by those who collect wild herbs for a living. Particularly in France it was popular in salves for healing wounds, bruising and burns. It was also used to soothe and heal sore throats, in the form of a honey-based syrup, and for treating diarrhoea and bleeding stomach ulcers. This was the French version of the 'carpenter's herb', or bugle.

PARSLEY (*Petroselinum crispum*): This herb was grown in very large quantities for the medieval kitchen. Possibly even more was grown in Roman gardens, for in Roman times it was frequently included in chaplets as it was believed to absorb the intoxicating fumes of wine. Parsley found a wide range of medicinal uses. The root was used as a diuretic for infections of the urinary tract, for dropsy and for gout. Parsley also found use for treating jaundice and eye problems, and it was used as a poultice for many minor problems, such as sprains, cuts and bruises, stings and burns. Like dill, it was administered as a distilled water to children suffering from wind.

PELLITORY-OF-THE-WALL (*Parietaria officinalis*): This is a perennial with sticky, scented leaves that grows on exposed ground and in old walls. The entire plant has a pinkish tinge. It is an ancient herb described by both Pliny and Theophrastus, and it was used in the medieval period for the treatment of urinary tract infections and as a diuretic.

PENNYROYAL or PUDDING GRASS (*Mentha pulegioides*): Pennyroyal is particularly used now for deterring fleas in and around pet bedding. It has been used as a flavouring for puddings and as a weak tea for treating flatulence and nausea, but it has a long history of use in inducing abortions, so that it should be avoided by pregnant women, and it is also not recommended for those with a history of kidney disease. Peppermint (*M. x piperita*) found herbal use in treating hysteria and nervous headaches, for flatulence and upset stomachs, and to promote the appetite. Spearmint (*M. spicata*) also had similar herbal uses to peppermint.

PEONY, MALE PEONY or ROMAN PEONY (*Paeonia officinalis*): Peonies were widely grown in the infirmary garden, the kitchen garden and the pleasure garden. Peony is said to be the oldest of all ornamental cultivated plants. The seeds were used as a hot peppery spice in the medieval period, and the roots were used in the treatment of nervous complaints, epilepsy and madness. Pliny advised taking fifteen black grains (seeds) in wine to counter the 'mocking delusions that Fauns bring on us in our sleep', perhaps not the commonest of complaints. The plant is native to southern Europe but not to England, where it is believed to have been introduced by the Augustinians at their monastery at Steep Holm Island in the Bristol Channel.

POT MARIGOLD or POORMAN'S SAFFRON (*Calendula officinalis*): As suggested by its alternative common name, the petals of pot marigold were used in the medieval period to colour butter and cheese. The plant found a number of herbal uses, many of which have been substantiated today. It was used in salves to treat stings, skin inflammation, eczema and ulcerated skin, as well as to promote wound healing. The

crushed stems were applied to both warts and corns. The type with deep orange coloured flowers is considered the most valuable medicinally. A very old form, Hens and Chickens, has many tiny marigolds growing around the rim of the main flower.

QUEEN ANNE'S LACE or WILD CARROT (*Daucus carota*): It is thought that the Romans introduced this plant into England. With its exquisite large, lacy, white umbels of tiny flowers, it was a very ornamental addition to the medieval garden. It was used for the treatment of kidney complaints and liver problems, and the root pulp was used to soothe irritated skin. The essential oil extracted from the whole plant is still used by expert herbalists on Corsica and in other areas of the Mediterranean.

ROSEMARY (*Rosmarinus officinalis*): Gerard, echoing earlier medieval beliefs, considered this to be a herb that 'comforteth the hart and maketh it merrie, quickeneth the spirits and maketh them more lively'. It was used to treat nervous conditions, to improve blood circulation and liver function, as a tea to improve digestion and in a syrup for coughs. Rosemary was also used externally in salves and poultices to relieve rheumatism and heal sores and wounds. Even the smell of rosemary wood was said to be marvellously beneficial. 'Smell it oft and it shall keep thee youngly', said Richard Banckes in his early sixteenth century herbal. The oil was first distilled c. 1330.

According to a well-known story, a hermit, said to be an angel in disguise, invented a recipe for Queen Elizabeth of Hungary, who was paralysed. The preparation was rubbed into her legs every day and, according to many witnesses, she was completely cured. Although seventy-two, she apparently also regained much of her beauty by bathing in the water every day. Certainly, she did marry again. This preparation became very well known, particularly around Montpellier in the south of France.

Hungary Water

1 gallon of brandy
1 handful of rosemary
1 handful of lavender
1 handful of sweet myrtle

Measure a 'handful' by holding as many stems as possible in your grasp. Cut up the branches into 5 centimetre (2 inch) pieces and place in the brandy to infuse. Cover and leave for several weeks. Filter and bottle for external use.

RUE or HERB OF GRACE (*Ruta graveolens*): Rue, with its lacy, blue-green foliage and golden flowers, is native to southern Europe and the Mediterranean basin. It was primarily used to treat eye strain (both Michelangelo and Leonardo da Vinci claimed to have used it), and it also found uses in treating indigestion and colic, and for expelling intestinal

worms. In poultices and salves, it was used to treat the pain of gout and rheumatism, sprains, chilblains and bruising. It was used as a bitter in drinks, and was a symbol of repentance for Christians. It was worn as a protection against plague, and magistrates would have it placed on their benches as a protection against gaol fever. Some people are allergic to the touch of this plant and develop contact dermatitis.

SAGE or DALMATIAN SAGE (*Salvia officinalis*): The name *Salvia* derives from the Latin word *salvere*, meaning to be in good health. Sage was widely consumed, in cheeses, salads, stuffings, teas and ales, to prolong life, to cut the greasiness of foods such as poultry, to cleanse the blood and to treat female sterility. Plague victims were also treated with it. Gerard said:

'No man need doubt the wholesomness of Sage Ale, being brewed as it should be with Sage, Scabious, Betony, Spikenard, Squinanth [*Juncus odoratus*, also known as 'Camel's Hay'] and Fennel seeds.' There are some very pretty varieties for the medieval herb garden, such as the golden-variegated 'Icterina'; the 'Purple Leaf' sage; 'Tricolor', with pink, purple, sage and cream variegated leaves; the very broad-leafed 'Berggarten'; and narrow-leafed 'Willow'. There are also some charming flower forms such as 'Provence' (with large, frilled, lavender flowers), 'Provence Lilac', 'Pink' and 'Alba'. In Greece, the very closely related wild Greek Sage or Three-Leaved Sage (*S. triloba*) finds similar uses, both culinary and medicinal. Lavender Sage (*S. lavandulifolia*) from Spain is also used to some degree for medicinal purposes.

SALAD BURNET or DRUMSTICKS (*Poterium sanguisorba*): This herb was largely used in salads for its cucumber-flavoured, fern-like leaves. The curious inflorescence is a rounded drumstick in form, closely set with small green flowers with protruding maroon anthers. A decoction made from the root was an excellent remedy for stemming the bleeding of cuts and wounds, and a tea made from the whole plant was used to treat diarrhoea and haemorrhoids.

SELFHEAL (*Prunella vulgaris*): Selfheal is an aromatic, perennial groundcover herb with small, dense spikes of lipped purple flowers with dark bracts. Its principal use was in staunching knife and sword cuts. According to the Doctrine of Signatures, its flowers had use in treating sore throats and diphtheria.

SOAPWORT, BOUNCING BET or LATHERWORT (*Saponaria officinalis*): This pretty pink-flowered, groundcover plant is a member of the carnation family and grows wild in Europe. It is one of the plants encountered around ancient monasteries. There is also an old, very pretty, double pink garden form. Soapwort flowers in the evening, pouring out its sweet fragrance, and remains fresh though the morning before looking rather dusty and forlorn in the afternoon heat. It has ancient use as a medicinal herb as a mild diuretic, for coughs, to reduce fever, as a tonic and as a purgative. A decoction of the whole plant was used to bathe itchy skin. Soapwort contains saponins, which create a lather with water, and has long been used as a detergent for delicate fabrics. The plant is poisonous when taken in excess.

SOLOMON'S SEAL (*Polygonatum multiflorum*): This beautiful plant was used for various healing purposes, among the more memorable being John Gerard's claim in his herbal of 1633 that 'the root of Solomon's Seal stamped while it is fresh and greene, and applied, taketh away in a night, or two at the most, any bruise, black or blew spots got by falls or women's wilfulnesse in stumbling upon their hasty husbands' fists or such like'. It was used in magic to ward off evil and in exorcism. The flowers were used in love potions. The rhizome is not used internally except under expert supervision, and then only after being dried and powdered and made into a decoction. It contains toxic substances that cause nausea, diarrhoea and tachycardia. The leaves and berries also induce vomiting if chewed.

SWEET BAY or BAY LAUREL (*Laurus nobilis*): With a neat, slow-growing habit, this plant has small cream flowers followed by black berries that yield an oil used as an antiseptic and to stimulate the appetite, as well as to flavour foods and liqueurs. A long soak in a hot tub to which bay leaves were added was considered excellent for aching muscles. The leaves and berries contain the essential oils eugenol, cineol and geraniol.

SWEET CICELY or BRITISH MYRRH (*Myrrhis odorata*): This member of the parsley family is a perennial, with much-divided, fern-like leaves and compound umbels of tiny white flowers followed by long brown seeds. The leaves are sweetly flavoured of anise and were an ingredient in salads, as well as pottages. Like angelica, Sweet Cicely was used to reduce the amount of sugar required in stewed fruits. The green seeds were highly recommended by Gerard, served with a dressing of oil, vinegar and pepper 'for the cold and feeble stomach'.

SWEET VIOLET (*Viola odorata*): Fragrant-flowered sweet violets were often featured both in *mille fleurs* tapestries and illuminated manuscripts. They were often dug from the wild for transplantation into gardens, and Gerard praised their modest virtue, 'for they admonish and stir up a man to that which is comely and honest'. Violets found many culinary uses, the flowers and young leaves being added to spring salads and used to flavour wine and syrup. The

crystallised flowers were used to ornament puddings and were nibbled after meals as a breath freshener. The flowers had a gentle, laxative effect and were also used in tisanes to relieve sore throats and cure mouth infections, as well as to treat fevers, headaches and epilepsy.

TANSY or GOLDEN BUTTONS (*Tanacetum vulgare*): Aromatic tansy was associated with Lent and the bitter herbs of the Passover. It was incorporated into a medieval pudding that was intended to invoke sombre thoughts of repentance. However, many recipes evolved to become rich in eggs, cream and sugar and were considered more of a delicacy than a penance. In England, pancakes flavoured with tansy were made at the end of Lent. The herb was used sparingly in salads and to flavour sauces and various sweet dishes, and

was also wrapped around meat as a fly repellent. Tansy found medicinal use in expelling intestinal worms, so that hearty helpings of tansy pudding may well have had health benefits. It was also used as a strewing herb.

THYME (*Thymus vulgaris*): Thyme grows very extensively around the hills and lower mountain slopes of Provence as well as in some other Mediterranean regions. While thyme played an important role as a culinary herb, it was also valued in fighting infections. It was used as a tea to treat fevers, sore throats, laryngitis and chest infections, as well as to calm digestive upsets. It was also used to expel intestinal worms. The common thyme of the eastern Mediterranean, Conehead Thyme (*T. capitatus*), found fairly similar uses. Serpolet or wild thyme (*T. serpyllum*) is native to south-western Europe and finds comparable use. The dried flowering tops were used to treat infections of the mouth, throat and chest, to prevent infection in wounds, and for treating indigestion and flatulence.

VALERIAN (*Valeriana officinalis*): Valerian was a favourite of the Arab physicians. This perennial plant has very fragrant white flowers (occasionally pale pink) and coarsely pinnate leaves. The rootstock is aromatic, and the dried rootstock was and remains very useful as a sedative to treat insomnia, anxiety and disorders caused by nervous stress.

WALL GERMANDER (*Teucrium chamaedrys*): This charming plant forms a hardy, evergreen subshrub with small toothed leaves and pink lipped flowers. In the Tudor period it was often used to outline knot gardens, but in the medieval period it was known as *Herba chamaedrys* and Quercula (in reference to its miniature oak-shaped leaves)

and was grown principally for its use in treating fevers and to improve digestion.

WALLFLOWER or JULY GILLIFLOWER (*Cheiranthus cheiri* syn. *Erysimum cheiri*): Wallflowers are intensely fragrant, and although they are now treated as annuals in gardens are quite long-lived perennials. They are native to southern Europe and naturalised, often in the cracks in old stone walls, in England. Wallflower was used to treat strained muscles, and Culpepper considered the yellow-flowered sort the most effective. The seeds were used in a heart tonic and the plant is now known to contain a compound, cheiranthin, which has an effect in supporting a failing heart similar to that of foxglove. The flowers and stems have been used to treat impotence and as an

aphrodisiac, as well as to treat paralysis. Wallflower is no longer used without medical supervision as it can be toxic.

WHITE HOREHOUND (*Marrubium vulgare*): The name 'horehound' came from the old English word 'harhune', meaning a woolly plant, but this plant comes from around the Mediterranean basin and Asia. It has been used since early times for coughs and was used as a tea, according to Gerard, to 'easeth those that have hard labour in childe-bearing'. He also recommended a syrup of horehound as a cough remedy.

WILD STRAWBERRY (*Fragaria vesca*): This is the wild strawberry of Europe. An infusion of the leaves and rootstock was used to treat dysentery, diarrhoea and infections of the urinary tract. The fruits were used to treat scurvy and constipation, and a decoction of the rootstock was used to treat diarrhoea. The wild plants are considered more potent than the modern cultivated strawberry.

WILLOWHERB (*Epilobium* spp.):
All the willowherbs found use
in staunching bleeding, for
urinary tract disorders and
migraine, and as antispasmodics
in treating hiccups, whooping
cough and asthma. Culpepper
favoured the Yellow Willowherb
(*E. lysimachia*) for herbal use,
but the Rosebay Willowherb
(also known as Persian
Willow or Blooming Sally,
E. angustifolium), the Great
Hairy Willowherb (or Codlins
and Cream, *E. hirsutum*) and
the Broad-Leafed Willowherb
(*H. montanum*) were used in
similar ways. Gerard added
that the smoke of burning
willowherb was an insect
repellent. The young shoots
were boiled and then eaten
like asparagus.

WORMWOOD (*Artemisia
absinthum*): Wormwood
contains the hallucinogen
santonin, as well as bitter
principles and a volatile oil that
promotes the appetite. Small
quantities of the seed were
taken to expel intestinal worms,
hence its common name. This is
one of the most bitter herbs
known and has been used in
the preparation of many
aperitifs and herbal wines,
such as absinthe and vermouth.
It also had a reputation as
an aphrodisiac and was used
to assist digestion, treat
jaundice, relieve constipation
and aid childbirth.

WOUNDWORT, WOOD BETONY,
HEAL-ALL or BISHOPSWORT
(*Stachys officinalis*): This herb
was held in the highest repute
as a kind of universal panacea.
It was said that even wild
beasts would seek it out to
cure themselves, and that
stags would use it to mend
injuries from arrows and
spears. It was used to treat
nervous conditions, including
palpitations, hysteria, neuralgia
and dyspepsia of nervous
origin. Gerard found it useful
for treating convulsions,
epilepsy, jaundice, coughs and
lung complaints, as well as
many other conditions. To
stimulate the appetite he
recommended a conserve made
from the flowers. This is a
creeping herb with simple
leaves and dense spikes of
reddish-purple lipped flowers.

YARROW (*Achillea millefolium*):
This herb has been used to
staunch bleeding, particularly
from knife and sword cuts, ever
since the ancient Greeks used it
in battle. It is native to Europe
and has finely divided, fern-like
leaves and tall dense
inflorescences of white
(occasionally pink) flowers
in summer. It spreads by
rhizomes. Yarrow also found
use in treating fevers, hyper-
tension and urinary tract
infections. It was a popular
remedy for feverish colds when
mixed with elderberry and
mint. The American Civil War
is said to be the last time
yarrow was used to treat sword
wounds suffered in battle.

Garden Design: The Abbess' Physic Garden

This physic garden is both ornamental and practical, and is based on French late medieval monastic gardens. The beds are raised and edged with wooden boards, and are of a width that allows for easy tending and harvesting. The garden forms a private enclosed space which captures the fragrance of the herbs and warmth of the sun. The garden is fenced on three sides with living willow grown in a traditional diamond lattice design. Alternatively, a wood pole fence in diamond design or, more elegantly, lattice carpentry, might be used. The fourth side may be hedged in three ways. In larger gardens, a mixed hedgerow of herbal shrubs such as elder, guelder rose and blackthorn would provide an authentic finish to give privacy and reduce wind on the site. Such hedgerows persist in the Shaker gardens of the United States today. Other alternatives include a hedge to 1.8 m (6 ft) of fragrant ancient Alba roses such 'Alba Maxima'

and 'Alba Semi-Plena', or of ancient Persian Damask Roses such as 'The Rose of Kazanlik', 'Gloire de Guilan' and 'Ispahan'. For small gardens, a hedge of the variegated pink and white ancient Gallica Rose 'Rosa Mundi' would be ideal.

Medieval herb gardens were usually restricted to one or two species in each individual plot to provide enough harvestable material, but this restricted planting also created a soothing simplicity, in contrast to our sophisticated modern and often complex plantings. In this garden the plots are dedicated to lavender, the Gallica Rose 'Officinalis' edged with Orris Root iris, rosemary, columbine and calendula, borage edged with wild strawberry, clove pinks, double Roman chamomile, marshmallow with hyssop, field poppy with cornflowers, angelica, sweet violets, and bronze fennel with golden-flowered elecampane. All internal paths are fully paved in stone using an attractive, and then

fashionable, diamond pattern. The outer walkway is turfed.

Each path is entered by passing beneath an archway of herbal flowers, either of eglantine roses, which have apple-scented foliage (or any single-flowered, fragrant, modest sized climber in pale pink or white) and two with the intensely fragrant wild pink honeysuckle of the English countryside, *Lonicera periclymenum*. A raised turf seat built with wood (treated railway sleepers are ideal for this task) and flanked with two pots of fragrant wild thyme provides a place to rest and and to meditate in the warmth and scented air of this *cordon sanitaire*, surrounded in summer by drifts of butterflies and the humming of pollen-heavy bees.

As designed, this garden woud be suited to a larger space. For smaller gardens, the design could be scaled down by up to thirty percent, or alternatively only the inner section of the garden created.

A little-educated and untravelled German nun named Sister Katherina Emmerich became seriously ill in 1811. Many witnesses saw her receive the stigmata, and from that time forward until her death in 1820 she fell into trance states, seeing vividly detailed visions. Many of those revelations were recorded in a book, *The Life of the Virgin Mary* by C. Brentano. In her visions, Sister Katherina saw the Virgin Mary leave Jerusalem with St John, as the persecutions of Christians became more threatening, and travel to Ephesus. She described how St John had built a small stone house for Mary, high above the city, in the mountains. It was rectangular in shape, with a round back wall and a hearth. There was a stream of water running beside it.

Wild white iris cover the woodland near Mary's house, high in the mountains above Ephesus, in spring.

In her visions, Sister Katherina, known now as the Blessed Anna Katherina Emmerich, described an early Christian encampment at the site. She told how Mary returned to Jerusalem for three years and fell very ill there, so ill that a grave was prepared for her. However, she recovered sufficiently to return to her tiny stone home above Ephesus, dying there at the age of sixty-four. The saints who had supported her performed the funeral and buried her some two kilometres (a mile) from the house, in a specially prepared cave.

The visions also revealed St Thomas mourning for Mary, and bitterly regretting that he had not been able to reach her funeral in time. St John led Thomas and his friends to the cave, where they knelt in prayer. St John then unbound the freshly sealed coffin and drew back the lid. The burial shroud was intact, but Mary's body was not inside. The saints and their followers sealed the cave, and the tiny house became a chapel.

In 1880, a French cleric named Gouyet, who had read Brentano's book, set out to discover the truth of the visions by attempting to locate Mary's house. He was supported by the Bishop of Izmir, who provided him with an assistant. Gouyet found Mary's house, and it did indeed correspond exactly to the description provided by Sister Katherina. He sent reports of his findings to Church authorities in both Paris and Rome, but they appear to have been ignored. The strongly held belief at that time was that Mary had been buried in Jerusalem, and that her tomb was in the Valley of Cedron. There are many records of pilgrimages to Jerusalem, to the Tomb of Mary, which was later enclosed by the Church of the Sepulchre of Mary.

In 1891, two additional investigations took place at the house above Ephesus. They found that the tiny home had in the long distant past been converted into a chapel but had fallen into disrepair. When questioned, local people said the place was well known to them and had been a place of worship for many centuries. A fairly recent report has been made stating that the stonework of the building dates to around the first century AD. The building was restored by 1894.

The waters of the nearby spring have been credited with many miracles, and the tiny building was declared a place of pilgrimage by the Vatican in 1914. It was visited by both Pope Paul VI in 1967 and Pope John Paul II in 1979. Today, thousands of modern pilgrims, both Christian and Muslim, visit this holy site, for Mary is also honoured in the Koran.

No official records exist of Mary living, and eventually dying, near Ephesus, but the home high in the mountains would have been a safe refuge. Jesus had commended his Mother to the care of St John before His death. Christians did flee from Jerusalem after Jesus's death and it is unlikely that St John, entrusted with her care, would have left the Virgin Mary in Jerusalem. There is a somewhat elliptical comment from the Third Ecumenical Council, which was held at Ephesus in 431, that there was at that time a Church of the Virgin Mary nearby, and yet the Marian cult with its many churches dedicated to the Virgin Mary did not begin until after this Council met.

The dedication of feast days to the Blessed Virgin appears to have begun in the Eastern Church, in Syria, in the fourth century. Ancient scripts from the fifth century speak of the Feast Day of Theotokos ('the god bearer', an alternative name given to Mary within the Orthodox Church) celebrated in Armenia and also Jerusalem on the fifteenth of August. Between the fourth and sixth centuries, all the main feast days for the Virgin Mary were established in the East, including the Conception, the Nativity (Christmas), the Presentation, the Assumption and the Annunciation. The Assumption became the most important of these festivals, and by decree of the Emperor Mauricius c. 600 it was celebrated throughout the Eastern Church on the fifteenth of August.

The Feast of the Annunciation in England became known as Lady Day and was celebrated on the old New Year's Day, the Vernal Equinox, which fell on the sixth of April. This custom was also carried to the American colonies. In 1752 the old Julian Calendar was replaced by the Gregorian Calendar, and the start of the year became the first of January. (A remnant of the old calendar remains in the start of the tax year in Britain on the sixth of April.) The Feast of the Annunciation, also called Lady Day, is now held on the twenty-fifth of March.

The cult in the West

Western Europe was slower to develop the cult of Mary. The first recorded Marian Feasts date to the end of the sixth century in France and Spain. Persian and Arab invasions of the East were responsible for displacing many monks, and those who fled to Rome are believed to have hastened the incorporation of Marian Feasts into the life of the Church in Rome by the seventh century. By the end of the ninth century, churches dedicated to the Virgin Mary could be found across the entire world of Christendom, together with the beautiful early art inspired by the Marian cult, and popular Marian pilgrimages took place to sites dedicated to the Virgin Mary, and to sites of miracles attributed to Her.

By the high and late medieval period, the Marian cult had resulted in outpourings of sublime music, literature and art, and had influenced and been influenced by the Doctrine of Courtly Love in France. Yet there remained a

A Mary shrine at a church in Parma, Italy. Shrines and churches to honour the Virgin Mary appeared rapidly after the Council of Ephesus in AD 431.

curious dualism in this period. The Virgin Mary had not lost her early role as the 'second Eve', and attitudes towards women were often notably misogynistic, a mixture of blame for Eve and the woes Eve was believed to have released on a fallen and wretched humankind, and a belief in the inferiority and innate sinfulness of women. Yet this attitude was simultaneously combined with veneration and celebration of idealised feminine traits divorced from sexuality. Even some of the most brilliant and mystical women saints of the period, such as Hildegard of Bingen, were inevitably affected by these social attitudes and on occasion suffered considerable humiliation and prejudice.

During the twelfth century a movement called theological scholasticism arose in France. Represented by intellectuals of the Church such as Peter Abelard, it sought a rational approach to divine understanding. St Bernard of Clairvaux, a conservative and powerful member of the Church, instead advocated an unquestioning faith and prayer directed to the Virgin Mary asking for divine intercession. He described the Virgin Mary as 'the royal way,

Detail of *Madonna and Child*, c.1315 (tempera on panel), Getty Images

by which the Christ comes to us'. St Bernard was perhaps the leading figure in the Church in Western Europe to promote the Marian cult. When Peter Abelard was later tried for heresy, the prosecutor was St Bernard.

By the end of the thirteenth century, the month of May had become devoted to the Virgin Mary, and the old pagan spring festivals were gradually displaced, although never lost. May Day had been a day of garlanding and of merriment, of wooing, of thinly disguised fertility rites around maypoles, and of declaring a pretty village girl Queen of the May. This now became a ceremony crowning the Virgin Mary with garlands of flowers. These lines from the poem 'May Magnificat' by the Jesuit priest and poet of magical, mystical words, Gerard Manley Hopkins, capture the spirit perfectly:

When drop-of-blood-and-foam-dapple
Bloom lights the orchard-apple
And thicket and thorp are merry
With silver-surfed cherry

And azuring-over greybell makes
Wood banks and brakes wash wet like lakes

And magic cuckoocall
Caps, clears, and clinches all—

This ecstasy all through mothering earth
Tells Mary her mirth till Christ's birth
To remember and exaltation
In God who was her salvation.

Marian plants

Wherever Christianity spread in Europe during the medieval period, plants that had previously been linked to the ancient gods and goddesses were renamed and dedicated to the Virgin Mary, or renamed for saints. Quite a few plants had folk legends attached to them, and these were sometimes new and sometimes a variation on an old myth. For instance, in Greek mythology the Madonna Lily was said to have arisen from the drops of milk that fell to the earth from the goddess Hera, but later it was said to have arisen from fallen droplets of milk as the Virgin Mary nursed the infant Jesus. Not only Hera (Roman Juno), but Artemis (Diana), Aphrodite (Venus), Persephone, the Celtic Brighid and German goddesses such as Bertha were among the many those who lost their ancient association with particular plants.

The rise of Protestantism and now a more secular world have seen quite a few of the old medieval plant names fall into disuse, although some survive. Just as Christianity renamed the 'pagan flowers', so did the secular world, in turn, rename the Mary flowers. The Reformation in England, for example, saw many of the common

The medieval beehive was symbolic of monastic communities and often included in Mary gardens.

old country names that referred to the Virgin Mary suppressed.

Many of the Mary flowers have been greatly changed by selection and hybridisation since the medieval period, dressed in brighter colours, altogether larger and sometimes doubled. Mary flowers are, by their nature, simple and innocent and gently coloured. Quite a few of the flowers listed here in 'A Marian Herbal' do remain close to their original form, but modern Hybrid Tea and Floribunda-style roses, large-flowered pansies, brilliantly coloured primulas and modern forms of calendulas are examples of plants that have changed considerably, and for which older and more authentic forms should be sought. At the height of the Marian cult, many hundreds of quiet and lovely plants had been named to honour the Virgin Mary.

What were the original Marian gardens like? We have abundant evidence of the flowers that were devoted to the Virgin Mary but far less knowledge of the form of the gardens. However, we do know from illustrations in old manuscripts that they were in the form of a *hortus conclusus*, usually a square, formal, geometrical and enclosed

The white lily is symbolic of the Virgin Mary, shown here in a recreated inspirational medieval garden by Ray Lynam at the University of Western Sydney.

space within walls or hedges. Many used the monastic plan, with the garden divided into four equal segments by two intersecting paths forming a cross. Seating would have been provided, perhaps turf seats or ones of wood or stone. We know the gardens were planted with flowers devoted to the Virgin Mary and that they contained simple ornamentation, such as a fountain or statuary. The gardens were raised with wooden boards or wattle edging. Wattle woven from grapevine trimmings would have been particularly meaningful.

Mary gardens often included bees and beehives, which had strong medieval symbolism and were closely associated with monastic gardens. Bees were symbolic of industrious habits, while the beehive was very much a part of the monastery garden and orchard, particularly for the Benedictine Order. The beehive became a symbol for a monastic community. It also represented the idealised selfless, diligent and hard-working community life aspired to by monks within medieval monasteries.

Above all, however, Mary gardens were intended to be places of rest and contemplation, somewhere to seek inner peace.

A Marian herbal

This herbal contains plants that were directly associated with the Virgin Mary, or were sanctified by close association. They are all planted in Mary gardens.

ANGELICA or ROOT OF THE HOLY GHOST (*Angelica archangelica*): A series of plagues devastated the medieval world. The development of trade routes and the wars of conquest that characterised the period allowed once-isolated pools of disease in various parts of the world to spread over large areas. The most fearful outbreak, the Black Death or bubonic plague, reached Europe in 1347 and major outbreaks continued for the next one hundred and thirty years. The bubonic plague was responsible for the death of a quarter of the population of Europe and fully half the population of London.

According to legend, the Archangel Gabriel revealed the medicinal value of angelica in treating the plague to the

Benedictine monks, and it was widely cultivated in European monasteries in the medieval period for this purpose. In addition to its connection with the Archangel Gabriel, angelica is also dedicated to the Archangel Michael, as it was usually in bloom on his feast day, which falls on the eighth of May in the old calendar.

Wild angelica, known as Shiny Angelica (*A. sylvestris*), is exceptionally handsome in the garden with its very shiny foliage. It goes by the medieval name of Mary's Church. It also finds herbal use.

CARNATION (*Dianthus caryophyllus, D. plumarius*): Carnations, with their deliciously spicy fragrance, were well known in the Near

East where they have been in cultivation for more than two millennia. The carnation was said to have grown from the tears shed by the Virgin Mary on the road to Calvary, and it became a symbol of motherly love during the medieval period.

Although no records exist of the carnation in Western Europe until the fifteenth century, a number of wild *Dianthus* species exist there. The cluster-headed Carthusian Pink (*D. carthusianorum*) was grown by the Carthusian monks, and the very fragrant Grass Pink (*D. plumarius*), the origin of our cottage pinks, was cultivated. In England, the Cheddar Pink (*D. gratianopolitanus*) once grew in profusion in Somerset's Cheddar Gorge, the Maiden Pink (*D. deltoides*) was widespread and the fragrant Deptford Pink was mentioned by John Gerard. The Superb, or Splendid, Pink (*D. superbus*) has very deeply laciniate petals and a glorious fragrance.

Clove pinks are exceptionally fragrant and bear dozens of small carnation flowers, forming neat, dense, low carpets of grass-like foliage. Old-fashioned clove pinks that are particularly suitable for a Mary garden include the ancient, very fragrant 'Sops in Wine', with double white flowers and a deep ruby centre; the double white 'Mrs Sinkins'; 'Old English Mauve'; and the small, double, fragrant 'Falstaff', deep red and laced white. Few old-style carnations exist, but one French heirloom variety, 'Blanc' (pictured), with intensely scented, single white blooms very closely resembles medieval carnations in illuminated manuscripts. Sweet William (*D. barbatus*) was once known as Mary's Tuft. Who William was has often been debated, but St William of Aquitaine and William the Conqueror are the most frequently proposed.

EYES OF MARY or FORGET-ME-NOT (*Myosotis sylvatica*): The exquisite pure blue flowers of woodland forget-me-nots in spring were said to resemble the eyes of Mary. This was one of the simple but charming plants often depicted in medieval manuscripts. Another richly blue-flowered herb, borage (*Borago officinalis*), was also compared to the eyes of the Virgin Mary and was given the name of Virgin's Face. The exquisite china blue of chicory led to it being known as Heavenly Way.

GIFT OF GOD, GREATER CELANDINE, JOSEPH'S LADDER, WITCH'S FLOWER, WARTWORT or SWALLOW HERB (*Chelidonium majus*): Celandine was planted in many gardens of simples in the medieval period, and it persists as a wildling around many ancient monasteries, along with Danewort, soapwort, fennel, comfrey, hollyhocks, Pellitory-of-the-Wall and alkanet. When the stem is broken it exudes an orange latex and the seeds ooze a powerfully staining golden-yellow juice. The name *Chelidonium* comes from the Greek word for a swallow, referring to a belief that the juice or latex was used by mother swallows to restore eyesight to injured fledgelings.

GRAPE or VINE (*Vitis vinifera*): Grapes and the vine were symbolic of Bacchus in Roman times, but they became a deeply significant symbol of Christ in medieval Europe and the Near East. Wine from the grape was associated with the blood of Christ and there are many allusions to the vine in the Bible. In the Old Testament, Jeremiah spoke of Israel as a vine, while Isaiah described Israel as a vineyard. The fourth century Syrian theologian St Ephraem wrote many hymns that described Christ as the true vine.

LADY-BY-THE-GATE, SOAPWORT, BOUNCING BETT, GILL-RUN-BY-THE-STREET or HERB PHYLYP (*Saponaria officinalis*): This delightful evening-scented plant with exquisite pink flowers has leaves that contain saponins. Soapwort was used as a medieval detergent, very gentle in action, and one of its medieval names in England, perhaps unfortunately, was Soapy Dick. Another of its names appears to dedicate the plant to St Philip. In early medieval times it was used to soap new cloth, and it is still used for cleaning delicate ancient tapestries, and in parts of the Near East for cleaning woollen garments.

LADY'S CANDLE, LADY'S FLANNEL, OUR LADY'S TAPER, LADY'S CANDLESTICK, VIRGIN MARY'S CANDLE, WOOLLY MULLEIN or HAG'S TAPER (*Verbascum thapsus*): As its folk names indicate, this plant is associated with both Christianity and medieval beliefs in witches. The plant forms a large rosette of very soft, silvered, densely hairy, woolly leaves within its first year and produces a tall stem growing to 1.2–1.5 metres (4–5 feet), with spikes of dense yellow flowers. As with many flowers dedicated to Mary, mullein had herbal value, being used in a sweetened tea to treat congestion of the lungs.

LADY'S CHEESES, COMMON MALLOW, FAIRY CHEESES or BREAD AND CHEESE (*Malva sylvestris*): Although it is a plant of wastelands, this species is nonetheless beautiful, forming a low shrub that is covered in single, richly rose-purple flowers. The fruits resemble tiny truckles of cheese, or buttons. The whole plant is very rich in mucilage and was used in medieval times and later in poultices and salves for its soothing properties.

LADY'S CUSHIONS, LADY'S PINCUSHION, SEA THRIFT, CUSHION PINKS or SEA GILLIFLOWER (*Armeria maritima*): Found on the very edge of sea cliffs in England and France as well as the Scilly Isles, these quaint and delightful flowers found their way into gardens by at least the sixteenth century, probably earlier. They form very dense,

spreading cushions of fine, grass-like foliage in the manner of clove pinks, and the pink, or occasionally white, flowers are borne in a very dense, spherical inflorescence at the top of the stem, resembling a drumstick. Mature plants often bear dozens of inflorescences.

LADY'S FRILLS or ENGLISH PRIMROSE (*Primula vulgaris*): The flower symbolic of the Feast of Corpus Christi, held on the twenty-sixth of May, is the primrose. Given the many admonitions about the dangers of walking the primrose path with all its temptations and sensual delights, it is perhaps odd that the primrose in this context represented the love of labour. The wild primrose, with its pale gold flowers, is the flower best suited to an authentic Mary garden. The ancient Laced Primrose, with clusters of small, exquisite flowers in deep brown or maroon, finely embroidered at the petal edges with silver or gold, is also appropriate and looks as if it were lifted from a medieval tapestry.

LADY'S MODESTY, HUMILITY or SWEET VIOLET (*Viola odorata*): The sweet violet has long been the symbol of modesty. According to legend, the violet drooped its head in sadness when the shadow of the cross fell upon it. St Bernard described the Virgin Mary as 'the violet of Humility', and in sending violets to the Abbess Hildegard of Bingen did not refrain from reminding her of its symbolism. The violet was frequently embroidered in tapestries and used to ornament manuscripts.

LADY'S SMOCK, MILKMAIDS or CUCKOO FLOWER (*Cardamine pratensis*): This is one of the prettiest of English wildflowers and was mentioned by Shakespeare. It is a perennial with graceful racemes of silvery mauve flowers, finely striped with a deeper mauve, and cress-like foliage that was used in salads. There is a rare and very old form still available with double flowers. The name is said to have arisen from the resemblance of the flowers to a row of little smocks hung out to dry. As it blooms in England at Ladytide, on the twenty-fifth of March, it was dedicated to the Virgin Mary. It loves a dampish but gently sunny place.

LADY'S UMBRELLA, OUR LADY'S NIGHTCAP, LADY'S SHIMMY or BINDWEED (*Convolvulus arvensis*): Both the Greater and Lesser Bindweeds have been dedicated to the Virgin Mary, but it is the Lesser Bindweed that is so common around old monastery sites today, particularly in France. It is a short-growing vine, bearing in summer many small, parachute-shaped, milky white flowers striped with rose-pink. Blooming over the meadow grasses of midsummer, it often resembles delicate medieval embroidery. It was included in illuminated manuscripts.

MADONNA LILY or ANNUNCIATION LILY (*Lilium candidum*): In the Christian tradition, lilies were a symbol of purity and innocence, and this exquisitely scented, white, open-trumpeted lily brought back from the Near East by the Crusaders was soon planted in monasteries throughout Europe. It found a ready association with the Virgin Mary. This flower was grown, in particular, to decorate the high altar. It was one of the first two flowers (the other being the rose, in particular the herbal rose *Rosa gallica* 'Officinalis') that Charlemagne the Great commanded be grown in every monastery in the Carolingian Empire. Until the sixteenth century, the Madonna Lily appears to have been the only lily in cultivation in Western Europe.

It is said that the Archangel Gabriel held a lily in his hand when he announced to Mary that she would conceive and bear a son to be called Jesus, and this has led to the alternative name, the Annunciation Lily. This lily was often a fertility symbol in the ancient civilisations of the Near East, such as Sumer, and in Abyssinia. In early medieval paintings of the Annunciation the olive, long a symbol of peace, was frequently depicted in the hand of the Archangel Gabriel but later, by decree of the Church, all paintings of the Annunciation were required to show a spray of lilies, usually with three flowers to represent the Trinity.

MADONNA'S HERB, WHERE-GOD-HAS-WALKED, GROUND IVY, GILL-GO-BY-THE-GROUND, ALEHOOF, TUNHOOF or ST JOHN'S GIRDLE (*Glechoma hederacea*): This humble herb, with its bitter-flavoured, heart-shaped leaves, has spread from Europe to North America and Australasia, naturalising in

areas with moist, rich soils. It makes bright purple pools of colour when it flowers. According to Gerard, in places like Wales and Chester it was long used to add a bitter note to ales. It was used in salves to treat wounds and to make gill tea. The colour purple is associated with spirituality, mysticism, religion, wisdom and miraculous healing, giving rise to some of its folk names.

MAIDENHAIR FERN or MARIA'S HAIR (*Adiantum* spp.): This plant, with its elegant and delicate foliage, is frequently used to ornament the altar for the feast of Corpus Christi, held in honour of the Eucharist. Nowhere does it grow more beautifully than in the ancient monastery at Kaisariani, near Mount Hymettus and modern Athens. Set among cypress trees, the monastery was founded in the eleventh century and built over the ruins of a Roman temple. Kaisariani was dedicated to the Presentation of the Virgin in the Temple, and it is pleasant to think of generations of monks tending their hives to produce

the famous Mount Hymettus honey. The fortified monastery contains the Chapel of St Anthony, and on the road, accessible to pilgrims of the past, is a walled fountain fed by a cool spring and surrounded by symbolically lush maidenhair fern.

MARY-LOVES, TWELVE DISCIPLES, DAY'S EYE, DAISY or SHEPHERD'S DAISY (*Bellis perennis*): With their cheerful, innocent little white faces, rosy buds, golden hearts and lowly place among lush green meadow grasses, it is not surprising that the little field daisy, which flowers in the month of May, the month devoted to the Virgin Mary, was seen as a symbol of Christian humility and figured in illuminated manuscripts. It was used as a medicinal herb, mainly for healing wounds. This plant seems to have been much loved by St Augustine, who spoke of its purity and goodness. It also seems to have been Geoffrey Chaucer's favourite flower of May, as he described in the 'Prologue: The Legend of Good Women':

... That of alle the floures in the mede
Than love I most these floures white and rede,
Swiche as men callen daysies in our toun.

MARY'S CROWN, CORNFLOWER or BACHELOR'S BUTTONS (*Centaurea cyanus*): The florets of the cornflower, in the rich blue colour used to represent the mantle of the Virgin Mary in many medieval paintings, are arranged around a central dark disc in the form of a coronet, hence the name 'Mary's Crown'. These simple flowers of the cornfield were much loved in medieval times and often illustrated in manuscripts. Cornflowers are frequently included in both Mary gardens and recreated medieval flowery meads.

MARY'S FLOWER, WALLFLOWER, WALL GILLIFLOWER or BEE FLOWER (*Cheiranthus cheiri*): The wallflower of the medieval period was the simple golden or gold-and-tawny brown, single-flowered, tall form with its ineffable fragrance and great attraction for bees. Wallflowers grow happily in the cracks of old stone walls and can be found in the ruined walls of ancient monasteries such as Lindisfarne Abbey, on the Holy Isle in Northumberland. There, the simple single, golden-flowered form blooms with the white-flowered sea campion (*Silene maritima*). The connection of wallflowers to the Virgin Mary may seem distant, but whereas today the term 'wallflower' refers to someone who lacks social success, in early times it represented the quality of faithfulness.

In the past, beekeepers who took pleasure in spreading a feast of fragrant flowers before their bees planted wallflowers in quantity. Gervase Markham in *The English Husbandman* (1613) wrote of the wallflower: 'The Husbandman preserves it most in his Bee-garden, for it is wondreth sweet and affordeth much honey'. Sir Francis Bacon wrote of wallflowers in 1625: '... Then wall-flowers, which are very delightful, to be set under a parlour or lower chamber window'. Clearly, by the early seventeenth century the older country name had prevailed over the Marian name.

MARY'S GIRDLE, LADY O' THE MEADOW or MEADOWSWEET (*Filipendula ulmaria*): Meadowsweet is widely distributed in Europe in damp meadows and produces soft, cloudy masses of almond-scented, tiny white flowers in summer.

The powerful goddess Aine appeared in many guises in Europe. Her names, translated from many places, included 'Richness of Light', 'Shining', 'Sweet Goodness', 'Abundance' and 'Strength of Light'. In Ireland, she is pictured as a beautiful woman with a voice of wonderful sweetness and a lily-like complexion blushed with rose, wearing a golden crown and carrying three golden apples. Her sacred flower was the hawthorn and her sacred herb Meadowsweet, and it is not surprising that both of these plants were rededicated to the Virgin Mary. Aine's brother, Bel, was said to be the first oak tree, and from two of his acorns arose the god Dagda and the goddess Brighid. It is said that Aine created the Tuatha Dé Danann, the ancient magical race of Ireland, from flowers.

MARY'S GOLD or POT MARIGOLD (*Calendula officinalis*):

The name of this plant became shortened over time and it is now known simply as 'marigold'. The satiny orange petals are an excellent natural food dye (they were a cheap substitute for saffron, as Gerard noted) and are used to this day to colour some cheeses in Holland. They are also used to add a spicy note and warm colour to soups and stews, and the young shoots and leaves were cooked as a potherb. These usages led to the name 'Pot Marigold'. In medieval times, the marigold had a single row of ray petals so that their round faces were reminiscent of the sun. In England they acquired many cheerful names such as Golds, Sunne's Bride, Publican-and-Sinner, and Husbandman's Dyall. A very old but still available form of marigold described by Gerard is called Hens and Chickens. It has many miniature-stalked calendulas protruding around the rim of the main flower.

In the old calendar, the 'Mary-golde' was named as the flower for Lady Day, the twenty-fifth of March. It was said that anyone who wished to pick the flowers must first say three Paternosters and three Aves, and be 'out of deadly sin'. The flowers were to be picked when the moon was in the sign of the Virgin (Virgo). Calendulas were widely used to decorate statues of the Virgin Mary during the first centuries of Christianity, and one story of the Virgin Mary tells how, during their flight into Egypt, Mary, Joseph and the baby Jesus were set upon by a gang of brigands. When they grabbed and opened Mary's purse, golden marigolds apparently fell out.

The Corn Marigold of Mediterranean countries (*Chrysanthemum segetum*) was also associated with the Virgin Mary, as was the Marsh Marigold (*Caltha palustris*).

MARY'S HEART, CHRIST'S HEART, HEART OF JESUS or BLEEDING HEART (*Dicentra*

spectabilis): This lovely plant for a cool, moist position bears pendulous heart- or locket-shaped flowers along its arching flower stems. The pink sepals form the heart while the little flower protruding below is white. Together they are said to represent the blood and water that flowed from Christ's side when it was pierced by the lance of a Roman soldier after His death on the Cross.

MARY'S MILKDROPS, VIRGIN MARY'S TEARS, OUR LADY'S TEARS, JERUSALEM COWSLIP, LUNGWORT, VIRGIN MARY'S COWSLIP, JOSEPHS AND MARIES, SAGE OF BETHLEHEM, ABRAHAM-ISAAC-AND-JACOB, or CHILDREN OF ISRAEL (*Pulmonaria officinalis*): This plant had many different country names, far more than listed above. Most were based on the silvery white sprinkling of spots and speckles on the

deep green leaves, which were variously compared to drops of milk or teardrops, but some were based on the contrast between the rosy pink buds and the rich blue flowers. Such an unusual colour contrast led to country names such as Adam and Eve, and Josephs and Maries. The name Lungwort, on the other hand, derived from the alchemical belief in the Doctrine of Signature, that the spots on the leaves indicated a supposed use for curing lung diseases.

MARY'S MINT or MENTHE DE NOTRE DAME (*Mentha spicata*): More commonly known today as spearmint, this herb was widely associated with the Virgin Mary. In Italy it was also known as Mary's Herb. The cool sweetness and purity of its fragrance and the fresh green of its foliage make it welcome in a Mary garden.

Mint was one of the plants of the Greek gods appropriated by the Marian cult. Menthe was a nymph and the lover of Pluto, King of the Underworld. When Persephone, Pluto's wife, discovered his infidelity she turned Menthe into a lowly creeping plant. Pluto was unable to lift the spell, but he gave Menthe a sweet scent that would be loved by all.

MARY'S SWORD OF SORROW or FLEUR-DE-LYS (*Iris pseudacorus, I. pallida* 'Florentina'): The leaves of iris are sword-shaped, and at least two iris species are planted in Mary gardens in memory of the prophecy of Simeon to Mary when Jesus was presented in the temple as a child. He foretold the sufferings of Jesus, and that Mary's heart would be pierced with the sword of sorrow. The ancient *I. pseudacorus*, which was planted in many medieval gardens and became the symbol of the royal house of France, is often chosen for Mary gardens. In dry, sunny gardens, the Florentine iris, which was often depicted in ancient paintings and illuminated manuscripts, is preferred.

MARY'S TEARS, OUR LADY'S KEYS, HERB PETER, HERBA PETRI, SAYNT PETERWORT, PAIGLE or COWSLIP (*Primula veris*): Our modern name Cowslip is derived from the old word 'cowslop', referring to the belief that cowslips grew up wherever a cow had left droppings in the meadows. In his herbal written in 1525, Richard Banckes referred to cowslips as 'cowsloppe' and 'Herba Petri' (Peter's Herb) and one year later Gerard referred to them as a 'cowslyp', 'pagle', 'Saynt Peterworte' and 'Herbe Paralysy'. This plant was used in the treatment of

palsy from the medieval period through to the eighteenth century. In Wales, the cowslip gained the name of Mary's Tears. It was said that St Peter dropped the keys to Heaven and where they fell to earth, the cowslip emerged. A variation on the story told that it was the Virgin Mary who dropped the keys.

OUR LADY'S BEDSTRAW, LADY'S BEDSTRAW, LADY'S TRESSES, LADY'S BED or YELLOW BEDSTRAW (*Galium verum*): This plant was a popular strewing herb in medieval times. It was also used in the same manner as rennet to curdle milk for cheese making. According to legend, the flower was white until Jesus was born, when it turned to gold in the light of His presence. Another legend has it that this plant was used by the Virgin Mary to create a mattress for the infant Jesus. The tiny

yellow flowers, borne in midsummer, are honey scented, and the foliage, in whorls of fine green leaves around the stem, releases the scent of new-mown hay when it is dried.

OUR LADY'S BELFRY, LADY'S SEAL, SIGILLUM SANCTAE MARIAE, SOLOMON'S SEAL, LADY'S LOCKETS, SEAL OF ST JOHN, SEAL OF THE VIRGIN, DAVID'S HARP, JACOB'S LADDER or SCALA COELI (*Polygonatum multiflorum*): This is one of the most graceful of flowers, sending up arching stems to around 80 centimetres (30 inches). These bear pairs of deep green leaves at intervals along their length, with twin nodding, narrow, white bell flowers tipped with green suspended below each pair of leaves. A very attractive variegated form exists. The plant prefers light shade and a moist soil. It had ancient uses as an aphrodisiac, as a salve for bruises and wounds, and as a distilled water in expensive cosmetics, especially in Italy. The ladder-like appearance of the paired leaves led to the names Jacob's Ladder and Scala Coeli.

A number of other species of *Polygonatum* would be appropriate for a Mary garden, including the Giant Solomon's Seal (*P. canaliculatum*), the Dwarf or Japanese Solomon's Seal (*P. humile*), the Smooth Solomon's Seal (*P. biflorum*) and the sweet-scented *P. odoratum*, including its variegated form 'Variegatum'.

OUR LADY'S DELIGHT, HEARTSEASE, TRINITY FLOWER, LOVE-IN-IDLENESS or PANCY (*Viola tricolor*): This plant was dedicated not only to the Virgin Mary but also to St Euphrasia, whose feast day is the thirteenth of March, and to St Monica, whose feast day is the third of May. In the medieval period, a pancy would have referred to the kitten-faced Heartsease, *V. tricolor*, also known as Johnny-Jump-Up. It was also Shakespeare's Love in Idleness, a flower reputedly much loved by Queen Elizabeth I of England. This tri-coloured wild pansy also became a symbol of the Holy Trinity. The large modern pansy, which takes its name from the medieval Pancy (derived from the French word *pensée*, meaning a thought), is the result of nineteenth and twentieth century hybridisation and selection.

OUR LADY'S FINGERS, LADY'S FINGERS, WILD HONEYSUCKLE or WOODBINE (*Lonicera periclymenum*): This is Shakespeare's 'luscious woodbine', the deliciously fragrant, pink-flowered, wild honeysuckle of English hedgerows. The tubular flowers are borne in a cluster, a little like fingers held out from the palm of the hand. They are white within, blushed pink on the outside and open from rosy buds. The fragrance is warm and delicious in the day, but at night intensifies with pure, high, sweet notes. It is a woody climber and was exceptionally popular from medieval times as a plant to train over bowers.

OUR LADY'S GLOVES, GANT DE NOTRE DAME, MARY'S THIMBLE, FOXGLOVE, FAIRY FOLK'S GLOVES, FAIRY BELLS, GOOSEFLOPS or FAIRY'S PETTICOATS (*Digitalis purpurea*): Foxglove flowers have always proved irresistible to children, who place them on their fingers to create gloves. In France, England and Germany foxgloves were renamed Our

119

Lady's Gloves during the medieval period, but country names inferred that they were also a perfect fit for foxes and fairies. The flowers are borne densely up tall spikes and are pink, mauve or white, speckled and freckled in the throat, and much loved by bees.

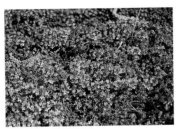

OUR LADY'S HERB, WILD THYME, SERPOLET or CRADLEWORT (*Thymus serpyllum*): Wild thyme was believed to have been one of the fragrant herbs chosen by the Virgin Mary to make a mattress for the baby Jesus. This is a creeping thyme found in southern Europe. It has tiny, fragrant leaves and it forms pink- or rose-coloured flowering carpets in summer. In Russia, thyme was used to decorate icons of the Virgin Mary. Most creeping thymes sold in nurseries are forms of *T. praecox*, but they are suitable substitutes.

OUR LADY'S LACE, LADY'S LACE or SWEET WOODRUFF (*Galium odoratum* syn. *Asperula odorata*): This dainty plant has clusters of tiny, starry white flowers, and while it has almost no scent when fresh, it develops a delightful scent of new-mown hay when dry owing to the presence of the compound coumarin. For this reason, it also found use in medieval times to stuff mattresses, to scent stored clothing and as a strewing herb. The sweet scent of hay was also transferred to the 'Maibowle', a drink celebrating the arrival of spring in northern Europe. It was made by adding a handful of Sweet Woodruff in flower to a white wine punch. The plant flourishes in moist situations.

OUR LADY'S MANTLE (*Alchemilla mollis*): Two plants are known to have had the name Our Lady's Mantle in the medieval period, the heavenly blue-flowered morning glory and this one, still generally known as Lady's Mantle. The pleated, fan-like leaves with their fine, silken hairs were said to resemble the homespun cloak worn by the Virgin Mary. *Alchemilla* was also credited with mystical properties. The leaves form droplets at even intervals around the edge of the leaf during the night (by the process of guttation) and these apparently miraculous drops were gathered for various alchemical uses. The plant is delightful in bloom, and produces airy clouds of tiny lime-yellow flowers.

OUR LADY'S NEEDLEWORK, QUEEN ANNE'S NEEDLEWORK, KISS-ME-QUICK, PRETTY BETSY, WALL VALERIAN and RED VALERIAN (*Centranthus ruber* syn. *Kentranthus ruber*): This perennial has large, dense panicles of tiny, fragrant, tubular flowers in rose, pink or white, and rather fleshy, fresh green foliage. Unlike the true valerian, it was not used for medicinal purposes, but the young leaves were used in salads and as a potherb in medieval times. It grows happily in old stonework and thrives beside the sea. The flowers are immensely attractive to bees and butterflies. John Gerard described it as growing in his garden in 1597. The flowers look almost as if they were created by needlework with alternate long and short stitches.

OUR LADY'S SHOES, DOVES AROUND A PLATE, DOVES AT THE FOUNTAIN, DOVES IN THE ARK, COLUMBINES (*Aquilegia vulgaris*): This beautiful European wildflower can be planted in a Mary garden in its wild form (the seeds are readily available from specialists) or in many entrancing cultivars, including a very double white form, 'White Victoriana', that actually dates from the seventeenth century, exquisite blue-flowered forms such as 'Bluebird' and the species *A. alpina*, and pure white single forms such as 'Kristal'. All are appropriate to a Mary garden. The coloured sepals (technically 'tepals') of aquilegias are spurred, so that the six spurs arranged at the top of the flower in a ring do indeed resemble doves around a dish or fountain. As doves are the symbol of peace, these flowers are a particularly appropriate choice for the Feast of Pentecost.

OUR LADY'S TEARS or LILY-OF-THE-VALLEY (*Convallaria majalis*): According to legend, this beautiful plant, with its nodding bells of purest white and delicious fragrance, sprang from the ground where the Virgin Mary's tears fell when she heard Jesus condemned to death. May is the month dedicated to the Virgin Mary, and it is the time when this plant flowers in northern Europe. In Germany, little bunches are often brought to decorate shrines dedicated to the Virgin Mary.

POMEGRANATE (*Punica granatum*): Few plants have more widespread and complex meanings than the pomegranate. It became a symbol of the Christian Church and represented eternal life. In earlier times, it was linked to the myth of Persephone, the daughter of Demeter, the goddess of wheat. Persephone was abducted and taken to Hades. She refused to eat, but eventually succumbed, eating six pomegranate seeds. She was thus condemned to spend six months each year in Hades, mourned by the earth, which turned cold without her joyous presence. In the Jewish tradition pomegranates were symbolic of virtuous deeds and of fertility.

ROSE (*Rosa gallica, R.* x *damascena, R. alba*): The rose became a symbol both of the Virgin Mary and of divine love. While both red and white roses were used, varieties of *R. alba*, such as the White Rose of York and the Jacobite Rose, were particularly favoured as symbolic of the Virgin Mary. The red rose planted in monasteries in the medieval period was *R. gallica* 'Officinalis', known by many names, including the Red Rose of Lancaster in England and the Rose of Provins in France. The rose was a pagan symbol of a more earthly form of love and was also dedicated to Venus and

Bacchus. In the medieval period, the red rose took on many other symbolic meanings, such as the blood of the Christian martyrs, chivalry and courtly love. The Damask Rose, called the Castilian Rose in Spain and its former colonies, is the rose that St Juan Diego found flowering on the mountain when he encountered Our Lady of Guadalupe.

Where long-flowering roses are required for a Mary garden, many of the David Austin roses offer the charm, fragrance and form of the old Gallica, Alba and Damask roses. 'Mary Rose', 'Winchester Cathedral', 'Brother Cadfael', 'The Nun', 'Canterbury', 'Chaucer', 'Glastonbury', 'The Friar', 'Sharifa Asma', 'Eglantyne', 'St Swithun', 'Wildflower' and 'The Herbalist' would all have medieval Christian associations. Suitable fragrant climbing roses for bowers or a garden backdrop include the double white Noisette Rose 'Lamarque', the tiny-flowered Rambler Rose 'Aglaia', Shakespeare's Musk Rose (*R. moschata*), the milky white Noisette 'Autumnalis', the

violet-scented 'Lady Banks Rose', and the arching, almost treelike 'Lady's Bower', with posies of small, powerfully sweet, musk-scented, pale pink blossoms wreathed along every branch. All these roses have exceptional fragrance and all are reliably healthy and floriferous.

According to tradition, the rosary was created by St Dominic from beads made of compressed rose petals. Mary appeared to St Dominic, a monk of the twelfth century, promising that if he spread devotion to the rosary his Order would flourish. The rosary is a prayer counter, something that exists in many religions where repetitive prayers are offered. It is thought that in the eleventh and twelfth centuries, prayers to the Virgin Mary were counted on stones, bones or dried berries threaded onto a string. Lady Godiva of Coventry bequeathed in her will c. 1075 a rosary of precious stones to be placed at the feet of a statue of the Virgin Mary. Strings of ornamental beads used for rosaries became known on the Continent as paternosters. One pleasant story, which apparently helped to spread the use of the rosary, told of a young monk who was seen praying with his rosary beads, with roses rising from his lips towards Heaven.

ROSEMARY (*Rosmarinus officinalis*): The name of this herb is not, as some believe, a corruption of 'Rose of Mary' but is derived from the Latin *ros marinus* meaning 'dew of the sea'. This intensely resinous and invigoratingly scented shrub is commonly found on sea cliffs in the Mediterranean. So prolific was rosemary once in southern France that John Evelyn, the seventeenth century writer, stated that the great numbers of bushes 'are credibly reported to give their scent above thirty leagues off at sea'.

As an evergreen, and as a symbol of remembrance, rosemary is often used in decorating the church at Christmas, at memorial services for those who fell in battle and on coffins. A charming myth links the Virgin Mary to this fragrant herb. It is said that the flowers of the rosemary were originally white. During her perilous flight to Egypt with Joseph and the infant Jesus, she cast her blue mantle over a rosemary bush to dry while she rested. From that day the rosemary flower took on the blue shade of her cloak. Writes Sir Thomas More:

As for rosemary I lette it runne all over my garden walls, not onlie because my bees love it, but because it is the herb sacred to remembrance and to friendship.

ST JOSEPH'S STAFF or HOLLYHOCK (*Alcea rosea*): Medieval towns, particularly in southern France and Italy, often have extensive stands of hollyhocks along the roadside, and they are found around ancient monasteries. The plant forms a large rosette of leaves from which emerge tall, dense spikes of large, silken, single flowers in a range of colours. Double hollyhocks are a quite recent invention. The Antwerp or Fig-Leaved Hollyhock was introduced into cultivation in the sixteenth century, resembling the common hollyhock but with fig-like leaves. Many modern strains of hollyhock are martyrs to rust, and heirloom varieties or plants grown from seed gathered around ancient sites are ideal for a Mary garden.

SNOWDROP (*Galanthus nivalis*): The exquisite nodding white flowers, tipped with green, of the snowdrop emerge when winter still grips northern Europe and shine bravely in melted patches in the snow as a harbinger of the coming spring. Snowdrop is usually in flower at Candlemas, on the second of February. In an old tradition, the altar was scattered with snowdrops symbolic of the purity of the Virgin Mary, and little bunches are still picked in many parts of Europe to lay before her shrines on Candlemas. Very large colonies exist around some old monasteries and castles in England.

STAR OF BETHLEHEM (*Ornithogalum umbellatum*): A member of the lily family, Star of Bethlehem is a bulbous plant with strap-like, deep green leaves and exquisite, glistening, starry white flowers striped green on the outside of the petals. The bulbs are nutritious and were eaten in ancient times, either raw or cooked. According to legend, after the star that led the Three Wise Men to Bethlehem had completed its task, it burst into a million fragments, falling to earth to become the Star of Bethlehem plants that carpet the Holy Land. The plains of Syria and Palestine have been described as being covered in sheets of these flowers in springtime.

STRAWBERRY (*Fragaria vesca*): There is a touching belief in some parts of Europe that the

Virgin Mary accompanies children who go strawberrying on St John's Day. Another belief ensured that no mother who had lost a child would eat a strawberry on that day lest her child have none to eat in Paradise.

The strawberries planted in Mary gardens are the intensely flavoured wild strawberry of the European woodland, first recorded growing in gardens, in the Louvre Palace in Paris, in the fourteenth century. In earlier times, wild berries would have been picked in the woods in summer. The large modern strawberry arose from hybridisation with two species from the New World.

Strawberries were often used as a decorative motif in the borders of medieval illuminated manuscripts and embroideries, and they were also used as a device on the coat of arms of various medieval families. Strawberries were considered to be a symbol of temptation, but in tapestries and medieval paintings a combination of the purity of the white flower and the luscious

ripeness of the red fruit symbolised the chaste bride and the pleasures of the marriage bed. They make delightful garden path edgings with their deep green, trifoliate leaves. The problems of regular replanting and the removal of runners usually associated with growing strawberries is overcome by planting a form of the wild strawberry called the Alpine Strawberry or Four Seasons Strawberry (*F. vesca* var. *semperflorens*), which has extremely short runners so that a clump appears to do no more than increase slightly in diameter each year.

SWEET MARY, COSTMARY, BIBLE LEAF or ALECOST (*Chrysanthemum balsamita var. tanacetoides*): This hardy, soft-leafed herb with frosted green leaves has a delightfully sweet and refreshing mint scent and was tucked into bibles to sustain listeners during those long and thunderous orations that were once the standard for pulpit deliveries. Discreet sniffs of costmary fortunately revived flagging senses, and gained the plant the name of Bible Leaf. It has small, golden button flowers and today is more likely to be used in iced tea, to flavour ale and to charm the senses in tussie-mussies and potpourri.

TEARS OF MARY, EASTER BELL or GREATER STITCHWORT (*Stellaria holostea*): This wildling has satiny white flowers and, according to legend, sprang from the ground where the tears of the Virgin Mary fell as she wept for Jesus when he was condemned to death.

This is a delightful plant for a lightly shaded area, at its best when planted in a mixture with ancient meadow plants, such as Red Campion or Red Riding Hood (*Silene dioica*), Ragged Robin (*Lychnis flos-cuculi*), Moon Daisies (*Leucanthemum vulgare*, also associated with the Virgin Mary), pink- and white-flowered forms of Musk Mallow (*Malva moschata*) and bluebells, in a flowery mead.

VIRGIN MARY'S THISTLE, OUR LADY'S THISTLE, MARIAN, ST MARY'S, MARY'S THISTLE, CHARLEMAGNE'S THISTLE, BLESSED THISTLE, VIRGIN'S THISTLE (*Silybum marianum*):

The Milk Thistle, with its bitter white latex, was valued from Roman times as a treatment for liver problems. It is a tall plant with smooth, light green leaves that have dots of white along the mid-rib, said to be droplets of the Virgin Mary's milk. The flowers are reddish purple. This plant was considered 'a great breeder of milk' and advised for the diet of wet nurses.

Another herb, *Cnicus benedictus*, also went by the name Blessed Thistle, and it was also known as St Benedict's Thistle or Holy Thistle. It has yellow flowers and white veining, although this is seen under the leaf. It was considered a cure-all, and was a specific treatment for smallpox.

VIRGIN'S BOWER, OUR LADY'S BOWER, TRAVELLER'S JOY or OLD MAN'S BEARD (*Clematis vitalba*): This flower is

commonly used to celebrate the Feast of the Assumption on the fifteenth of August. Virgin's Bower is a woody climber often found in hedgerows and on roadsides, earning it the name of Traveller's Joy, both for the beauty of its abundant, fragrant white flowers, which appear between July and September, and its habit of creating a shady bower with interlaced arching stems. The flowers are followed by delicate, silky, long-feathered balls of seeds, which persist well into winter, leading to its name Old Man's Beard. This is one of those ambivalent plants associated with both good and evil. In some places it was associated with the Devil, probably because of its habit of strangling other plants in its rush to grow into the sunlight.

Garden Design: The Mary Garden

This is a garden which employs simplicity, privacy, and the mind stilling properties of symmetry and geometry to create a meditational space. It is enhanced with gentle colours, a feeling of space and light, and sweet fragrance. The use of recycled bricks creates an instantly aged feeling to the garden, and the runner bond pattern employed here leads the eye into the distance. Three wattle arbours with seats are provided to offer different visual perspectives and a retreat from the sun at any time of the day. The deliciously fragrant woodbine or wild English honeysuckle *Lonicera periclymenum* could be planted over the arbours. If wished, the arbour at the far end of the garden could be replaced with a statue of the Virgin Mary, perhaps surrounded by a simple circular garden of Madonna lilies or alternatively fragrant white-flowered *Lilium longiflorum*.

Planting for this garden is very restrained. In cooler climates, apple, crab apple, cherry or pear trees are suggested. The crab apple 'Floribunda', with its deep rose pink buds and pale pink blossom, is very floriferous and particularly adaptable. Ornamental cherry trees recently bred for warm temperate climates such as the beautiful mid-pink 'Yvonne Matthies' will create the same effect in areas with milder winters. It is important that all four trees should be of the same variety. In warmer climates, olive trees, lemon trees, or a tall variety of orange tree such as 'Seville' would be appropriate. The trees are underplanted with turf which could, if wished, be studded with bulbs of snowdrops in cooler climates and snowflakes in mild climate areas. The four rectangular rose beds are planted with pale pink Damask roses which should be pruned, if necessary, soon after flowering.

A central feature is provided to mark the centre of the axial paths. A large urn with a topiary bay tree has been suggested. The art of topiary, inherited from the Romans, was particularly popular in the medieval period. A simple wellhead or a modest fountain or birdbath might equally be chosen for this position.

To enhance the ease of maintenance of this garden and reduce invasion by weeds and grass, a 0.5 m (20 in) paved pathway surrounds the garden. Simple stone pillars or strong wooden gate posts to around 2.0 m (6 ft 6 in) mark the entrance, and the garden is enclosed by either stone or brick walling, or alternatively by a formal clipped hedge of bay, cherry laurel, or yew (if not exposed to livestock to which it is poisonous). The proportions of this garden add to its restful effect, but to accomodate the smaller garden the dimensions might be scaled down by up to thirty percent, provided care is taken to select small tree varieties. Alternatively, the rear quarter segment of the garden could be eliminated.

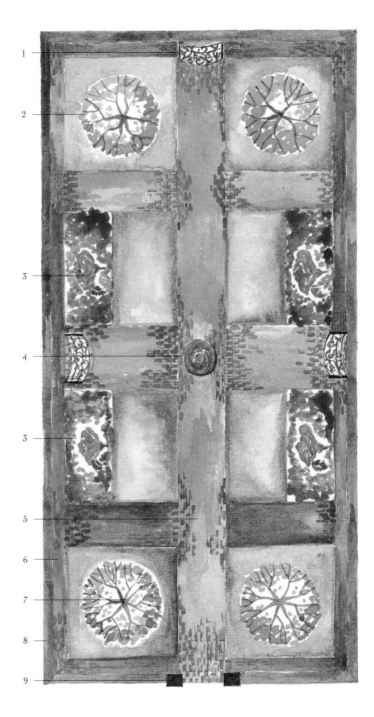

Chapter 5

The Pilgrim's Garden

Give me my scallop shell of quiet,
My staff of faith to walk upon,
My scrip of joy, immortal diet,
My bottle of salvation,
My gown of glory, hope's true gage,
And thus I'll make my pilgrimage.

SIR WALTER RALEIGH, *The Passionate Man's Pilgrimage* (1603)

Pilgrimages

All religions have sacred places that draw the faithful on a pilgrimage, a journey to make contact with the inspirational sources of faith. Yet, in an era when travel was exceptionally difficult even for the rich, for many there was also an undoubted element of excitement and adventure in setting out upon a pilgrimage with like-minded people, sharing trials and joys, exchanging stories and breaking free from the limited personal world that was the lot of many in the medieval period.

A pilgrimage was a major event in life, never to be forgotten, and often undertaken just once. Many died en route to the Holy Land or on the long journey to Santiago de Compostela, the result of privations (sometimes self-inflicted as acts of religious penitence), brigand attacks, drownings (including those deliberately caused by murderous and greedy ferrymen), illness, accidents and frailty. Few pilgrims were deterred by such dangers. Many undertook pilgrimages because they were weighed down with a sense of their own sinfulness and believed that the penance of pilgrimage would aid their salvation. To die on pilgrimage made the way to Heaven more certain.

The Church acknowledged three great Christian pilgrimages that would result in all sins being forgiven. They were the pilgrimage to Santiago de Compostela, the pilgrimage to Jerusalem and the Via Francigena to Rome. A fourth, considered to be a penance for certain crimes, was the pilgrimage to the tomb of St Thomas à Becket at Canterbury.

Long before the time of Jesus, pilgrimages were made to tombs of Jewish prophets and leaders, and these provided a model for Christian pilgrimages. Remarkable numbers of pilgrims made their way to Palestine, Syria and Egypt in the first centuries after the death of Christ. Syria, a great centre of early Christianity, became a portal through which both Italy and France accessed the arts, culture and religion of the Near East. Italy, in particular, traded heavily with Syria, particularly for the beautiful silks and fragrant spices that came overland from China on the Spice Route.

Many of these large-scale pilgrimages were organised by the Church, which also provided armed escorts as protection. There was even an early travel guide to the Holy Land, *The Pilgrim of Bordeaux*, prepared in 333. Some pilgrims, on reaching their destination, remained and took up a religious life with the monks of Sinai or Thibaid. A much needed hospice for pilgrims was erected in Jerusalem in 600, and Charlemagne the Great funded a major hospice in the early ninth century. In comparison with modern travel, a pilgrimage was not only fraught with danger but often occupied a very long time. In the eighth century, St Willibald took seven years to complete his pilgrimage to the Holy Land.

Within Western Europe, pilgrimages to local sites of sacred significance also began quite early. A number of these sites were sacred both to the old religions and to Christianity, and many pilgrim routes overlaid those trodden by countless pagan feet. As routes became better established, they were increasingly lined with chapels and shrines, and with places dispensing hospitality to the faithful. It was quite common for rooms in castles to be set aside to accommodate pious pilgrims. Lodging and food were supplied in return for tales of the pilgrims' exotic experiences. In this way, many were kept well informed about happenings in the wider world.

Wells and springs are among the sacred sites that attracted early pilgrims. For some time, the Church was intent on stamping out veneration of these sacred sites, many of which were reputed to have healing waters and carried the names of the old gods and goddesses. Over time, a number were renamed or became associated with Christian saints and miracles, but nevertheless the Church frowned on well worshipping. In 789 Charlemagne went so far as to issue a decree against well worship. In the previous century, the Council of Rouen had even ruled that offerings made at a well were made to the Devil, and two English kings issued decrees similar to that of Charlemagne. 'Well dressing' was common in the countryside and consisted of hanging a strip of clothing, or 'clootie' in Ireland, on surrounding trees. Despite the official attempts at suppression, the practice survived, and wells and springs continued to be places of mystical power that attracted pilgrims, particularly those seeking healing. Both Ireland and Wales were notable for large numbers of sacred wells.

Wells were widely considered to represent the female principle, and after the rise of the Marian cult many sacred wells were rededicated to the Virgin Mary, or to a female saint. Probably the most visited healing well in England is Chalice Well on Glastonbury Tor, sometimes called the Lourdes of England, and Holywell is the most visited in Wales. In parts of England, sacred wells were ceremoniously visited on the saint's day and dressed ornately with flowers. Intricate floral pictures representing scenes from the Bible were created in some areas, and this tradition can still be seen, particularly in the Peak District in England.

Perhaps the earliest Christian pilgrimage within Western Europe was associated with Mary Magdalene. There is a strong belief in France that Mary Magdalene spent the remainder of her life, after the death of Christ, in Provence. This story, closely intertwined with that of Glastonbury in southern England, relates how after the death of Christ one group of His followers escaped the early Christian persecutions, leaving the Holy Land c. AD 40 by boat. Among those on board were Mary Magdalene, Joseph of Arimathaea, St Maximinus, Lazarus, the myrrh bearer St Salome (Mary Salome), Martha, Mary Jacobe, Sarah (the servant of Mary Salome and Mary Jacobe), St Saturnius and St Cleon. The boat took the already long-established Phoenician route to Marseilles and landed at the place now known as Saintes-Maries-de-la-Mer, on the coast of the Camargue, the great wetland delta of the Rhône River. It is said that while Martha went to Tarascon, Mary Salome, Mary Jacobe and Sarah remained and preached in the area where they landed. An early name for the town was Villa de Mari and in the seventeenth century it was known as La-Ville-des-Trois-Maries (the town of the three Marys), before receiving its current name in the nineteenth century. The Camargue was a very remote area, yet in the ninth century the Church of Notre-

Dame-de-la-Mer was built in the town, followed by a priory in the eleventh century, and the church was rebuilt and fortified against the Saracens in the twelfth century. It is now know as L'Eglise des Saintes Maries. The tomb of the three saints, Mary Jacobe, Mary Salome and Sarah, lies within the church and has been the object of pilgrimage for nineteen centuries, as it continues to be today. A festival is held at the church every May.

Mary Magdalene is said to have preached all through Provence, where many sites are associated with her, before finally withdrawing into a cave at Ste-Baume to live the life of a hermit. Mary Magdalene's last home was in an extraordinarily peaceful and beautiful place. The Massif de la Ste-Baume lies to the north-east of Marseilles, reaching almost 1150 metres (3770 feet) in altitude with brilliant white limestone cliffs. Mont St Victoire is nearby. The remarkable ancient forest contains huge ancient lime trees, giant beech, red-berried holly, yews and maples, a mixture quite unlike the typical Mediterranean flora. The woods have been considered sacred for many thousands of years, a belief that has saved them from timber cutters.

A tale of two wells

Gwenfrewi was born c. 615 at Treffynoon in Gwynnedd. She entered a different world from that of most early medieval women. Women in Wales were accorded by law an assurance of personal dignity and considerable independence. No woman could be compelled to marry against her wishes, violence against women was prohibited and their financial independence was guaranteed.

Wales was also notable for its remarkably generous hospitality, a keystone of their society. Giraldis Cambrensis expounded in some wonder at the generosity and obligations of hospitality in Wales:

> No one of this nation ever begs, for the houses of all are common to all; and they consider liberality and hospitality amongst the first virtues ... The young men move about in troops and armed bands, each under the direction of a chosen leader, ever ready to defend their country. And so, also, they have free admittance into every house as if it were their own.

St Winifred's Well at Holywell in Wales.

At fifteen, Gwenfrewi already planned a life as a nun. Her uncle, St Beuno, destined to become the Abbot of Clynnog at Caernarvon, had constructed a church on a grant of land given by her parents. It was unthinkable for hospitality to be abused, so when a young prince and neighbour named Caradoc, thirsty from hunting, came by and requested a cool drink, it was natural for the young girl to provide one. But Caradoc then made sexual advances towards her. The terrified girl escaped and ran towards the church. He caught her at the entrance and, enraged by her refusal of him, hacked off her head with his sword.

St Beuno, emerging from the church and taking in the horrific scene, called on God to witness the horrendous crime. Caradoc was struck dead instantly and his body swallowed by the earth. Where Gwenfrewi's head had rolled a spring of purest water flowed. The saint then prayed for his niece to be returned to life. His prayer was answered and the only sign of her injury was a fine white scar. As St Winifrede (or Winifred), she became a famous abbess, renowned for her sanctity, and ended her days in a remote mountain valley at Gwytherin.

The spring became known as Holywell and it was famous as a place of healing and the scene of many miracles. Holywell became a very important site of pilgrimage and counted many famous names among its pilgrims, including Richard II in 1398; Henry V, who walked the Pilgrims' Way from Shrewsbury in 1416 to give thanks for his extraordinary victory at Agincourt; and Lady Margaret Beaufort, mother of Henry VII. In 1487, King Henry VII issued an edict to the Abbot of Shrewsbury to establish the Guild of St Winifred. Of all the holy wells recorded in Britain, Holywell is the only one to attract pilgrims more or less continuously from the medieval period until the present, and it is still venerated as a place of healing.

The healing water of Chalice Well at Glastonbury Tor.

Chalice Well, sacred and timeless, surrounded by white hawthorn and apple orchards, lies high above ancient Glastonbury Abbey on the ascent to Glastonbury Tor in Somerset. It was dedicated to an ancient goddess and has been sacred for thousands of years. The never-failing spring that feeds the well finds its source in the Mendip Hills. It is known as the Blood Spring, and the water is cold and clear with a faint tang of iron. Red sediments from the iron have given it its name. The water was piped down to the abbey in 1220.

Glastonbury is the centre of Camelot country, and there is a story that after King Arthur died, Lancelot and the surviving knights encamped around the spring to recover from their wounds and exhaustion. A long-held story also claims that the Holy Chalice lies somewhere at the bottom of the well.

Close by there is a second spring, the White Spring, which is iron free but was capped in Victorian times as a water source for Glastonbury. Both wells were frequently visited in the medieval period by those walking the Pilgrims' Way and Chalice Well, with its Red Spring, was regarded as the Lourdes of England. It attracted huge numbers of people to its healing waters in the nineteenth century.

Chalice Well and the adjoining land were purchased by an extraordinary man, Wellesley Tudor Pole, soldier, mystic, seer and honest businessman, who created the Chalice Well Trust in 1959 so that pilgrims of all beliefs might visit the well in peace and seek what they needed. Today the healing well has been surrounded by one of the most beautiful, peaceful and inspirational gardens in England.

Mary Magdalene is said to have lived her hermit existence of prayer and contemplation for thirty-three years. When she felt her life was drawing to an end, she descended from the cave to receive final communion from St Maximinus. Today, the place of her final communion is marked by the Petit Pilon, near the Abbaye de St-Maximin.

The cave was venerated and the story was supported by a number of early, although not contemporary, manuscripts. In the fifth century, the monks of St Cassien camped around the cave, as well as settling in the Abbaye de St-Maximin. The site became a focus of regular pilgrimage. In the eleventh century the relics of Mary Magdalene were reported to have been stolen and removed to Vézelay, which in turn became the focus of pilgrimage. In 1279, the missing relics were finally located, still in the Abbaye de St-Maximin, by Charles of Anjou, and from that time the pilgrimage has focused on the Abbaye de St-Maximin and the cave at Ste-Baume. In the intervening years the sites have been visited by millions, including a number of popes (particularly those of nearby Avignon) and French kings. The Dominican Order became the guardians of the cave in 1295. Today, pilgrims celebrate at this sacred site on the eve of the feast of Mary Magdalene, on the twenty-first of July, and celebrate Mass there on the twenty-second.

Santiago de Compostela

If what was perhaps the earliest pilgrimage in Western Europe was inspired by Mary Magdalene, the most important medieval pilgrims' route was the Camino de Santiago de Compostela, or Route of St James. This pilgrimage route was like a great river fed by many tributaries in Western Europe, flowing inexorably to a grave reputed to be that of St James in the north of Spain. James and his brother John, fishermen on the Sea of Galilee, were among the first apostles called by Jesus. As attested in the Bible, James was beheaded by King Herod Agrippa c. AD 44, possibly on a charge of sedition, as beheading was the normal punishment for political crimes. There is no mention in the New Testament of James becoming a travelling evangelist, and his recorded death at the hands of the state in Jerusalem suggests that he remained in, or at least around, the Holy Land during his life.

An early fifth century manuscript written by Jerome is the first to suggest that St James and St John were responsible for the evangelisation of Illyria (an area occupying the western half of the Balkan Peninsula) and Spain. However, the only apostle, on available evidence, who may have evangelised in Spain was St Paul, who mentioned this intention in his Letter to the Romans written c. AD 57. As he was arrested in that same year in Jerusalem and taken under escort to Rome in 61, it seems unlikely that he would have had the opportunity then to visit Spain. On his release in 63, according to Apocryphal sources as well as Clement of Rome, he finally made his way to Spain, before visiting Crete and Greece. Paul was beheaded in AD 67 in Rome.

Santiago de Compostela is the capital of Galicia in north-western Spain. 'Santiago' is the Spanish for St James, while 'compostela' may be derived from the Latin *campus stellae* (field of the star) or *composita tella* (burial ground). The city has been occupied for a long time and is of pre-Christian origin. There is evidence that it was a centre of ancient Celtic culture and later a Roman necropolis. The Roman Empire included the Iberian Peninsula from the second century BC, and the Romans were not displaced until a group of Western Germanic tribes, collectively known as the Ostrogoths, crossed the Pyrenees and occupied Spain in AD 409.

The discovery of the tomb of St James is said to have happened in 835, in the time of Theodomir, Bishop of Iria Flavia. According to tradition, a hermit named Pelagius was informed by angels of the existence of the tomb and Theodomir was then guided by a star to a site where, under dense brambles and associated with ruined marble arches, he discovered what he believed to be the tomb of St James. No real explanation seems to have been given of how the saint's relics were found entombed in the north of Spain, when his martyrdom was recorded in Jerusalem, although a story was later told that his relics were carried there.

Some believe this is the grave of a Galithean saint, Priscillian of Avila, a severely ascetic mystic who won support for his ideas from at least two influential bishops and had many followers. He advocated a strict life of deep piety and celibacy even within marriage, together with abstinence from meat and wine, ideas that challenged the teachings of the Church. He appears to have had the dubious honour, together with six of his followers, of being the first Christian 'heretic' to be put to death. The charges were politically motivated and loaded with particularly ludicrous assertions of the practice of magic and participation in orgies. He was beheaded in Trier in Germany in 385. His death did nothing to reduce his popularity in some quarters, and the cult of Priscillianism spread widely through Spain and Gaul. In Galithea (today northern Portugal and the Spanish province of Galicia), Priscillian has long been honoured as a martyr, far from being dishonoured as a heretic.

Regardless of which saint lay in the tomb to which Theodomir was directed, a monastery was built on the site and the monks were instructed to guard the tomb. (The monastery was later moved in order to build the cathedral.) A pilgrimage route, the Way of St James, which has endured for a thousand years, took shape. The official gathering points in France for the French Way to Compostela were at the great abbey at Cluny, Saint-Jean-Pied-de-Port, Le Puy, Vézelay, Tours and Arles. Pilgrimage routes from yet farther afield, in Ireland, England, Germany, Belgium and Switzerland, fed into these centres. On the Spanish side of the border, pilgrims often assembled for the long walk at Roncesvalles.

Some pilgrims continued onwards after their stay at Santiago de Compostela to Finisterre on the Atlantic coast. The scallop shell is very common on the beaches there and became the symbol of the whole pilgrim route to the tomb of St James. At Santiago de Compostela, pilgrims purchased replicas of the shell and attached them to their hats and clothing to show that they had completed the journey. Many churches, chapels and hospices along the pilgrim route adopted and displayed the sign of the scallop shell to indicate that their doors were open to the pilgrim weary in body and soul.

This pilgrim route was again popularised in the late 1980s when it was declared the first European Cultural Route, and in 1993 it was listed as a UNESCO World Heritage Site. Today the beautiful cathedral of Santiago de Compostela, with its rich Spanish Baroque facade and original barrel-vaulted Romanesque cruciform interior, represents journey's end for the more than one hundred thousand who travel the pilgrim trail each year. A golden scallop shell adorns the altar above the crypt in which the remains of St James are said to lie. The cathedral also houses what is said to be a piece of the true Cross. Beside the cathedral on the Plaza del Obradoiro is the pilgrims' hospice, the Hostal de Los Reyes Catalicos, founded in 1492.

The scallop shell, symbolic of the entire pilgrim route to St James, is displayed in the church of Abbaye de Valsaintes.

Along the route to Santiago de Compostela a cross marks the path for the pilgrims at Abbaye de Valsaintes.

A green cloistered walk lined with gently soothing lavender is true to the medieval spirit in Orsan's famous garden.

had already been restored. We wanted a ruin. And we wanted a ruin with the right kind of atmosphere, the right spirit, the right kinds of ghosts. And in Orsan, we found just that. We stumbled by accident on this place that was, as we say in France, 'in its own juice'. It had kept its past atmosphere. This is what attracted us, plus the location. Here you have four buildings that make a large courtyard, a valley that is lovely and surrounded by woods, a small river that runs through the valley, and magnificent trees because we are surrounded by a forest with large oaks that grow up to 30–40 metres (100–130 feet) tall. So all this created a protected rural and farming scenery that we loved. Orsan had water, a forest and four buildings with roofs that were beautiful to look at, steep, covered by tiny tiles, and running nearly down to the floor.

The four buildings that remain at Orsan are only ten percent of the original monastery, which was burned down by Protestant armies in the sixteenth century and then partly rebuilt when the Catholic monarchy was restored. After the French Revolution, it was sold by the state as a farm, then many of Orsan's buildings were sold as stone in 1860. There used to be a 75 metre (250 foot) long basilica dating to the early twelfth century, two enclosed retreats for the monks, many monastic buildings, nine defensive towers, and 4.5 kilometres (3 miles) of enclosing stone walls.

All this had been sold and demolished. Only these four buildings remained, and these had also gone to ruin. In the first year we emptied the buildings, cleaned them out, and shored them up by replacing rotten timbers, fixing roofs and restoring walls. In this way we stopped any further deterioration. Outside, we demolished pigsties and poultry sheds. We cleaned the hedges and removed tens of tons of rubbish that had piled up everywhere. The site could not have been cleaned for three hundred years. After a year of heavy labour, we ended up with seventy-five hectares of clean land, woods that had been rejuvenated with the dead wood removed, and all non-original farm buildings removed. Then we decided to work on the four buildings and the garden, slowly and in parallel. Each winter since 1993 we have worked simultaneously on a small part of the buildings and a small part of the gardens. We open to the public for seven months each year, then for the remaining five months we renovate.

The garden is not a restoration. No-one can tell what the garden of the monastery of Orsan was once like, simply because there is no trace left. Our source of information has been literature and monks' paintings because this is a period for which a lot of documents remain. And we were lucky, since at the time we had the idea of making a garden with a medieval and monastic inspiration, there was an exhibit at the National Library in Paris entitled *When Painting Was in Books*. This library contains hundreds of thousands of volumes displayed to the general public. So we were able to absorb many drawings from that period which proved to be useful in redesigning Orsan. It is true when I say this garden is not a medieval garden. That is simply impossible. It is a garden of medieval inspiration. In France we are very involved in conservation whereby we keep things of the past as they were. What I find more interesting is to build onto tradition because it takes into account the thousands of people who have existed before us. We are continuing their work. We are now in the twenty-first century. We make progress by using as a foundation what has been done before us.

In designing the garden, we made use of what existed, the remaining buildings, three old pear trees and one *Buxus*. These were the backbone of the new garden.

Medieval style willow fences divide sections of the garden.

Vegetables grow in traditional woven fenced plots.

First we designed the alleys and large spaces. Then we began the planting. To use the human body as an example, we first made the bones, followed by the skin, then fleshed it out year by year by putting in more plants.

Early on we had planned to make, for example, a vegetable garden. But we first planted our hedge trees (of hornbeam, beech and hawthorn) and grassed areas. Not until three years later did we make the vegetable garden. I'm a firm believer in structured plans. For me, the skeleton does everything. I start from the overview, then gradually zoom in. The design for the seventy-five hectares took into account slopes, roads and solar orientation. The entire garden is integrated within a template. It is a structure that allows us to evolve indefinitely into the future. This is the way I work as an architect.

Of course, we must also maintain what we have created. Three gardeners are here now. They work intensively on the inner plot of 4 hectares (10 acres). Then there is a 15 hectare (37 acres) plot containing flowering meadows, stands of oak trees, and rural hedges of maple trees and blackthorn. Then there is a third area of 60 hectares (150 acres) where we are creating four biotopes: grazing land, hedge, wood and river. We work on the flora, the fauna, the insects and the mammals to make sure that the whole chain of life is recreated.

The disciplined, structured gardens of Orsan are in evidence here, with straight lines, perfectly maintained hedges, trained and topiary soft fruits with abundant berries, and beyond an orchard of ancient varieties of apples and pears.

We have an exceptional master gardener named Gilles Guillot. During the first year we worked alone, and we were still living in Paris and travelling three hours to get here by car. We knew we could not continue working alone. We built our team of gardeners around Gilles who came here at the end of 1993. He is still heading the team, and they work together very cohesively. Everything done in the garden is planned on paper. Planning is established for the whole year. Everything possible is predicted. Work is broken into two-hour blocks of time per gardener to correspond to a given task. To deal with unexpected disasters such as a tree falling down, several time blocks are left free in each month.

We re-evaluate our time allocations each winter. We may also modify garden designs, discuss changes in the way we work or the tools we work with. The objective is always to reduce the workload because labour costs are our most expensive item in budgeting. In a place like this every task is done with great precision. Everything we do must be purposeful. There is a lot of work to do and there really should be more gardeners.

I think that the medieval garden must not so much be a garden of charm and pleasure as a garden that is useful. What is beautiful must also be functional, and what is functional must also look beautiful. Beauty is not the objective, it is the result.

Garden Design: The Garden of Joyous Contemplation

This restful garden has at its heart a single large silver-grey olive tree symbolic of peace. Marking the intersection of the axial paths is a two-tiered structure, the lower tier with a diameter of 3.0 m (9 ft 9 in) forming a circular turf seat, the upper level a circular garden of smaller diameter, 2.0 m (6 ft 6 in) with a centrally planted olive tree and turfed surface. While wattle fencing was traditionally used to edge such gardens, it would need replacement at regular intervals due to rotting in contact with moist earth. For this reason the garden is constructed with brickwork cemented into place and then disguised by wattle edging around both tiers. Very old, even ancient, olive trees can be successfully transplanted, and some specialist nurseries stock such plants, often removed from old olive groves. They can be expensive, but an olive tree that is already a century or more in age can create a magnificent effect within a year of being installed.

Four entrances to the garden are provided, each approaching the turf seat with its olive tree canopy via a short 3.0 m (9 ft 9 in) tunnel arbour over which old grape varieties have been trained. It is suggested that the tunnel arbours be constructed with strong wooden posts and steel arches and finished with a wattle construction. The paths are lined with recycled bricks in runner bond pattern, the turf seat being surrounded by a circular path/edging of 0.5 m (approximately 20 in) diameter. The plantings for this garden are intentionally very simplified, the border garden being filled with the beautiful pale lavender Florentine iris which is exceptionally cold, heat, and drought hardy, while the four circular beds are filled with pink Damask roses such as 'Ispahan' and 'The Rose of Kazanlik'. For a garden that is required to be in bloom for many months of the year, there are a number of suitable roses of old fashioned appearance, graceful habit and charm bred by David Austin in England that would be entirely suitable including the well proven 'Mary Rose' and the exquisite 'Sharifa Asma'. 'Winchester Cathedral' would be an excellent choice if white rose gardens are preferred.

The garden is surrounded by a square patterned pole fence with espalier-trained apple and pear varieties alternating, providing fragrant blossom in spring and fruit in autumn. Two plants should be established on either side of each entry point. Plants should be grafted onto dwarfing stock, and specialist fruit tree nurseries will be able to offer advice on suitable varieties for your area. For additional significance, ornamental moulded scallop shells might be placed to either side of each entrance to the garden.

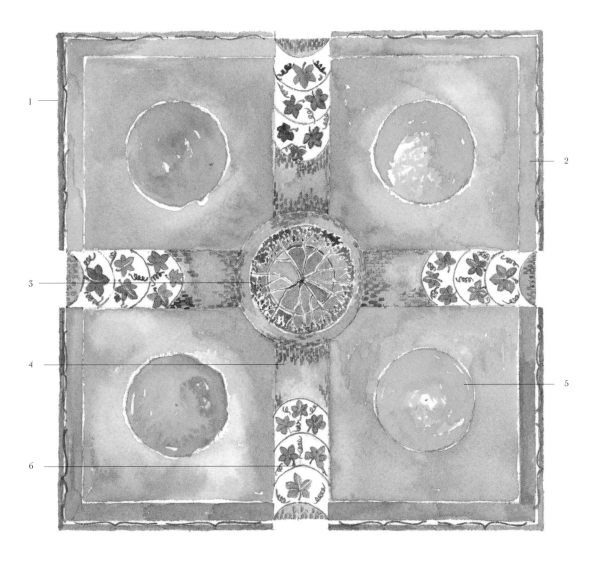

 Legend

1 CARPENTRY TRELLIS WITH ESPALIER APPLE AND PEAR TREES ALTERNATING (4 PER SIDE)

2 FLORENTINE IRIS (LAVENDER COLOUR)

3 TWO-TIER FOCAL STRUCTURE

OF A CIRCULAR TURF SEAT SURMOUNTED BY A TURF GARDEN PLANTED WITH AN OLIVE TREE, BOTH LEVELS CONSTRUCTED OF BRICK, THEN DISGUISED BY WATTLE.

4 RECYCLED BRICK PATH

5 CIRCULAR BED OF DAMASK ROSES (4 IN TOTAL)

6 STEEL FRAME TUNNEL ARBOUR WITH WATTLE COVER, PLANTED WITH OLD GRAPE VARIETIES

With their love of the fantastic and amusing, medieval banqueters were not above enjoying entirely mythical roasted animals. The cockentrice was one such, a dazzling creature with the front end of a suckling pig sewn to a rear devised from a capon. The mysterious animal was well filled with a stuffing made from bread, eggs, spices and suet, and then painted with a mixture of lightly beaten egg, parsley juice, saffron and ginger so that it emerged from roasting with a gilded appearance. A more expensive version of the dish involved a Persian-style stuffing that included pine nuts, currants and various spices, and the creature was encased in fine gold foil before it was presented.

Ingenious menus for fast days

The influence of the Church permeated every aspect of life in Europe in the medieval period in a way that is unimaginable in our more secular times, and the Church decreed what might be eaten during the numerous fast days. The Church saw abstinence from meats as an act of piety, but that belief seems to have been influenced by the Doctrine of Humours (see Chapter 3), which dictated that the consumption of

meats of whatever kind caused excessive anger and lechery, not to mention general intemperance.

The most significant medieval fasting periods were Lent, which preceded Easter, and Advent, which consisted of approximately four weeks, including four Sundays, leading up to and including Christmas Eve. Lent coincided with the hungry gap, the period when winter supplies had almost run out and new season crops had not started to yield, so Lenten fasting was often as much a matter of necessity as virtue. Fish dishes were permitted during fasts, and herring with mustard sauce is typical of the dishes served in the late medieval period. In all, more than half the year was set aside for religious fasting.

Freshwater fish and various seafoods, including many different shellfish, were essential for varying the diet during the lean days of fasting. The medieval taste for variety and attempts to avoid the boredom of religious culinary restrictions led to menus of unimaginable adventurousness by today's standards, and gave indisputable evidence of the ingenuity and creativity, not to mention downright deviousness,

Highland breed cattle are of ancient origin.

Medieval riddles and double entendres

Riddles were much appreciated in the medieval period, and so too was a ribald sense of humour. When the two joined together, the riddle was inevitably a social success. The tenth century *Book of Exeter*, ironically left to the library of Exeter Cathedral by Leofric, the first Bishop of Exeter, on his death in 1072, contains one of the bawdier and certainly one of the cleverest medieval riddles. Almost one hundred of these riddles were included at the end of the book, which also contains the most important collection of literature of its period. The riddles are filled with double entendres. The exceedingly popular English *Carry On* series of movies are clear descendants of the style.

> A young man came over to the corner where he knew she stood. He stepped up, eager and agile, lifting his tunic with hard hands, thrust through her girdle something stiff, worked on the standing one his will. Both swayed and shook. The young man hurried, was sometimes useful, served well, but always tired sooner than she, weary of the work. Under her girdle began to grow a hero's reward for laying on the dough.

Translation by CRAIG WILLIAMSON, *The Old English Riddles of the Exeter Book*

And the answer? A butter churn.

of medieval cooks. The barnacle goose (see Chapter 1) was a good example of this ingenuity, but certainly not the only one. Beavers were hunted to extinction in England as they were deemed to be fish because they used their tail in swimming. Artificial 'animals' created by cooks from vegetables were popular to relieve the tedium. For Lent, when eggs and dairy products were forbidden, a fifteenth century recipe calls for eggs that had their contents blown out and were then filled with almond paste, a forerunner to the modern Easter egg.

Fish dishes included freshwater pike, eels, tench, lamprey, whale, dogfish and porpoise, as well as the more obvious cod, plaice, shad, trout, mackerel, tuna and haddock, and shellfish such as periwinkles, mussels, oysters (which were very cheap by modern standards), scallops, cockles and clams, crabs, lobsters and shrimps. The good cook had an astonishing repertoire of recipes for these ingredients and they were further varied with many different sauces. None of the ubiquitous modern cod and chips for the medieval diner! Castles, monasteries and manors were often equipped with a stewpond, a large pond that acted as a living larder. Fish caught in streams and lakes were transported live to the stewpond and kept there until required by the cook.

Green vegetables

Vegetables were the backbone of the medieval diet, although they were seen as rather lower class, particularly in the late medieval period, and were often disguised or enhanced by expensive spices for grander occasions. Most types of medieval vegetables would be more or less recognisable to a cook today, but centuries of selection have developed newer varieties that may be more tender, have slightly different flavours or be differently shaped or coloured. As with meats and seafood, people were generally more adventurous and ate seasonally from a much wider range of vegetables and salad greens than now.

Cabbages and their near relatives (*Brassica* spp.) were known in medieval times as coleworts. During the period of the Roman Empire, various coleworts were developed and grown. The Romans, ever considerate of their digestive systems, believed the raw juice of coleworts to be useful in lining the stomach before a drinking spree.

Some coleworts were open in form and they have changed little in the last two thousand years. Today's kale and collards are representatives of this type. Kohlrabi belongs to a different line of breeding in which the stem swelled to become tender and rounded. Headed cabbages resembling those known today were gradually created by selection for compressed intervals (internodes) between leaves and were already known in Roman times. Red cabbages were recorded in Germany by the twelfth century and in England by the fourteenth century. Savoy cabbages, with their puckered leaves, reputedly originated in Italy. The Portuguese cabbage, usually called Couve Tronchuda or Braganza, is yet another ancient colewort, resembling a tender and large-leafed collard with small broccoli-like sprouts in spring.

Fava beans (*Vicia faba*) were one of the mainstays of the medieval diet in Europe. The modern green or French bean, shell beans, field or dried beans such as haricot and kidney, and horticultural beans originated in the New World and were unknown to medieval Europe. Fava beans are one of the most ancient crops in cultivation as well as being the most cold-resistant of all beans. They have been found in excavations of ancient Jericho, and there is a record of them growing in Egypt in 1800 BC. A black-seeded form first described by Homer was excavated in the ruins of the ancient city of Troy.

Fava beans were distributed widely across Europe two thousand years ago, but by the first century AD the fava bean was already steadily descending the social scale. Their well-founded reputation for causing flatulence was incompatible with an upper-class lifestyle, but they remained a very important part of the medieval diet, particularly in monasteries. While they were sometimes grown in gardens, favas were usually grown as a field crop and dried to supplement winter dishes. Four varieties of fava bean, all of ancient origin, are recognised: the broad bean (*V. faba* var. *faba*), the horse bean with small, pale brown seeds (*Vicia faba* var. *equina*), tic beans (*V. faba* var. *minor*) and a Central Asian variety (*V. faba* var. *paucijuga*).

Various kinds of peas (*Pisum sativum*) were grown in the medieval period, and like fava beans they were usually grown as field crops along with cereals, although the more sugary garden pea was raised in vegetable gardens. The grey or field pea (*P. sativum* var. *arvense*) was very widely used as a staple food, as this lament by a Benedictine monk in the eleventh century records:

> Yesterday I had peas and pot herbs, today pot herbs and peas; tomorrow I shall eat peas with my pot herbs and the day after pot herbs with my peas.

The grey or field pea was usually dried and reserved for winter dishes

Coleworts, forerunners of modern cabbages, were developed by the Romans.

Modern kale and collards resemble open-hearted coleworts.

or simmered down to a sauce of 'mushy peas'. The field pea had a number of common names (and no doubt some unprintable ones, as the monk's complaint was by no means atypical), and in medieval accounts it was also called the Mutter Pea, the Dun Pea and the Partridge Pea. It is native to the eastern Mediterranean area and eastwards into Turkey and Iran.

The pea was domesticated about the same time as barley and wheat. Archaeological discoveries in ancient Jericho, dating to approximately 8000 years ago, and also in Tell Azmak and Erbaba, included smooth-seeded peas. An incredible but true story is told about Heinrich Schliemann's famous excavation of the fabled city of Troy. The team found what was described as an immense hoard of dried peas dating, as they thought, to the era of the legendary King Priam of Troy, and it was recorded that visitors to the site 'supped from peas from Priam's larder'.

The pea appears to have been widely distributed in Western Europe by 2000 BC, yet there is no clear reference to this vegetable in England until after the Norman Invasion, and then it appears that the field pea was by far the more commonly grown form. Peas were certainly among the Lenten foods eaten at Barking Nunnery in the twelfth century. These were most probably field peas as even in the seventeenth century Parkinson noted of the soup pea 'they serve to boyle into a kind of broth or pottage much used in Town and Countrey in the Lent time, especially of the poorer sort of people'.

Some very old cultivars of field peas are still grown, including 'Blue Pod Capucinijner', developed by the Capuchin monks in either France or Holland in the sixteenth century, and the English 'Carlin', possibly the oldest European pea cultivar we have left, with very ornamental two-toned fragrant purple to crimson flowers on vines up to 1.8 metres (6 feet) tall. The name came from Carlin Day, the second Sunday before Easter, a Church festival celebrated in northern England. It was a day on which peas were given to the poor, a tradition dating to the twelfth century.

Ancient 'Carlin' peas have a distinctive flavour. They were soaked for twenty-four hours before sugar was added and the pot simmered very slowly until the peas were soft.

'Blue Pod Capucinijner' were developed by Capucin monks in the sixteenth century.

Old varieties of vegetables, such as 'Red Epicure' broad beans, are the most appropriate for medieval gardens.

Like the fava bean, the field pea was progressively downgraded socially to the level of the poor and the long-suffering religious, but the sweet and dainty garden pea became a symbol of wealth and social standing. This attitude was reinforced when Catherine de' Medici married Henry II in 1533 and brought to France the sophisticated cuisine of the Tuscan court, along with seeds of the now famous and delicate 'Petit Pois' cultivar from Florence.

The first recorded mention of a named garden pea in England appears to have been made by an ecstatic and gourmet Benedictine monk named John Lydgate from Bury St Edmonds. He exclaimed in a poem about London street life in the mid-fifteenth century: 'Fresh gathered peas, young Hastings!' The 'Hastings' pea was recorded by Parkinson in that best of all gardening books, *Paradisi in Sole*, first published in 1629. 'Hastings' appears to be identical with a cultivar named 'Hastyngez' grown in France for the Archbishop of Rouen in 1486. This pea travelled to the New World with settlers in the seventeenth century but now appears to be extinct in both the Old and the New Worlds.

Thomas Tusser, in his much loved book so relied upon by good housewives, *Five Hundred Points of Good Husbandry* (1572), a blockbuster bestseller of its day, considered 'runciuall pease' to be 'a daintie'. This famous old garden pea was bred in the grounds of the Hospital of St Mary of Roncesvalles at Charing Cross in the second half of the fifteenth century. It appears to have become extinct somewhere in the first quarter of the nineteenth century. The 'Rounceval' was famed for centuries, prized as the last garden pea of the season, with large seeds that earned it an alternative name, the 'Egg Pea', but it was gradually ousted by the newly developed, very large, late season and sweeter 'Marrowfat' pea. Edward Lear's nonsense rhyme 'The Owl and the Pussycat', in which two highly unlikely lovers pursue their ill-advised affair by going 'to sea in a beautiful pea green boat', included a reference to a 'runcible spoon'. Lear loved inventing language, and it is thought likely that this imaginary utensil was based on the 'Rounceval' pea.

Sugar peas were also known in medieval Europe but appear to have reached England quite late, c. 1600.

Many medieval gardens have been recreated on a grand scale but this delightful smaller example at Gordes in Provence is filled with medieval flowers in simple raised gardens, a place of peace and pleasure.

'Peascods' is an old word for pea pods and John Gerard wrote of peas 'whose cods are to be eaten with the Pease when they be young ... [and] are exceedingly delicate meat'.

In the medieval period peas were most often referred to as 'peason' or 'peasun' (spelling in the medieval period was creative bordering on the anarchic). The fourteenth century masterpiece *Piers Plowman* by William Langland, for instance, refers to 'a potful of peasun'. By the Elizabethan period, 'peason' had become 'pease', a name that continued into the eighteenth century, when it gradually became 'pea' due to an excessive concern with refinement and the incorrect assumption that 'pease' was the plural form of the vegetable and, therefore, unacceptable in educated society.

Chickling peas (*Lathyrus sativus*) were also grown in medieval times. They continue to be grown today, largely as fodder for ruminants, and are drought resistant. Related to the sweet pea and the vetches, they can be nutritious in small amounts provided they are thoroughly cooked. This pea goes by many names, most of them ancient, including Chickling Vetch, Dogtooth Pea, Grass Pea, Wedge Pea, Spanish Lentil and White Vetchling. Chickling peas contain a number of neurotoxic compounds called lathyrogens. When the peas become a significant proportion of the diet (over thirty percent), which has happened in times of scarcity, a paralysis of the lower limbs called lathyrism occurs, and long-term effects include skeletal damage. The price is even higher for children, who may suffer abnormal physical and brain development. These effects were well known to medieval people, but they were sometimes faced with a terrible choice between immediate death from starvation or long-term irreversible effects for themselves and their children. The last recorded outbreak of lathyrism was in Ethiopia in 1997–98, and it is certainly not a disease left behind in the medieval world.

Wild green garlic, featured in a fourteenth century manuscript, may have referred to three-cornered garlic (pictured).

Tempting salads

Salads were popular with the Romans and continued to be popular in the medieval period. Many potherbs were included in salads and lettuce was commonly used, although cabbage-headed cultivars like 'Iceberg' were yet to be developed. Instead, several varieties of open-headed lettuce, the kind now favoured in gourmet leaf mixes, were popular. The simple, tossed green salad dressed with oil and vinegar and a touch of salt was recommended for everyday meals in Gerard's herbal and the recipe differed in no way from that of Roman cuisine or, for that matter, modern French cuisine. In the appropriately titled *De Honesta Voluptua* of 1474, Platina recommended his Italian readers try a similar salad, modified with a little mint and parsley for additional interest. However, Platina also recommended more intricate salads. His recipe for a salad of several greens contained not only lettuce, mint and parsley, but also the tender leaves of plants such as the perennial Blue Sow Thistle (*Sonchus alpinus*), which added a slightly bitter note, bugloss, catmint, fennel, oregano, plantain and chervil, together with 'several other fragrant greens'. Other ingredients used in medieval Italian salads included basil, rocket, sorrel, salad burnet, lemon balm, violets and the tender leaves and flowers of borage and tarragon.

A fourteenth century English manuscript provided a recipe that included a far more complex mixture of greens, including cresses, purslane, wild green garlic, onions, leeks, spring onions, borage, mint,

fennel, sage, parsley, rosemary and rue, all shredded into small pieces and dressed simply with oil, vinegar and salt. The wild green garlic mentioned in this recipe was almost certainly ramsons (*Allium ursinum*), or alternatively the Three-Cornered Garlic or Snowbells (*A. triquetrum*) with its pretty clusters of nodding white star flowers, both of which grew wild in woodlands. Garlic-flavoured rocambole might also have been used.

A medieval vegetable used in salads as well as pottage and now returning to favour is the strawberry blite (*Chenopodium capitatum*). It produces small, red, sweet fruits and the leaves are a spinach substitute, although they do contain oxalic acids and should be eaten in modest quantities. Those who suffer from gout, kidney stones, arthritis or rheumatism should be additionally cautious about eating strawberry blite. Both the fruits and tender young leaves were used in medieval salads.

By the late medieval period, these healthy salads were very prettily presented and made with ever increasing care. Edible flowers such as periwinkle, borage, primrose and cowslip, violets and their tender leaves, rose petals,

Salads were often intricate compositions, and particularly in Italy and France tarragon was added for its sweet anise fragrance and complex taste.

clove pink petals and sprigs of flowering thyme were arranged over salads.

The Elizabethans were to create the most diverse and charming of all salads, developed from the medieval recipes. Gervase Markham's *The English Housewife*, first printed in 1615, included a salad for great feasts that included blanched and roughly chopped almonds, raisins, figs, capers, olives, currants, red sage, spinach, oranges, lemons, pickled cucumbers and finely sliced cabbage lettuce.

Darina Allen, famed cook from the Ballymaloe Cookery School in County Cork, Ireland, has done much to resurrect traditional Irish cookery, as well as the use of artisanal produce, and creates just such salads in springtime from the resources of her large potager garden and formal herb garden, as well as wild-gathered plants. Darina's spring salad contains rocket, sorrel, wild watercress and the dainty wild miner's lettuce (or 'Spring Beauty', to give it its Elizabethan name), *Claytonia perfoliata* syn. *Montia perfoliata*. The salad is dressed, tossed and decorated with the deliciously edible flowers of primroses. How Gerard would have approved!

Harvesting the strand

For those who lived near the sea, two other vegetables, seakale (*Crambe maritima*) and samphire (*Crithmum maritimum*), were also harvested from the wild. By the sixteenth century, the tender green springtime shoots of seakale, or *chou marin*, as the French called it, were gathered in such quantities from shingle beaches that they were sold in the marketplaces

of cities. Seakale did not come into popular cultivation until the eighteenth century, when the shoots were blanched beneath pots in early spring to remove any bitterness. Seakale achieved gourmet status with any number of cognoscenti in the food world, from the Francophile Thomas Jefferson by way of the great French chef Carême (who thought it tasted somewhere between asparagus and celery) to the great English cookery writer Jane Grigson. It continues to be grown as a delicacy in Europe.

Samphire was sometimes called Poor Man's Asparagus. It grows close to the sea, and the tips of the plant are tender, crisp, slightly lemon flavoured and salty. It is surging in popularity in top restaurants these days and is being cultivated in the United States as well as gathered from the wild in Europe.

In places like Ireland, Scotland and Wales, wild-gathered seaside vegetables also included a seaweed called laver, which was traditionally rolled in oatmeal crumbs and fried, another poor man's dish that has again become fashionable.

Root crops

The European medieval garden contained a number of root crops of particular value during winter months. These included parsnip, turnip, radish, skirret, rampion, vegetable oyster or salsify, mallow root and scorzonera.

Carrots (*Daucus carota*) originated in the eastern Mediterranean and were domesticated in Iran and the Balkans. They do not appear to have been grown in their modern form, with its well-thickened, straight taproot, until the tenth century when they were recorded in the Near East. Early varieties were in many colours: white, ivory, purple, red or orange. Even today, in Afghanistan, India and the Far East, there are both purple and red cultivars that remain very popular, and the white and yellow forms retain their popularity in northern France and Belgium. Our modern carrots were probably taken to Western Europe by the Crusaders. Gerard, in his famous herbal, recorded growing yellow, purple and red varieties. The mild-flavoured purple carrot remained the most popular in England into the seventeenth century, when it was largely supplanted by the Dutch-

bred orange carrot. An old red English heirloom cultivar that remains particularly popular in North Africa is 'Red Muscade', a very large, unfashionably misshapen but wonderfully sweet, juicy and tender carrot ideal for juicing.

Turnip (*Brassica rapa* subsp. *rapa*) originated in Eastern Europe and the Near East. While it was largely bred for its sweet bulbous root in Europe (the Romans had several root turnip cultivars to choose from), it was selected for tender, tasty leaves in Asia, and for its seeds, from which colza oil is extracted, in India. A seemingly quite different vegetable was created by Italian gardeners who, patiently selecting for tightly bunched, broccoli-like flowering buds borne in spring, created a vegetable known variously as broccoli raab, *Rapini*, *Sparachetti*, *Cima di Rapa* or Turnip Broccoli. In medieval Europe, root turnips were widely cultivated, as much for their hardiness and ease of cultivation as for their frequent use as an animal fodder crop.

A root vegetable that is rare today but was popular from the medieval period onwards was the

Medieval grains

Under medieval agricultural practices barley far outyielded wheat in many areas. Around half the crop was used to make malted barley for ale.

almost every monastery, manor and castle possessed demesne farm fields where most grain crops were grown. Various forms of wheat, as well as rye, barley, rice and cultivated oats, a relatively new grain dating back little more than two millennia, were grown depending on soil and climate. Oats particularly favoured a cool, moist climate, such as that of Scotland, and could thrive on thinner soils. Wheat, on the other hand, required a sunny area with drier climate.

Breads, cakes and pastries were as important to those who lived in the medieval period as they are today. Huge numbers of recipes have survived, including variations on gingerbread, tarts and wafers. Peasants were forced to eat heavy, coarse breads made from the most common grains, and after poor harvests they were often compelled to dilute what flour they had with ground acorns, and sometimes pulses. Wheat bread was preferred, and the rich particularly enjoyed white bread milled from the central, white part of the grain. At the tables of the rich, courses were sometimes served on a flat disc of baked bread called a trencher, which soaked up gravy and juices. A less elaborate trencher in more widespread use was a thick slice of stale bread. It is with reluctance that one records that the trenchers were quite often gathered up at the end of the meal and distributed to the poor.

There are various wheats, all hybrids from species of the grass genus *Triticum* and another grass, *Aegilops*. Einkorn wheat (*Triticum monococcum*) is probably ten thousand years old, and although it gives a low yield compared to modern wheats, it has very good resistance to heat, cold, drought and disease, will grow on poorer ground than modern wheat and matures over a shorter season. It is still grown in high altitude areas of Europe such as Switzerland. Einkorn wheat retains its glumes after threshing, making it more difficult to mill, and it is most commonly ground and used as a cereal rather than for bread making as it has a low gluten content. The stems were used for thatching and to make paper. The wheat known as 'wild einkorn' is *T. monococcum* var. *aegilopoides* and it, too, is ground for use as a cereal.

Emmer wheat (*Triticum dicoccum*) was reputedly first grown by the Babylonians nine millennia ago and is thought to have originated in Palestine.

Grains of emmer wheat, together with barley, were also found in the pyramids, and it literally fuelled the Roman army. Its use has continued today in parts of Turkey and Syria, and in Germany and Russia. This hard red wheat makes a heavy, coarse-grained bread and is also used in some areas as a stock feed. Other names for it include two-grained spelt and starch wheat. Emmer is closely related to modern durum wheat, which is used to make pasta.

Spelt (*Triticum spelta*) is thought to have been cultivated in Europe since about 5000 BC. It has a hard outer layer and was grown extensively in medieval times. In the Italian region of Umbria, varieties of spelt have been grown for millennia, and it is also grown in parts of neighbouring Tuscany and Marche. Its mellow, nutty flavour is currently ensuring it a comeback in European restaurants. It is also valued in the health food industry for its high vitamin B content, as well as its digestibility for those with wheat allergies.

Our more modern bread wheat (*Triticum aestivum*) is free threshing with shorter stalks, is cold resistant and requires a more fertile soil than the various ancient wheats. It has a complex breeding history, with two sets of chromosomes from three different parents.

Under medieval conditions, crops of barley (*Hordeum vulgare*) yielded more than twice as heavily as wheat. About half of the barley harvest was dedicated

Spelt wheat was grown extensively in medieval Europe, and in France was sometimes called mother of wheat. It is once again very fashionable.

Rice was once grown quite extensively in Europe. Today northern Italy remains a producer, particularly of short-grained arborio rice for risotto.

to making ale, the main drink served to monks. The seeds were germinated first to produce malted barley before being fermented. Pearl barley, consisting of the grain stripped of its outer coat, was used in soups, pottages and stews. The unremitting gruel of the medieval peasant and monastic table was also sometimes made from barley, although more commonly from oats.

Oats (*Avena sativa*) also outyielded wheat and were a staple medieval food, although they had a very unsophisticated image. Oats were also the staple of northern European monasteries in the form of gruel. Dr Johnson, writing in the seventeenth century, expressed the continuing antipathy and disdain of the well-to-do towards oats, describing oats as 'a grain which in England is generally given to horses, but in Scotland supports the people'. However, the medicinal value of oats was appreciated early. The roasted grain was used to make an effective drink for constipation and haemorrhoids, and oat porridge, biscuits and bread were all used to restore appetite and strength, and to reinvigorate those with nervous exhaustion.

eryngoe or sea holly (*Eryngium maritimum*), which grows wild along seashores in Europe and Scandinavia. The candied roots of sea holly had quite a reputation as an aphrodisiac, and it was said that all prudent housewives grew it in their gardens. Such was the aphrodisiac reputation of this plant that a booming trade in eryngoe roots candied in orange flower water and sugar emerged in the sixteenth century, centred on Colchester in Essex. The eryngoes referred to by Falstaff in his passionate pursuit of Mistress Ford in Shakespeare's *The Merry Wives of Windsor* were these reputedly potent candied roots.

Like eryngoes, rampions were commonly eaten in the medieval period and through to the Elizabethan Age. They are the white roots of the bellflower (*Campanula rapunculus*). The leaves were used in salads, while the roots were boiled, sliced and served cold, dressed simply with vinegar, salt and sometimes oil, as a salad to stimulate the appetite. Another bellflower (*C. rapunculoides*) was used for the same purpose. Like many medieval foods, rampions are again receiving interest from innovative chefs.

Parsnips (*Pastinaca sativa*), a very cold-hardy root vegetable, were as popular in medieval Europe as they had been in Roman times. They are suffering something of a popularity slump, yet they have many virtues for sophisticated palates. Like carrots, parsnips are high in sugars, they have a starchiness akin to that of the potato, which did not reach the European world until the Renaissance, and they have a decidedly nutty taste and complex spicy aroma. Resembling large white carrots, they were not only appreciated for

their culinary virtues but, at least in medieval times, were credited with some useful side effects, such as increasing men's libidos and repelling snakes. In the ancient Roman cookbook by Apicius a number of recipes are provided for parsnips, including a delicious vegetarian sausage and parsnips simmered in wine. Medieval recipes included a quite excellent parsnip pie. As an aside, pigs in northern Italy destined to become the finest Parma ham are to this day often fed on parsnips in order to ensure their delicate, sweet flavour, a practice widespread in the medieval period.

Onions, both bulbed and leafed, added flavour to medieval dishes, along with garlic and leeks. Leeks (*Allium porrum*) were almost as much a part of the omnipresent monastic pottage as were peas and coleworts. They have been cultivated for at least five thousand years, and the Romans popularised their use in Western Europe. Chaucer mentioned leeks in *The Canterbury Tales*, and they were included in many herbals. The leek was the alternative national symbol for Wales and has been associated with the Festival of St David's Day since at least the seventh century, when St David, patron saint of Wales, persuaded his followers to wear the leek in their hats to distinguish them from the Saxons in the Battle of Heathfield.

The Serpent Leek or rocambole (*Allium sativum* var. *ophioscorodon* syn. *A. scorodoprasum*) is a dramatic and intriguing plant of medieval gardens. The tall plants have chive-flavoured leaves, the base is used in much the same way as a leek, and the flower heads are a mixture of purple flowers and bulbils that have a mild garlic flavour. However, the dramatic effect of this plant in the garden is due to the way the flower stalk coils and loops like an over-amorous swan's neck or, as its common name suggests, a serpent. The beak-like unopened inflorescence only adds to the illusion of a besotted swan.

Some kinds of onions grown in the medieval period are rare today but still available from specialist nurseries. Walking Onion, Tree Onion, Topset Onion or Egyptian Onion (*Allium cepa* var. *proliferum*) is among the quaintest of these old onions and forms a number of small bulbils the size of baby pickling onions (for which purpose they are often used) at the top of the tall, hollow stems in place of a flower head. The bulbils frequently put forth green shoots so that the plant looks mop-headed. The weight of the growing bulbils finally weighs the head to the ground where the bulbils take root. In this way the plants progress across the garden patch to earn their name of Walking Onion. Potato onions (*A. cepa* var. *aggregatum*), both white and yellow kinds, proliferate around the base of the parent bulb, resembling a nest of tiny onions. They have survived and remained popular in places fortunate enough to retain traditional gardens, such as Tasmania and Somerset.

Herbs and spices

The cook's garden would not have been complete without herbs. Medieval dishes were by no means all highly flavoured and some would seem very bland to modern tastes, but herbs were readily grown in most gardens and added flavour to even simple dishes. Among the herbs that might be stocked in a kitchen garden or rural household garden were smallage (a forerunner to modern celery with a more intense flavour and very much easier to grow), thyme (both narrow-leaf French Thyme and broad-leaf English Thyme), tarragon, hyssop, lemon balm, sage, rosemary, sweet marjoram (introduced to England from the Mediterranean in the fourteenth century), parsley, mint, dill, fennel, anise, cumin, caraway, cress, lavender, coriander and chervil.

Most spices, such as cinnamon, nutmeg, mace, pepper and ginger, were imported, and many spices that are considered exceptionally cheap and readily available today were far less accessible then to ordinary people. A great deal of nonsense has been talked about the heavy use of spices to disguise the smell of rotting meats. Medieval noses and stomachs were no more pleased by or tolerant of rotten meat than are our own, and spices were only used to enhance the flavour of dishes and to impress guests with the wealth and sophistication of the host (they were one of the conspicuous consumption items of the time). There is very good evidence that larger towns, and many smaller ones, had strict food control laws that were enforced by inspectors.

was a place in which to see the moral precepts of nature.

That bees were needed to pollinate orchards was well known by medieval times, and Lawson, who was an enthusiastic and experienced amateur apiarist, provided extensive advice on the subject in his book for the benefit of the country housewife. Lawson's affection for bees, which as a clergyman he could not resist using as a model of industry and 'cleanly and innocent' behaviour, led him to view them as very much more than a useful adjunct to the orchard, contributing honey (which was still the most important sweetener in cooking) and its fermented products, mead and spicy metheglin, as well as beeswax for candles. He saw bees as an integral part of the living beauty of an orchard and spoke very fondly of them making 'a pleasant noise and sight'.

Lawson's perfect orchard, in keeping with long-held late medieval ideas, is one protected from winds by a double plantation of woods, and it contains many different varieties of fruit trees in patterned array, together with bee skeps to ensure pollination. For the rich landowner he suggests the

inclusion of devices such as mounts for viewing the beauty of the orchard and gazebos for resting, and additional ornamentation in the form of knot gardens and topiary. He envisioned extensions such as a maze, a bowling alley or an archery butt to provide recreational sports suited to an Elizabethan gentleman, but his orchard remains a perfectly English garden, with no reference to the stylish and highly contrived designs of Renaissance Italy that were already supplanting earlier gardens on the great estates. Lawson was in many ways a traditionalist: his interpretation of the paradise orchard bridges the medieval and Elizabethan worlds and is of the countryside rather than the city.

Medieval orchards were places of pleasure wherever money and labour permitted, containing both shade and productive trees. The choice of trees was dependent on the climate. Pietro de' Crescenzi instructed that gardens of middle size should be enclosed by ditches and protective 'hedges of thorns or roses ... in warm places make a hedge of pomegranates and in cold places of nuts or plums and quinces'. Such a mixed rather than uniform hedge was described at

Two engravings from the *Livre des Profits Champetres et Ruraux* 'Love of the Vine' c. 1500: Farm workers planting a young vine (top) and harvesting the grapes (bottom). Getty Images

Hampton Court in 1599. It was made of shrubs such as hawthorn, roses, juniper, box and English Elm. In the warm climate of southern Europe, Crescenzi recommended that in the orchard: 'Trees are to be planted in their rows, pears, apples, and palms, and in warm places, lemons. Again mulberries, cherries, plums, and such noble trees as figs, nuts, almonds, quinces, and such-like, each according to their kinds, but spaced twenty feet apart more or less.'

Cider, wine and ale

The medieval attitude to fruit was ambivalent. There was a widespread belief, thanks partly to the prevailing Doctrine of Humours and partly to inherited Roman fears, that eating raw fruit was dangerous. To eat fresh pears without a doctor on hand, or at the very least a glass of wine, was thought in some quarters to be courting death. Cooked fruits were very popular, however, and apple sauce, fruit tarts and pies, fruit fritters, preserved fruits, fruits in spiced syrup and conserves of fruit were as popular then as they are today.

The production of apples and grapes before the medieval period was largely devoted to making fermented drinks. The Romans made both cider and perry, although wine was their most popular drink. For a Roman connoisseur, apples scored very low as a fruit, but pears (and the perry made from them) were better valued. The Romans appear to have spread their prejudice against cider through Western Europe and for centuries even monks favoured ale or wine. One of the first reliable mentions of cider in medieval Europe was by Charlemagne in the ninth century.

The Normans carried their love of the apple and its fermented juice to England after the Norman Conquest, and monasteries often featured pomeriums, or apple orchards, housed their own presses and sold cider for additional income. Workers in monasteries were often paid in part with an allowance of cider. By the fourteenth century cider was a popular drink in England.

Kent was the centre of medieval cider making in England and famed for its strong spicy brew. Somerset, Sussex, Gloucestershire, Hampshire, Cornwall, Devon and Herefordshire were also important for their cider, and Herefordshire would later take a leading role in the sixteenth and seventeenth centuries, partly because of the famous apple cultivar 'Herefordshire Redstreak'. Neither cider nor perry, however, rivalled ale in the affections of English workers, and circumstances combined with taste preferences to see cider production much reduced between the fourteenth and sixteenth centuries. The revival of cider drinking only came about with the introduction of better cider cultivars from France.

Heritage and old cider cultivars that are still available, many of them creatively and quaintly named, include 'Stack Me Girdle' (worth growing for the name alone), 'Genet Moyle', 'Redstreak', 'Bushy French', 'Brown Thorn' (or 'Argile Gris'), 'Dymock Red', 'Foxwhelp', 'Gros Hagloe Crab', 'Kenchy Pippin', 'Kill-boys', 'Medaille', 'Michelin', 'Royal Wildling', 'Upright French', and 'Styre' or 'Stiar' (a great favourite for rough cider).

Rome protected her export wine industry for centuries, using an imperial decree to bar other countries within the Roman Empire from growing commercial vineyards of grapes. It was not until AD 280 that this decision was reversed by Emperor Probus in order to encourage local wine production in France, England and Spain.

France became a leading producer of quality wines in the medieval period, as it is today. Burgundy, with its proximity to Paris, was a large producer, but it was Bordeaux with which England traded heavily. From the time of Henry II, in the twelfth century, England imported a great deal of its wine from the Bordeaux region, which at that time was under English control. By the fourteenth century, a wine fleet of around two hundred ships was sent to France twice a year, the first time for the new season's wine, which was required in time for Christmas celebrations, and the second time in spring for the now older wine of the same vintage. This light red wine became known in England as claret.

Vineyards in France were the property of the Church in medieval times. Some of the surviving vineyards date from the third century, and medieval vineyards in Burgundy include Clos de Vougeot, Meursault, Le Romanée, Montrachet, Clos de Bèze and Corton-Charlemagne. To those who love French wines, these names will still be familiar. Many of the grape varieties grown are equally familiar, including Pinot Noir, which was cultivated in Burgundy from the first century AD and used by the monks in the sacraments, Grenache, and Verdelho from fifteenth century Portugal. Chardonnay came from Mâconnais in Burgundy and was first recorded in 1330. The Cistercian monastery at Vougeot planted Chardonnay exclusively, protecting the vines behind stone walls. One of the oldest wine varieties is Shiraz, known in France as *Syrah*, which originated in the northern Rhône district where it was grown during the Roman era. Muscat of Alexandria is the world's oldest known grape variety, presumed to have reached Roman France from either Greece or the Arabian Peninsula. By Charlemagne's reign, Muscat wine was being shipped out of Frontignan in southern France. Pliny called it 'the grape of the bees'.

Only a few specialised wine producers, mainly centred in Umbria, Tuscany and Trentino in Italy, still produce the famous medieval raisin wine. For this, grapes are dried until they have lost up to sixty percent of their moisture, and the resulting wine has the most intense and delicious flavour. Germany produces a variation on raisin wine, the delicious *Eiswein*, by harvesting and pressing grapes immediately after they have been subjected to frost and shrivelled. These wines are remote descendants of raisin wines made by the

Greeks and later by the Romans, a technique spread widely around the Roman Empire and perpetuated in parts of Europe during the medieval period.

England had vineyards growing in the south during the medieval period. There is some archaeological evidence that attempts were made to take advantage of Probus's edict and plant vineyards in England, although no industry seems to have resulted. The first reliable reference to vineyards there was in 731 by Bede, who described vines grown in a number of places in England and Ireland, most often in association with monasteries. The most significant vineyard is likely to have been at the Abbey of Ely, which earned the name 'Isle des Vignes' in Norman times.

The eleventh century Domesday Book mentions a total of thirty-eight vineyards in England. The yields, where they are recorded, appear very low by modern standards. Some vineyards apparently yielded no fruit at all, although whether that was to avoid paying taxes we will never know. The book recorded vineyards at Holborn (then Holeburne), now a part of the central business district in London but outside the city walls in the eleventh century, and Kensington, which had 'woodland for two hundred pigs and three arpents of vineyard'. The largest vineyard recorded was at Bisham Abbey.

Perhaps stimulated by the apparent dearth of vineyards in England as demonstrated by their census, the newly occupying Normans imported superior wines into the monasteries from France,

Ancient wine grape varieties, some dating to the Roman era, are still grown in wine producing areas of France and Italy.

How to create espaliers

Espaliers are shrubs or small trees trained to grow in a two-dimensional plane, usually against a wall although they can be free standing. This is a popular technique for growing fruit trees as it is space saving, fruit ripen more rapidly, and harvesting is easier. Ornamental effects can be achieved by training the trees into various shapes such as fans and candelabras. Apples, quinces and pears with their flexible branches are classic subjects, covered with fragrant blossom in spring and ripening fruits in autumn. Other suitable subjects include crab apples, cherries, peaches, plums, and citrus.

Espaliers should be sited in a sunny position and are trained against a framework usually constructed of several rows of horizontal training wires strained between vertical posts. The lowest wire should be around 40 cm (16 in) above the ground.

The highest training wire should be at the desired height of the mature espalier. The space between successive wires should be around 35 cm (14 in). It is easiest to start with a one-year-old single-stemmed tree. Plant it just in front of the frame. The basic process involves removing all branches that emerge behind or in front of the tree to achieve a flat, two-dimensional shape. For a formal espalier, remove all branches that do not conform to the chosen pattern.

The illustrations provide an example of how to create a simple formal espalier. Soft ties are used to hold the branches in place along the wires.

An impressive espalier can be achieved in five years.

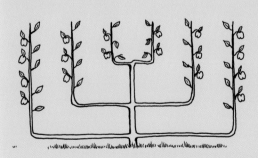

Espalier plants are trained to grown in two-dimensional planes, usually against walls.

Espalier is a popular technique for growing fruit trees as it is space saving, fruit ripen more rapidly, and harvesting is easier.

The medlar is a member of the rose family and is closely related to the pear and hawthorn. It is a small, slow-growing tree, living up to three or four hundred years. It bears clusters of exquisite, large, single white blossoms, blushed with pink, in late spring. The flowers are followed by curious fruits a little like small russet pippins. The fruit is formed in the same way as an apple, but the blossom end remains wide open, creating a flattened base. After the first frosts, the medlars are gathered and placed on straw in a cool, dry place. Damaged by the cold, the cells break down and the fruit begins to slowly ferment, a process called bletting. The perfect time to eat medlars is when they are soft and brown and the pulp can be sucked. They have a sweet, slightly acidic flavour, a texture like apple sauce, and a scent of cinnamon. Medlars have long been served with port as winter winds howl. The fruit are high in pectin and make a delicious jelly for hot buttered crumpets or toast, as well as a very desirable cider and medlar wine.

Medieval Orléans was famous for its preserves of medlar, and it is said that Joan of Arc was presented with medlar preserves when she triumphantly entered Orléans at

the head of her troops. The high tannin content of medlars also made them popular for treating gastroenteritis in the medieval period, and the fruit was made into a syrup for this purpose.

Medlars bear good crops from three years after planting. The varieties available now are almost all many centuries old. These are 'Nottingham', 'Dutch' (in narrow-leafed and broad-leafed forms, with very large flowers) and 'Stoneless'. 'Royal', of French origin, was imported into England by the great fruit breeder Thomas Rivers in 1860. Another very well-flavoured variety, 'Senlac', was gathered near Battle Abbey and is believed to be a seedling only a few generations removed from those planted by the monks. The glowing autumn foliage of many medlars adds to their considerable ornamental qualities. Medlars are self-pollinating, so only one tree is necessary to obtain fruit.

Plums

The sloe or blackthorn (*Prunus spinosa*) is native to Europe and Britain and the fruit were largely used to make sloe wine, as they are very sour if eaten raw. Another native plum, far more acceptable for fresh consumption, was the bullace

The Damson plum takes its name from Damascus in Syria and was well known by the Roman era.

Closely related to the pear, the medlar, with its exquisite bloom, was very popular.

of Britain, known as the Mirabelle in France. Domestic or garden plums arose from hybridisation between the myrobalan or Cherry Plum (*P. cerasifera*, commonly used as a rootstock today), which is not native to Britain, and another *Prunus* species. Domestic plums were widespread during the Roman period. Pliny provided the names and descriptions of twelve plum varieties, although he included the peach, which he referred to as the 'Persian Plum'. Among the plums he described was the Damson Plum, named for Damascus in Syria. He said it had already been long in cultivation.

France seems to have embraced the plum very early and produced excellent quality fruit. The Orléans type appears to have been a very early development. In England there are records of plums being cultivated in monastic orchards, including those of Glastonbury Abbey in the tenth century and Westminster Abbey in the twelfth century. The varieties were grafted onto sloes. However, most people continued to gather their plums from the countryside. It was only in the thirteenth and fourteenth centuries when royalty led the fashion for creating orchards filled with choice varieties that plantings of selected plums, mostly imported from France, were boosted.

Throughout the medieval period, dried plums, or prunes, were very extensively used in cooking, and the word 'plum' appears to have been generic for a number of dried fruits, including cherries. Prunes were gradually replaced in many recipes during the sixteenth and seventeenth centuries with raisins. Our

Christmas plum pudding is an example of a recipe in which plums were later replaced by raisins, as are plum cake and plum duff. The words 'raisin' and 'plum' remained confused in meaning for some time, and we will never know whether Little Jack Horner pulled out a plum, a raisin or even a dried cherry. Some prune plums typical of the medieval period, such as the 'Blue Perdrigon' used to produce Brignon prunes, are still available.

Apart from the Damson, several very old plums are still available. These include 'Reine Claude', known in Italy as 'Verdoccia', which probably came from Greece and before that almost certainly from Armenia. This plum, with its translucent pale green fruits, is filled with exquisitely flavoured, nectar-like juice. It reached France in the fifteenth century and in England it became known as the 'Green Gage'. It needs a pollinator and the luscious eighteenth century 'Coe's Golden Drop', which had 'Green Gage' as one parent, is commonly used for this purpose. 'Catalonia' is believed synonymous with 'Amber Primordian', which was listed by Parkinson in England in the seventeenth century. It is believed to be considerably older than that. The 'Black Bullace' is considered to be the same as the seventeenth century variety 'Winter Creke'. Among the old Mirabelle plums still available and treasured for making conserves, as well as a potent liqueur, are 'Mirabelle de Metz' and 'Mirabelle de Nancy'.

Stephen Switzer in his book *The Practical Fruit Gardener* (1724) had memorable advice for modern fruit breeders: 'A good plum should have a sweet sugar'd Juice, a tender melting Pulp, and a rich and Exquisite Taste something perfum'd'. Alas, without an orchard of our own, we may never know such a delight.

Peaches and nectarines

Peaches originated in China but they were cultivated very early by the Babylonians and Assyrians, and there is a record of them in Egypt in 1400 BC. Nectarines, known to the ancient Romans as *duracinus*, differ by only one gene, that which controls the skin of the fruit, which can be smooth or downy. They both belong to the same species (*Prunus persica*). This was recognised very early, and Pliny described the existence of different types from France and Asia.

Peaches appear to have reached France at about the same time as they reached Italy, according to Columella who wrote in the first century AD, and the fruit from France was considered to be very large compared to the Persian peaches. The well-flavoured, heavy cropping variety 'Nutmeg' (mentioned by Gerard under the name 'avant') was grown for centuries in England and was of the Persian type. The climate would have proved difficult for peaches in England and there are no early references to them, although various monastic records in France show they were in very early cultivation there.

The milder climate in England during the twelfth and thirteenth centuries would have provided more favourable growing conditions for peaches. Probably the first real mention of them, and a dramatic one at that, occurred in this time frame. In the Wendover Chronicle, a severely depressed King John is recorded as having eaten a surfeit of green peaches (helped by a surfeit of ale), leading to severe diarrhoea and his subsequent death in Newark, Nottinghamshire, in 1216. A less sensational mention of peaches in England comes from records of the plantings made for Edward I at the Tower of London gardens in 1275, although the price of the two trees was notably scandalous. Other nobles followed the king's lead, and peaches appear to have been espaliered against the walls of many enclosed gardens. Chaucer and the Benedictine monk John Lydgate both mentioned that peaches were common by the fourteenth century.

Long and intensive peach breeding has replaced the early varieties of peaches and nectarines, and reconstructed medieval orchards are planted with the oldest heritage varieties available. One worth seeking is the old French variety 'Pêche de Vigne', a very dark skinned peach with deep crimson, melting flesh filled with intensely flavoured aromatic juice. It was traditionally placed to mark the end of grape rows in vineyards.

Among the oldest surviving nectarine varieties are 'Elruge', first described by Switzer in 1723, and 'Violette Hative' ('Early Violet'), which is a French variety first recorded in 1659. 'Elruge' has a pale skin and palest green, delightfully aromatic, melting flesh still sought after by connoisseurs, while 'Violette Hative' is a freestone, white-fleshed variety, pale gold blushed with crimson, with wonderful flavour and sweetness.

Cherries

Cherries were in cultivation by the eighth century BC in Mesopotamia, in the time of the Assyrian King Sargon II. Wild cherries (*Prunus avium*), known as mazzards, and the Morello cherry (*P. cerasus*) were indigenous to Europe, including Britain. They were a particularly popular fruit in the medieval period and were regularly mentioned in association with monasteries. Larger monasteries possessed orchards for separate fruits, for instance an area devoted to apples was known as a 'pomerium'. A 'cherruzerd' (surely a name worth bringing back into the language!) or 'orto cersor' was similarly an orchard devoted solely to cherries. Although the cherry season was brief, coinciding with midsummer, it appears to have been a merry one, and much of the harvest found its way to local markets. By the sixteenth century large cherry orchards were concentrated in Kent to supply the London markets. The orchards of cherries in Provence are similarly legendary and have survived far better.

Morello cherries are cooking cherries with acidic, deep red, juicy flesh, ideal for cherry pies, for pickling, juicing and preserving in spiced brandy or syrup. 'English Morello' is a very old, aromatic variety with all the culinary virtues. Another group, called *griottes* in France and Amarelle or Kentish cherries in England, are another form of *P. cerasus* but differ from Morello cherries in producing colourless juice. They include 'Flemish', 'Kentish Red' and the famous old 'Carnation', first mentioned by John Rea in 1665 (although it is thought to be much older)

and later treasured by Thomas Jefferson, who planted it at Monticello in Virginia. 'Carnation' is a freestone, red-skinned, white-fleshed, very high quality cherry particularly valued for confectionery and, in France, for making the superb liqueur Cerise Eau de Vie.

Sweet cherries were cultivated from early times, although Pliny described some, for instance 'Junian', as being so delicate that they had to be eaten beneath the tree. Pliny rated most highly a cherry called the 'Bigaroon' or 'Duracina', which has been identified as the firm-fleshed, heart-shaped 'Bigarreau' ('Spanish Cherry' or 'Spanish Amber'). 'Black Heart' dates to at least the seventeenth century and is quite likely older. Although 'Bigarreau Napoléon' (later known as 'Napoléon') belongs to the early nineteenth century, it has much of the look of the original Roman cherry to which it is related, and it is still found piled high in Provençal markets in midsummer.

Berries

Berries were mainly gathered wild from the countryside in the medieval period. The Woodland Strawberry or *fraise des bois* (*Fragaria vesca*) has a delicious fragrance and intense flavour in the delicate flesh, which compensates for their Thumbelina size. The first recorded use of strawberries in the medieval period was medicinal rather than culinary. They were used to treat gout and also digestive problems. The fruits were avoided for a considerable time as people shared older Roman beliefs that they were contaminated by their proximity to the ground or might have been infected with the plague as a result of contact with snakes and rats.

In some areas, the strawberry was considered an aphrodisiac, and a creamy soup of strawberries and borage was served to newlyweds. By the thirteenth century, the French took up cultivation of the woodland strawberry, although the Romans are known to have cultivated this species many centuries earlier, probably from c. 200 BC onwards. Another very fragrant species, the pale pink, delicate fleshed Musk Strawberry or *hautbois* (*F. moschata*), which has more than a hint of raspberry in its flavour, came into cultivation in the fifteenth century. Another European species that was known then, although not cultivated, was the Green Strawberry (*F. viridis*).

Those who long for strawberries that melt in the mouth and have the sweetness and intense wild fragrance of the medieval strawberry should seek out a French variety introduced in 1991 called 'Mara des Bois'. With small to medium fruit it is now considered the premium gourmet strawberry in France. Specialist nurseries supply the Woodland Strawberry in red, yellow and white varieties that are

authentic to medieval gardens. The latter two colours attract little attention from birds. These strawberries also make delightful edges to paths and potager gardens, particularly the non-running Alpine Strawberry variety. Each fruit will remind you of why the strawberry was a metaphor for sensual pleasures in the medieval world.

Other berries gathered in the countryside were blackberries, raspberries and cloudberries. Blackberries, or brambles as they were also called, were widely used in Europe to make wine. The leaves of raspberries were drunk as a tea by expectant mothers, and the fruit used for raspberry syrup and, on the Scottish island of Skye, to flavour spirits.

Gooseberries (*Ribes uva-crispa* syn. *R. grossularia*) are native to parts of Europe where they were gathered wild. Gooseberries appear to have been appreciated on the Continent for their ornamental garden value as well as food and, according to the German author Herebachius in 1578, the bushes were commonly used 'for encloasying of Gardens, and makyng of Borders and Herbes'.

Varieties of gooseberries were first cultivated in England in the

Blackberries were gathered wild and used to make wine.

Gooseberries were appreciated as much for their ornamental qualities as their fruit in Europe.

The black mulberry is ancient in cultivation and was made into wine and medicinal syrup.

thirteenth century when bushes were planted in the royal gardens of the Tower of London for Edward I. By the sixteenth century, gooseberries appear to have become quite common in England and John Gerard described several sorts in London gardens, including some red coloured forms, the 'Pale Gooseberry' (first grown for Henry VIII), some common smaller sorts, one perfectly round and cherry sized and one that was as large as modern varieties. He was of the opinion that the gooseberry had not been commonly grown in the time of older writers in England, or alternatively they 'esteemed it not'. Gerard mentioned that gooseberries were used in place of verjuice in broths and in a variety of sauces for meats, and that the tender young leaves were included in salads. 'Honest' Tom Tusser advised in his sixteenth century bestseller *Five Hundred Points of Good Husbandry*:

> The Barberry, Respis and Gooseberry too
> Looke now to be planted as other things doo,
> The Gooseberry, Respis and Roses al three
> With strawberries under them trimley agree.

Mulberries are very ancient in cultivation. The Black Mulberry (*Morus nigra*), which is native to Iran, and the White Mulberry (*M. alba*) have been in cultivation in Europe for a very long time. The Black Mulberry was traditionally used to make a medicinal syrup for sore throats and was fermented for wine. The Black Mulberry tree is exceptionally long lived and known to bear fruit for hundreds of years. It is slow growing to around 10 metres (30 feet) and the fine-grained wood was used for musical instruments as well as furniture. Among the most ancient mulberry varieties is the Black Mulberry 'Shah', originally held in the Persian royal gardens and used to supply the royal family with honey-sweet fruits. 'Black Tartarian' was introduced into Europe approximately 1500 years ago.

Garden Design: A Paradise Orchard

This enclosed orchard garden is both productive and a pleasure to rest within. Medieval orchards were usually planted to the quincunx pattern in which all trees are equally spaced and each row is offset by fifty percent from the previous row. The pattern has been echoed here both for practical purposes and to create a subtle symmetry for the eye. The trees may all be similar in type, for instance an orchard of apple trees planted in an array of old varieties would look authentic and charming. However a mixed orchard would also be successful, including for instance apple, quince, cherry, pear and medlar. Trees grafted on to semi-dwarfing rootstock would allow for easier tending and harvesting. In warmer climates, an orchard of various citrus trees such as sweet orange, Seville orange, old varieties of lemons, mandarins and citron would provide fragrance in late winter and early spring as well as months of colour with their

fruit. Olive trees would be another suitable choice and very beautiful with their silver-grey leaves creating light patterns with every breath of wind.

The axis of the garden is defined by a tunnel arbour constructed of strong wooden posts, metal arches and a wattle construction finish to disguise the metal frame. The arbour has three paired arched exits to allow ready internal access and views into the orchard, and is covered with four plants of old grape varieties, evenly spaced. Two narrow beds, interrupted by the paired exits, might be included down the sides of the tunnel arbour, the edges bricked, and planted with fragrant wild strawberries.

A pathway also circles around the circumference of the garden to allow for an all weather walkway. The paths, in recycled brick, might also be created in stone in a diamond pattern. Four bench seats are provided to rest and view the orchard.

The orchard is enclosed by a pole fence to 1.5 m (5 ft) high in diamond pattern, against which are trained soft fruits suited to the area, among which might be both red and yellow raspberries, boysenberries, blueberries and gooseberries. In warm climate gardens these might be replaced with passionfruit vines trained along the fence. Their flowers, said to represent the passion of Christ, would be appropriate.

Medieval orchards usually contained bee skeps so that the fruit trees would be pollinated and honey could be harvested to cater to those with a sweet tooth at a time when sugar was rare and costly. If wished, hives might be included, located around the periphery of the garden and within the protection of the pole fence. If bee keeping seems a pleasant but too daunting prospect, a local amateur bee keeper might supply the household with honey in exchange for keeping some hives within the orchard.

 Legend

1 ORCHARD TREES SUCH AS APPLE, QUINCE, CHERRY, MEDLAR

2 EXIT APRON OF BRICK

3 CENTRAL TUNNEL ARBOUR WITH THREE PAIRS OF EXITS INTO THE ORCHARD

4 A SELECTION OF ANCIENT GRAPE VARIETIES

5 ALL WEATHER WALKWAY LAID WITH RECYCLED BRICK

6 BENCH SEAT, PREFERABLY OF STONE

7 HEDGE OF SOFT BERRY FRUITS, SUCH AS BLUEBERRY, RASPBERRY AND GOOSEBERRY

Chapter 8

The Knight's Garden

In March and in April, from morning to night,
In sowing and settling good housewives delight;
To have in a garden, or other like plot
To trim up their houses, and furnish their plot.

THOMAS TUSSER,
Five Hundred Points of Good Husbandry (1572)

The Crusades

When the western Roman Empire crumbled under successive
invasions from the north in the fifth century, the centre of
power in the empire shifted eastwards to Constantinople and
the largely Christian, Greek-speaking empire of Byzantium.
This eastern half of the Roman Empire was to survive for
another thousand years.

Islam arose in the seventh century, becoming a great conquering force.
After the death of Mohammed in 632, his followers set out from Medina,
taking and occupying one country after another. Within forty years the rest
of the Arabian Peninsula, Palestine and Syria, then Mesopotamia, Egypt,
northern Africa and Persia fell. Only Anatolia remained in Christian hands.
The conquests were amalgamated under the Caliphate and within two
generations most of the population had converted to Islam.

The great cities of the East continued to thrive, including Cairo and
Alexandria in Egypt, Damascus in Syria, Basra, and above all Baghdad,
which became immensely rich as the capital of the Abbasid Dynasty. While
these cities and the surrounding areas were flourishing, Western Europe
was beset by unrest and its population and economy were in decline.
However, by the eleventh century a resurgent Western Europe had
emerged and the stage was set for a clash of civilisations that would take
place, from the end of the eleventh century to the end of the thirteenth, with
a series of military campaigns known as the Crusades.

One woman, Eleanor of Aquitaine, was intimately connected with both the Second and Third Crusades. With her brilliant court, she also did much to shape medieval culture, and she was an eloquent advocate of the codes of knightly chivalry and courtly love. Eleanor was indisputably extraordinary, both magnificent and magnificently flawed, passionate, visionary, fearless, independent, beautiful, romantic, powerful, possessed of a remarkable intellect and an indefatigable energy. It is not too much to claim that she changed the path of European civilisation. She was certainly the most powerful and influential woman of the twelfth century, the wife of two kings and mother of two kings, and a force in her own right the equal of any of them.

Eleanor was born in 1122, the eldest child of Guillaume X, Duke of Aquitaine and Count of Poitiers. She had a younger sister, Aelith, and a brother, William Aigret, but lost both her mother and brother while she was still young. Her father provided her with an excellent education befitting the heir, and he was very proud of his beautiful, spirited and highly intelligent daughter. It was during those years, surrounded by a cultured court, that she acquired her great love of books and music. She inherited her intellectualism and passion from her father, who was a patron of the arts, and from her grandfather, Guillaume IX. A considerable musician and poet of earthy tendencies (and even earthier love life), Guillaume IX died when Eleanor was five, leaving her father to inherit the duchy. He, in turn, died on Good Friday in 1137 while on pilgrimage to Santiago de Compostela,

and Eleanor inherited both Aquitaine and Poitiers, a domain stretching from the Loire Valley to the Spanish border. She was just fifteen and was placed under the guardianship of King Louis VI (Louis the Fat) of France.

Louis hastily arranged a marriage between Eleanor and his son, also named Louis. Less than three months after her father's death, Eleanor was visited by the younger Louis with a retinue of five hundred knights, and accompanied by the Abbot Suger and assorted courtiers. She was married a fortnight later in a vast wedding at the Cathedral of St-André in Bordeaux. Louis was a man of very serious bent and exceptional devoutness, in later life regarded by some as a saint. As the second son, he had been raised to follow an ecclesiastical path until his brother's unexpected death in 1131. Eleanor is said to have later commented that she had thought she had married a king only to find that she had married a monk.

When Louis VI died from dysentery just a month after the marriage, Eleanor's husband was crowned Louis VII of France. Fifteen-year-old Eleanor had now become Queen of France. She was apparently much disapproved of by her mother-in-law and was frequently criticised by the austere St Bernard of Clairvaux and Abbot Suger. She was not the modest, malleable, dutiful wife that they held as a model. In part it was her youth and confidence that annoyed them, but it was also the clash between the culture of the south and the far more ascetic culture of the north of France.

Clairvaux was a great and immensely powerful abbey founded in 1115 by the reformed

Benedictines (the Cistercians), and under Bernard's powerful leadership as abbot it was the major force behind the expansion of the Cistercian Order. Bernard was a conservative within the Church, in many ways the absolute model of a medieval monk, living a life of very strict observance and personal privation, though a man not without gentleness and kindness. In 1145 he was summoned to the court of Louis VII, who had been fired by the news of the fall of Christian Edessa, in southern Anatolia, to the Muslims. Bernard was consulted as to whether a Second Crusade should be launched. The king's advisers had tried to dissuade him, but the Faith burned very strongly in Louis. Bernard diplomatically withheld his decision until called on by Pope Eugene III to preach in support of a Second Crusade.

The First Crusade had begun in 1096 and lasted for three years. By the eleventh century, the Seljuk Turks had evolved into a force to be reckoned with and had progressively taken control of the Abbasid areas, much of Anatolia and the Holy Land, which they conquered in the 1070s. Christian access to Jerusalem became very difficult, and the Byzantine Emperor Alexius I sent a delegation to Pope Urban II appealing for military assistance.

In November 1095 Pope Urban II preached at the Council of Clermont in France to an audience of some fourteen archbishops, two hundred and fifty bishops and four hundred abbots, with a large contingent of knights encamped nearby on the Plain of Chantoin. He exhorted them to take up arms to regain the Holy Land, promising them that joining the Crusade would count as full penance for all their sins. Crosses were distributed at the meeting and the cross became the symbol of the Crusaders. Bishop Adhémar of Puy-en-Velay was appointed the Papal Legate for the Crusade.

The First Crusade was the only Crusade that could be counted a success militarily, although it could not be counted a moral success. The first group to depart for the Holy Land, mostly poor peasants, was known as the 'People's Crusade' and was led by Peter the Hermit, who claimed he had been inspired by a vision. They suffered terribly en route and the few who survived the journey to the Holy Land died at the hands of the Turks. The second group was composed largely of knights and soldiers. There was no clear line of command between the disparate groups when they finally met up in Constantinople, but the best organised among them were the ten thousand knights and thirty thousand foot soldiers led by Godfrey of Bouillon and his two brothers.

The Crusaders took Nicaea, Edessa and then Antioch, but this only after a seven-month siege that ended in a massacre of many of the inhabitants. They failed to take Arquah but after six weeks of fighting, in July 1098, took Jerusalem, the battle ending in another terrible massacre. A monk called Fulcher was an eyewitness to the event and described the sickening sight of blood running ankle deep in the city. The Muslims were to later say that seventy thousand died at the hands of the Crusaders.

was seen as a saint by many, but as a libertine by others. He never achieved the Church's benediction of sainthood but would undoubtedly have achieved Eleanor's approval.

Eleanor was by no means the only woman greatly affected by the Crusades. Her granddaughter Blanche of Castile held the reins of government while her husband Louis waged a series of campaigns against King John of England. Apparently always hungering for war and spoils, Louis set out on the Albigensian Crusade against the Cathars in 1219.

The Cathars held controversial ideas that involved considerable self-denial but were regarded by the Church as heretical. The nobility in the south were supporters of the movement, which was centred on the Languedoc. The Church initially attempted to suppress the Cathars by using diplomacy, but then called for a Crusade against them, offering Cathar lands as spoils to those who joined the Crusade, and pitting the nobility of the south against that of the north.

The Albigensian Crusade took place mainly from 1209 to 1229, with a level of violence and brutality so extreme that it was notable even in medieval times. It was said that

Eleanor of Aquitaine lies in Fontevraud Abbey in Anjou, where she died in 1204.

Louis's massacres of the Cathars, particularly that at Marmande in 1219, horrified even his own battle-hardened troops. In 1226, now crowned Louis VIII of France and directed by a new pope, Honorius III, Louis led a second campaign against the Cathars, this time capturing Avignon. He died that same year in the Languedoc, just three years after his coronation.

After her husband's death Blanche continued support for the Albigensian Crusade, and Languedoc came under the dominion of her son Louis IX. The Inquisition was established in Toulouse in 1229, invested by Pope Gregory IX with virtually unlimited power to destroy the Cathars, who were tortured for evidence and burned wherever they were found. However, small communities of Cathars survived in remote castles at the base of the Pyrenees, and the last Albigensian Crusade in 1244 resulted in a ten-month siege at Montségur, ending in a mass burning of two hundred professed Cathars.

Blanche of Castile was still in her thirties when, in 1226, she became the regent for her twelve-year-old son, Louis IX, her fourth child but the first to survive infancy. She was also appointed guardian of her six other children. In the same year, she arranged Louis's marriage to Margaret of Provence, thereby bringing Provence into France. Later she suppressed a rebellion of the barons, largely by skilled diplomacy and determination, brought the Languedoc region into France, repelled an attack by King John's son in 1230, and created many significant alliances.

In 1248, history repeated itself, and Louis IX took up arms as a Crusader, at the age of thirty-five leading the Seventh Crusade to the Holy Land and leaving his mother once again as regent of France, and his children as her wards. At one stage Louis was captured by the Saracens and, like Eleanor of Aquitaine, Blanche raised the ransom and carried out the delicate diplomatic negotiations needed to gain her son's freedom. To her fury, he immediately returned to the battlefield, and she continued as co-regent with her son Alphonse until her death in 1252. Louis returned from the Holy Land the following year and led an almost monk-like existence until 1270 when, at the age of fifty-seven, he again set out on a Crusade, this time dying of plague in Tunis. He was canonised twenty-three years later.

If great queens were left to manage kingdoms as a result of the endless Crusades, then many other wives were left to manage the castles and estates of Crusader knights. It has been calculated that half a million men never returned after the Second and Third Crusades. Even if they survived, it was not unknown for husbands and sons to be absent for ten years, lost in the madness of futile wars. By the time of the Second Crusade, more aware of what might be entailed, many nobles and men-at-arms arranged for their property and wealth to be administered by their wives. It was a period of empowerment for women, particularly those of the upper classes. They often had full control of legal and financial matters, and were in charge of the defence of the castle, taxation of estates, the running of the castle and the raising of their children. Their competence would only too soon be forgotten by history.

Deep in a morass, the Crusades continued grimly onwards. The Fourth Crusade (1202–04), led by French and Flemish nobles, was diverted from its purpose, resulting in the sacking of the Christian city of Zara (now Zadar) on the Dalmatian coast and the equally horrific sacking and massacre of Constantinople. The sad Children's Crusade, which followed in 1212, was led by a French peasant boy, Stephen of Cloyes, who was inspired by his overwhelming faith. The children reputedly departed from Marseilles and most were never seen again, being sold into slavery. In the same year a German boy, Nicholas of Cologne, led a separate Children's Crusade, which reached Genoa. Again few returned home and none reached the Holy Land.

The Fifth Crusade had Egypt as its objective. Damietta was captured in 1219 but lost again in 1221. The Holy Roman Emperor Frederick II negotiated a treaty with the Muslims, but the treaty failed and Thibaut of Champagne and Navarre re-entered the fray in 1239 with a series of attacks that were then continued by the Duke of Cornwall. Three further Crusades took place, all failures. The last Christian strongholds of Tripoli and Acre fell by 1291 and there were no further Crusades, despite occasional agitation.

Life in the castles

Bloody though the Crusades had been, and seeding the future with resentment and fear as they did, the clash of civilisations did bring a prize without price to Western Europe. Generations of influential nobility and soldiers had been exposed to the great architecture, the gardens, the new and strange plants and fruits, the richness of literature and the great fund of ideas and knowledge possessed by the Near East. Western Europe, which had progressed little in a millennium and had been far too regimented in its thought, was flooded with new ideas in every possible area, from science to the arts and literature. In the field of medicine alone, progress was enormous: medical degrees were developed in universities, total anaesthesia techniques were much improved, a number of new and successful surgical procedures were developed, antisepsis was practised, and the use of plants containing cardiac glycosyides to regulate and strengthen the heart was introduced. The art of distillation

One of the last English medieval castles to be built, Bodiam castle in Sussex.

223

The influence of Islamic gardens

garden art is shaped by both physical and social environments. The hot, dry climate of many parts of the Near East strongly influenced garden design. Walled gardens provided protection from hot winds, the enclosure isolating the garden from the everyday world. Within these walls it was possible to create a beautiful, sensual, earthly garden of paradise, a place of peace and contemplation filled with the presence of water, the sweet fragrance of flowers, the cool shade of trees and the bounty of fruit. After the prophet Mohammed died in AD 632, Islam spread rapidly as the Arabs conquered the ancient lands of Egypt, Mesopotamia and Persia. All of these countries had been famed for their agricultural skills and engineering of water, as well as for their wonderful gardens. The Islamic empire absorbed the rich traditions and skills of its conquered lands and added to them.

The Sassanid Empire of Persia lasted from AD 226 to 651. Its once successful armies fought both the Romans and the Byzantines, before it came under the dominion of the Arab Caliphate. The paradise gardens of ancient Persia became

Opium poppy
(*Papaver somniferum*).

the starting point for gardens that would evolve to reflect subtly the teachings of the Koran. In these gardens it would be possible to enter an alternative space deeply overlaid with symbolism, where the mind might be healed and the soul refreshed. The Islamic garden became an expression of the highest art, living poetry embodied in intricate design, and an expression of the sublime.

In time, the ideal of the Islamic garden spread across the vast lands of the Arab conquest, which stretched from Andalusia in the Iberian peninsula and North Africa eastwards to the kingdom of the Mogul emperors in Pakistan. In each area the basic design was followed faithfully. The walled garden with its elegant entranceway was constructed around a canal of flowing water, which was intersected by a secondary canal to create a quadripartite garden. In larger gardens, each quarter might be further subdivided by intersecting canals. The idea of a fourfold garden design came from the Persians, but it was also an expression of the esoteric and sacred number four.

Jasminum officinale.

The Crusaders encountered flowers and fruits that they had never seen in the orchards and gardens of the Near East. The Oriental plane tree and the dark and sombre columnar cypress were used with great effect. By the eleventh century, other trees in these gardens included date palms, pomegranates, mastics or terebinths, almonds, apples, quinces, peaches, plums, Morello cherries, apricots, bananas, sweet cherries, jujubes, mulberries, figs, grapevines, olives and oranges.

The gardens of the Near East were also filled with flowers unknown to Western Europeans, and some of these flowers were brought back to Europe by returning Crusaders. The roses of the Near East were legendary, particularly those in the gardens of Syria and ancient Persia. The Damask Rose (*Rosa* x *damascena*) and the Gallica Rose 'Officinalis' are two that returned to Western Europe with the Crusaders. Other roses they would have encountered include the soft yellow Sulphur Rose (*R. hemispherica*) and the intensely and sweetly fragrant climbing Musk Rose (*R. moschata*), which was first taken to Italy and later found its way to England with Thomas, Lord Cromwell, in the reign of Henry VIII.

All the large yellow roses of the early world emanated from Persia. These included the clear yellow briar rose *Rosa foetida lutea*, a native of northern Iran, with large single flowers filled with a powerful incense-like fragrance and sea-green, ferny foliage, together with its double form (*R. foetida persiana*), the Persian Yellow Rose. The extraordinarily beautiful 'Austrian Copper' (*R. foetida bicolor*), known in France as 'Rose Capucine', was introduced into Europe via Austria some time before 1590. It is one of the most glorious blazes of colour in the rose world, being smothered in single blooms that are nasturtium red on the inside and golden yellow on the outside.

Fragrance was essential in the Islamic garden, and jasmines such as the pure white and intensely fragrant Poet's Jasmine (*Jasminum officinale*), used from ancient times in perfumes, and the yellow *J. fruticans* were grown. Al-Biruni, writing in 1050, provided lists of plants to be found in eastern Islamic gardens. These lists were interpreted by John Harvey in 1975. Among the flowers listed were the Opium Poppy, the spring-flowering *Anemone coronaria*, various species of *Narcissus*, violets and mallows. Madonna Lily would certainly have been grown. Herbs included Marshmallow, sweet marjoram, chamomile, elecampane, mints, southernwood, mugwort, alexanders (*Smyrnium olusatrum*), cumin, coriander, and the Persian or Conehead Thyme (*Thymus capitatus*).

Al-Biruni also provided lists of useful plants and vegetables that included asparagus, turnips, lentils, chickpeas, forms of carrots and cabbages, leeks, celery, cucumber, the saffron crocus, indigo and hemp.

'Rose Capucine'.

Eileen Donan castle, like a number of castles, used a strategic position surrounded by water to reinforce defences. It is located in Loch Ness.

also became known, widening the scope of plant-based medicine.

Most people during these dangerous times spent their lives closely associated with castles and fortified towns built strategically on sites that were difficult to attack. Castles and towns were protected by very strong, very high walls with immense gates. The walls were often exceptionally high, particularly after siege machines became more effective, and could be of the order of 10 metres (30 feet) high and up to 2.5 metres (8 feet) thick. A moat with a drawbridge provided an added barrier for an invading army.

The first major period of castle construction in England was initiated by William the Conqueror in the eleventh century, but it was Edward I who became known as 'the king who built castles'. His reign marked the high point of castle construction in Britain. The castles built at that time include the superbly designed Carnarvon (Caernarfon) Castle in Wales, based on concepts brought back by Crusaders who had encountered astonishing triple-walled fortifications in their travels. The walls were lined with flanking towers, each a fortress in itself. The Crusaders had learned only too well the effectiveness of such structures during the sieges of Acre and Antioch. Richard I implemented some of these ideas at Château Gaillard, but the finest example of their kind in Western Europe is Carcassonne in France.

Not even a king lived well by modern standards within a fortified castle. Castles were often cramped within and privacy was almost impossible. Earlier castles lacked passageways to permit entry into individual rooms. Instead rooms opened progressively, one into another, to save space. In larger castles, stone spiral staircases provided access to other floors. Sophisticated, later castles such as Carnarvon possessed passageways.

The castle was virtually a fortified town and had to include places for leisure, and places for sport for the young pages, squires and knights. These usually included an archery butt and jousting area. By the fourteenth century jousting had progressed from a way to develop and test the fighting skills and horsemanship of the knights to a major spectator sport comparable to modern football. The injuries in jousting were often appalling and the frequent deaths led to popes and kings placing ineffective bans on the sport. Less dangerous events that far better demonstrated knightly skills included knights on horseback negotiating intricate obstacle courses without the use of reins, and 'ring spearing', which required the mounted knight to negotiate a course while spearing as many rings as possible.

The pleasure gardens within castle walls, reserved for the use of the lord and his family and guests, were provided with pleasant grass walks and turf seats. Arbours covered with fragrant climbing plants and hedges provided shade and privacy. The gardens were based on the concept of an earthly paradise, designed to provide inspiration and quietude, and though many were often very charming indeed with their ornamental herbers, meads and small orchards, they lacked the complexity and sophistication of the gardens that would evolve in Renaissance Europe.

James I of Scotland, who was imprisoned in the Norman-built Windsor Castle, in the 1420s described the quite simple and predominantly green garden he saw each day from behind prison bars:

> Now was there made, fast by the Towris wall
> A garden fair; and in the corners set
> An arbour green, with wandis long and small
> Railed about and so with trees set
> Was the place, and Hawthorne hedges knet,
> That lyf was none walking there forebye
> That might within scare any wigh espy.

Few castles made many gestures towards comfort. Their prime purpose was survival. A poet in the French court in the fourteenth century, Eustache Deschamps, described the misery of life even in grand castles in winter, and strongly recommended being absent from the court.

Castle windows had only wooden shutters and iron bars for protection until the thirteenth

ancient symbol, thought to be more than four and a half thousand years old and to have originated in ancient Mesopotamia. It has also come to represent the rising kundalini in yoga.

In time, the centre of Western alchemy moved to Western Europe. The search for the Elixir of Life remained one of its constant objectives. A mysterious figure and alchemist, the Comte de St-Germaine, was said to have been in possession of the Elixir of Life. A nobleman of uncertain origins who lived during the eighteenth century, St-Germaine was rumoured then to be several thousand years old.

The count never revealed his early life, although it seems to have been taken for granted that he was of noble descent. He was said to have studied in the University of Siena as the protégé of the last of the Medici line, the Grand Duke Gian Gastone, but all is conjecture until a record was made of his arrest c. 1743 in London on charges of spying, charges that were soon dropped. Almost immediately afterwards there was a record of his giving virtuoso performances on the violin, and of a meeting with Horace Walpole who described him with apparently mixed feelings, noting that he 'played the violin wonderfully' and composed music but 'is mad and not very sensible'. According to rumour, Casanova claimed that St-Germaine was the violinist Catlini. A meeting between St-Germaine and the great Jean-Jacques Rousseau has also been reliably recorded.

A decade followed without any record of St-Germain before he appeared in the Court of Versailles and took up quarters in the Château de Chambord. He was known to Louis XV and his mistress Madame de Pompadour. He was said to have offered the French court formulae for various dyes, possibly developed through his alchemical research. Leaving France with the intention of travelling to England, he diverted to St Petersburg in Russia at the time when Catherine the Great was installed on the Russian throne. He was rumoured to have had more than a hand in that event.

Moving to Belgium and changing his name to Surmount, he is reputed to have demonstrated transmuting iron to gold, and to have offered the state various formulae. He again disappeared for over a decade, this time reappearing in 1774 in Bavaria as the Count Tsarogy and in 1776 in Germany as Count Welldone, with formulae for liqueurs, paper, cosmetics and other useful items. He then settled in Schleswig-Holstein, the guest of Prince Karl of Hesse-Kassel, where he identified himself as the Prince of Transylvania, a title he had been rumoured for several decades to genuinely hold.

St-Germaine was reputed to have died in 1784, and that might seem to be where the story ends: he was an apparently delusional charlatan who had received alchemical training, claimed to be a Freemason, perhaps had genuine royal connections and had managed to fool, at least temporarily, many of the crowned heads of Europe. But his story continues past his death. Reports of sightings of the count continued to surface. He was said to have been seen and clearly identified in Paris in 1835, in Milan in 1867 and in Egypt during Napoleon's campaign.

Napoleon III is reported to have actually kept a dossier on him. He was seen in 1896 by Annie Besant, a leader of the Order of the Temple of the Rosy Cross, and then reported in Rome in 1926. The Theosophical Society considers the Count of St-Germaine to be one of the great ascended masters. His mysterious story at least demonstrates that belief in the Elixir of Life continues and is the stuff of living legend.

The search for the Holy Grail in Christendom has also become a part of the story of the Elixir of Life. In the medieval period it was believed that the Grail could transmute water into the Elixir of Life. It has long been rumoured that it lies buried at the bottom of Chalice Well at Glastonbury in Somerset, and the story associated with this buried Grail claimed that it could confer powers of healing and the gift of immortality on those who drank from it.

The Crusaders may have failed in their quest to regain the Near East for Christendom, but Western Europe gained much through interaction with the intellectual and cultural wealth of the Near East. Universities were created in Western Europe in the twelfth century, receiving and translating the great texts of the ancient Greco-Roman world and the Muslim areas. Knowledge was no longer centred in the Church. By early in the thirteenth century, copies of those translations had been widely dispersed across Europe.

While alchemy in Western Europe focused on the transmutation of base metal to gold and the search for the Philosopher's Stone, it also inherited a wealth of chemical and metallurgical knowledge from the earlier civilisations of the eastern Mediterranean and Near East. Among the Egyptian alchemical discoveries were the art of embalming and the formulation of embalming chemicals, dyes, perfumes and metal alloys. Other Near Eastern peoples were very skilled in mining and refining metal ores, and added mathematical knowledge in which they were very advanced, as well as elements of philosophy.

The universal quest for the Philosopher's Stone was certainly of a different order from these more practical discoveries. The Stone was also known as the *lapis philosophorum* and the *materia prima*, a kind of universal touchstone or essence, a catalyst for both the creation of the

Jean Perreal, 'Dialogue between the Alchemist and Nature', 1516 (vellum). Getty Images

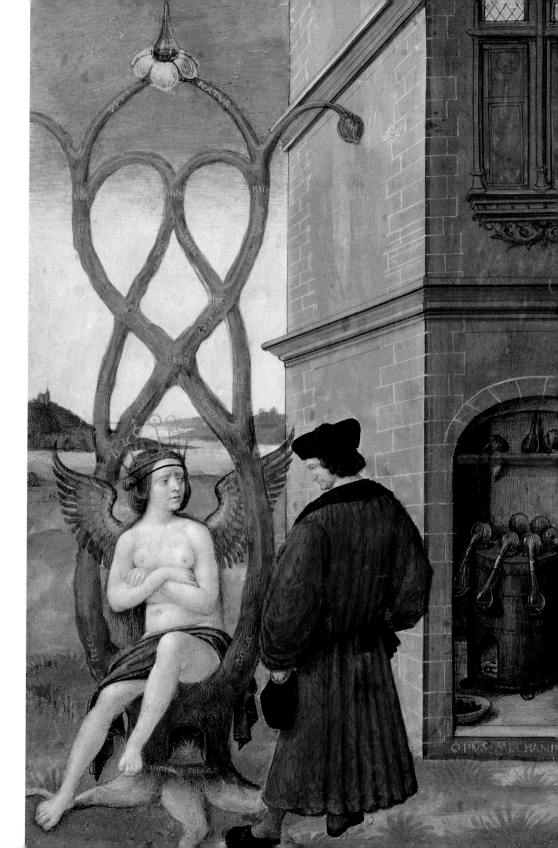

Planting by moon and stars

For country people in the medieval period, time was measured not so much in minutes as in sunlight and in seasons, following the earth's natural rhythms. Country people rose with the first rays of the sun and finished work with the last. The only exception was during the harvest season when the full moon, the harvest moon, allowed harvesting of the precious crops to continue after the sun had set.

Dandelion folk names reveal a widespread practice of telling the time by their flowers.

In an era when time measurement was less oppressive in daily lives, country people used nature's indicators to help them tell the time. Some of these indicators were fanciful, others quite practical. Children picked the rounded heads of feathery seeds of the dandelion and blew on them, counting the number of seeds left to tell the time. The shiny bare receptacle left after the seeds blew away reminded country people of the tonsured head of a monk, earning the plant its medieval name of *caput monachi* or Monk's Head. Other country names included Fairy Clocks, What O'Clock, Clocks and Watches, Old Man's Clock and Schoolboy's Clock. The calendula, or marigold, is a sun tracker that opens at approximately nine in the morning, beginning to close at three in the afternoon.

The Star of Bethlehem (*Ornithogalum umbellatum*), which John Gerard mentioned as being common in 'places that lie open to the aire', was associated with the journey of the Magi. Its white starry flowers opened around eleven in the morning.

The humble Scarlet Pimpernel acted as both a country clock and a barometer. It opens its petals at around eight o'clock in the morning and closes them at around four o'clock in the afternoon. This habit earned it country names such as Twelve O'Clocks and Shepherd's Sundial. The Scarlet Pimpernel is not only sensitive to sunlight but its flowers close up at once if rain is on the way, resulting in names such as Shepherd's Weatherglass, Weather-Teller and Shepherd's Warning.

The day was not divided into twenty-four equal parts until the mid-fourteenth century. Instead, the period of sunlight was divided into twelve equal parts, resulting in long hours in summer and short hours in winter, a perfectly sensible solution in an agrarian community. Bells were tolled to let communities know when it was time for a particular activity. All this was to change with the introduction of the mechanical clock, which counted out twenty-four evenly measured hours of time. The Romans, like the Egyptians

and Greeks, developed a calendar that was based on the moon. Their year was 355 days long, with an extra month added every second year. They had special names for three days of the month, related to the phases of the moon. These were *calends* or first day of the new moon, *nones* or day of the half moon, and *ides* or day of the full moon. It was this calendar that was inherited by the medieval world. The many Christian festivals were superimposed so that life was measured not only by the seasons but by the festivals ordained by the Church.

The tenth century Arabic treatise *Secretum Secretorum* seems to have been, at least in small part, responsible for an increasing preoccupation

with time in Western Europe. It was a book packed with information, demonstrating the Arabic love of mathematics and expertise in astrology. It ascribed the seasons to precise astrological positions and dates.

The idea of carrying out gardening activities according to the phases of the moon was well known to the Romans, and the idea long preceded them. It is a practice that is very widespread around the world. Francis Bacon seems to have been the first to propose scientifically testing the effect of the lunar cycle on the growth cycle of plants, and in the twentieth century some well-conducted trials were carried out, including those of Maria Thom in the 1950s and the rigorous trials carried out

Leafy vegetables such as cabbage are planted in the first quarter of the moon.

Eggplants are planted in the second quarter of a waxing moon.

Root crops like turnips are planted in the third quarter of the moon.

by Hartmut Spiess in Germany. Both found that the lunar rhythm influenced plant growth.

Just why the moon has an effect has still not been established, although many explanations depend on some aspect of the tidal effect of the moon on living cells, which are largely filled with water. Phases of the moon have well-established effects on many biological organisms. The landmass of Earth is calculated to rise as high as 30 cm (12 in) due to the moon's gravitational pull. Even ground water has been shown to be affected by the moon, being pulled upwards to fill the intercapillary spaces between soil particles, which then refill with air as the water drains back. Recent research has revealed what appear to be a number of plant rhythms dependent on the moon cycle. These include a fluctuation in the diameter of tree trunks, water uptake, water partitioning between the parts of a plant, oxygen usage and changes in DNA. The relationship of oestrus events in animals to the lunar cycle has

long been recognised by farmers, not to mention the effect of the full moon on hospital casualty intakes and police incident reports. In the wild, many events are timed by the lunar cycle, for example, the annual reproduction of reef corals is initiated by a full moon.

The first quarter of the waxing moon is considered to be the best time to plant the seeds of leafy annuals, particularly those that do not bear their seeds in fruits. Spinach, the cabbage tribe, celery, lettuce and endive are examples. During the second quarter of the waxing moon, seeds of twining annuals and plants that bear their seeds in fruits are planted, for example, melons, squash, peas, beans, cucumbers, peppers, tomatoes and eggplant. Other activities to be carried out during the waxing moon include all types of propagation, such as taking cuttings, budding and grafting, potting of rooted cuttings, repotting house plants, planting garlic and grain crops, sowing or laying turf, and planting roses and ornamental flowers. Fresh fruits are

thought to be at their juiciest during the waxing moon.

From the full moon to the third quarter of the moon is the time to plant root, bulb, corm and tuber crops such as onions, spring bulbs and potatoes, as well as rhubarb crowns, grapevines, berries, and fruit. Activities recommended during the third quarter include turning compost, weeding, harvesting and drying herbs (for ease of drying and potency), pruning, harvesting flowers for dried arrangements, and ploughing and hoeing. In the fourth quarter of the moon, nothing should be planted, although many gardeners consider it the best time to apply organic pesticide sprays.

The interaction of the Near East and Western Europe increased interest in astrology, and many gardeners used both the phases of the moon and astrological alignments, in combination with their own knowledge and experience, to determine farming and gardening activities. Farmers' almanacs and moon calendars for gardeners are widely published today.

Elixir of Life and the transmutation of metal to gold. It was the ultimate goal of alchemists in the Western world.

The closely related 'panacea', named for one of the daughters of the Greek god of healing, was a substance that could bestow immortality and heal all diseases, similar to the power of the Chinese Grand Elixir of Immortality.

As with all things alchemical, there was a mystical aspect to the Stone. While it was said to transmute entities in the physical world to a purer state, such as restoring the ageing human body to eternal youth, in the Hermetic tradition the Stone was also able to raise and purify the spirit to reach a state of enlightenment.

In the medieval period and beyond, the quest for the Philosopher's Stone continued and involved both the truly learned and charlatans. King Rudolf II of Bohemia attracted more than his fair share of both in the early seventeenth century when he decided to try and solve his plummeting financial situation by offering large rewards for the Stone. A number of alchemists flocked to the court in Prague, including some of impeccable repute such as the Danish astronomer and alchemist Tycho Brahe.

Another aspirant to the reward was John Dee, sometimes called an Elizabethan magus, a brilliant mathematician who received his first degree at St John's College, Cambridge at the age of seventeen and devoted his life to Hermetic philosophy, alchemy, the search for the Philosopher's Stone and divination. He and his assistant, Edward Kelley, who claimed to have discovered two extraordinary alchemical powders in a tomb in Wales, visited Prague and it is said that on several occasions Kelley demonstrated to Rudolf's court the use of a solution of the two powders to transmute mercury to gold. The gold was tested and found to be genuine. Kelley also claimed to hold the formula for the powders. However, Dee, dubious of his assistant's claims and feeling endangered, broke with Kelley and returned to England. Kelley continued to enjoy the king's benevolence until the powders ran out and could not be replaced. He was imprisoned and died of injuries sustained when he attempted to escape. Rudolf II died insane, and it has always been postulated that it was due to exposure to dangerous mercury.

Ancient liqueurs and alchemy

Liqueurs were the province of alchemists in the medieval period as their production required advanced chemical skills and technology. Recipes for liqueurs were often kept secret and liqueurs were considered to be divine gifts, capable of restoring health and promoting long life. Their alternative name, aqua vitae (water of life), reflects this belief. One of the earliest records of the creation of a liqueur is in a thirteenth century book, *Liber de Vinis*, by Catalan alchemist Arnaldus de Villa Nova.

The recipes of some famous liqueurs that are still available today were derived from alchemical formulations for the Elixir of Life. Various monastic orders were interested in developing these old formulae for their reputed health benefits. The Benedictines, Carmelites, Trappistines and other Orders all created herbal

The second half of the garden is screened by a series of gently billowing drapes reminiscent of the background screen for a knights' tournament. They give a theatrical feel to further exploration of the garden. Past the sequence of drapes lie three gardens in sequence, dazzling creations called the Work in Black, the Work in White and, finally, the Work in Red, representing upwardly seeking stages in human existence.

The Work in Black is a stark, almost ominous garden approached through a long, dark tunnel of hedged and clipped beech. The tunnel leads to a dark, chipped gravel path punctuated by pots of the dramatically stalked, black-foliaged succulent *Aeonium arboreum* and a sombre, square, slate-edged pool, all enclosed in high lime-green hedges that provide eerie contrast. This is the garden of the embryonic state, of the emerging consciousness.

From here the garden opens suddenly into breathtaking space and light, the Work in White, formed around sparkling water in a moon-shaped pool lined with white stone, surrounded by the massed white flowers of the Floribunda-style rose 'Iceberg' (in France, 'Fée des Neiges'), the light-coloured, wide gravel path lined with huge clumps of the Butterfly Bush (*Gaura lindheimeri*), with its long, graceful wands of delicate white flowers, and the ornamental Maiden Grass (*Miscanthus sinensis*), creating a misty softness. The Work in White represents the period of gaining knowledge and of emotional development.

'The Work in Red'
garden.

Entering the Work in Red is overwhelming. This is no subtle exercise in plums and deep velvety reds but a work of brilliant intensity. The garden centres on a pool designed as a pentagon, a five-pointed star drawn with five equal straight strokes, that has had associations with magic since it was used in ancient Sumer. In the garden its outline is coloured red. The garden blazes with great masses of fiery red roses, including the beautiful 'Prestige de Bellegarde'. Occult numbers of great alchemical significance are represented in this Work. Thirty-three pomegranates represent the rays of the sun, while two series of nine pots are planted with red-gold lantana and hibiscus. The mind takes fire with the energy of this last garden, representing the end of the spiritual journey, the soul aflame in the state of enlightenment. On the physical level, this last Work symbolises the gold formed in the flames of the cauldron.

Garden Design: The Garden of Eternal Life

This is a very theatrical garden reflecting the tastes of the late medieval and Renaissance periods. Enclosed on two sides by tall, formal dark hedges of clipped bay or yew, the centrepiece of the design, the 'Pyramid of Luna' is a raised hollow wooden tower, a feature often associated with medieval gardens, with a pyramidal roof.

The wide path that marks the long axis terminates at either end at a shallow circular pool, each of which is surrounded by a circular grey flagged edging path. The 'Cauldron of Sol' contains the alchemical symbol for the sun, while at the opposite end the 'Terra Scrying Pool' contains the alchemical symbol for the planet Earth. The symbols are inscribed on the bottom of each pool, most simply with pool paint. A more elegant finish can be achieved with mosaic, in either deep grey pebbles or small tiles, applied with a suitable waterproof adhesive. The path is finished with deep grey chipped gravel or slate to emphasise the drama

and the slightly darker vision of this garden design.

The gardens flanking the two pools contain the alchemical symbols for earth, air, fire, and water outlined in low brick cemented walls which are two courses high, primed, and then painted Chinese lacquer red. The garden and symbols are infilled with black Mondo grass. The beds on either side of the axial path contain strongly contrasting blocks of plants, silver-foliaged Artemisia or alternatively garden sage (*Salvia officinalis*), brilliant gold *Calendula officinalis*, and scarlet-flowered Maltese Cross (*Lychnis chalcedonica*) or alternatively scarlet-flowered *Verbena hybrida*, signifying respectively the noble metals silver and gold, and the fiery cauldron of the alchemist. The path and gardens are outlined in brick, cemented into position, primed, and also painted in Chinese lacquer red.

The open tunnel arbours are formed with paired, strong,

wooden, well seasoned posts at least 10 cm (4 in) square and preferably larger. A single metal arch spans each pair of posts and is strongly attached to them. Each arch is planted on either side with a climbing rose, and these are trained over the arch. It is important that the roses all be of the same variety to create maximum drama. White roses create a more open airy feeling and Climbing 'Iceberg' (also known as 'Schneewitchen' and 'Fée des Neiges') would be an excellent choice. Alternatively, 'Sombreuil' from 1851, one of the most glorious of all climbing roses with Bourbon, Hybrid Perpetual, and Tea Rose in its breeding, has clusters of creamy white, very double, old fashioned blooms of great beauty borne in profusion, and is a reliable flowerer over many months. It reaches 4.0 m (13 ft) and has the most delicious, rich, summery depths of fragrance. It has good, but not extreme, cold hardiness.

Legend

1 GREY STONE OR GREY TINTED CONCRETE SURROUND

2 GREY CHIPPED GRAVEL

3 RED PAINTED BRICK EDGING, TWO COURSES IN HEIGHT

4 GREY CHIPPED GRAVEL OR SLATE PATH

5 FORMAL 1.8 M (6 FT) HEDGE OF CLIPPED BAY OR YEW

6 BLACK MONDO GRASS

7 'THE CAULDRON OF SOL'

8 ALCHEMICAL SYMBOLS FOR EARTH, AIR, FIRE AND WATER OUTLINED IN CHINESE RED PAINTED BRICK, TWO COURSES IN HEIGHT

9 SINGLE METAL ARCH WITH SQUARE POST SUPPORTS, TRAINED WITH CLIMBING 'ICEBERG' (WHITE) OR 'ALTISSIMO' (CHINESE LAQUER RED) ROSE

10 CENTRAL CARPENTRY WORK TOWER WITH PYRAMID-SHAPED ROOF 'THE PYRAMID OF LUNA'

11 SAGE (*SALVIA OFFICINALIS*) OR ARTEMISIA (SILVER)

12 CALENDULA (GOLD)

13 'MALTESE CROSS' *LYCHNIS CHALCEDONICA* (FIRE)

14 THE TERRA SCRYING POOL

15 SYMBOL PAINTED IN BLACK ON BOTTOM OF SHALLOW POOL

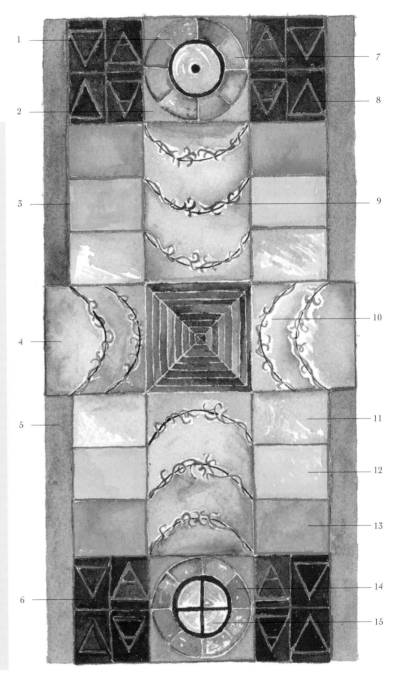

Further reading

Ashe, Geoffrey 1979, *The Glastonbury Tor Maze*, Gothic Image Publications, Glastonbury, Somerset

Bartlett, Robert 1994, *The Making of Europe*, Princeton University Press. (Reprint edition)

Biddle, Martin 2000, *King Arthur's Round Table: An Archeological Investigation*, new edn, Boydell Press, Woodbridge, UK

Black, Maggie 1992, *The Medieval Cookbook*, Thames and Hudson, New York (Reprinted 2003, British Museum Press, London)

Botineau, Michel 2001, *Les Plantes du Jardin Médiéval*, Belin, Paris

Brasey, Edouard and Gilbert Fabiani 2000, *La Cuisine Magique des Fées et des Sorcieres*, Editions de L'Envol, Forcalquier, France

Chamblas-Photon, Mic 2000, *Jardins Médiévaux*, La Maison Rustique, Paris

Coates, Alice M. 1968, *Flowers and Their Histories*, A. & C. Black, London

Codrington, John 1979, *The Plants of the Cloister Gardens*, Lincoln Cathedral, Lincoln, UK

Dowling, Alfred and E.P. Raymond 1900, *The Flora of the Sacred Nativity*, Kegan Paul, Trench, Trubner & Co. Ltd, London

Fournier-Rosset, Jany 1999, *From Saint Hildegard's Kitchen Foods of Health Foods of Joy*, Liguori/Triumph, Missouri

Gerard, John 1597, *The Herball or General Historie of Plantes*, rev. Thomas Johnson 1633, new edn 1985, Random House Value Pub, New York

Gillingham, John 2002, *Richard I*, Yale English Monarchs, Yale University Press

Grigson, Geoffrey 1958, *The Englishman's Flora*, Phoenix House, London

Harvey, John 1975, 'Gardening Lists and Plant Lists of Moorish Spain', *Garden History* vol. 3 no. 2, pp. 10–21

Harvey, John 1976, 'Turkey as a Source of Garden Plants', *Garden History* vol. 4 no. 3, pp. 21–42

Harvey, John 1981, *Medieval Gardens*, B.T. Batsford, London

Harvey, John H. 1985, 'The First English Garden Book: Mayster Jon Gardener's Treatise and Its Background', *Garden History* vol. 13 no. 2, pp. 83–101

Hill, Thomas 1558, *The Gardener's Labyrinth*, ed. Richard Mabey, Oxford University Press, Oxford, 1987

Jennings, Anne 2004, *Medieval Gardens*, English Heritage, London

Kaufmann, H.W., J.E. Kaufmann and Robert M. Jurga 2004, *The Medieval Fortresses: Castles, Forts and Walled Cities of the Middle Ages*, Da Capo Press, Cambridge, Massachusetts

Landsberg, Sylvia 1996, *The Medieval Garden*, Thames & Hudson

Lawson, William 1618, *A New Orchard and Garden*, reprinted 1983, Breslich and Foss, UK

Levi, Peter 1990, *The Frontiers of Paradise: A Study of Monks and Monasteries*, Paragon House Publishers, New York

Luckwill, L.C. and A. Pollard (eds) 1963, *Perry Pears*, J.W. Arrowsmith Ltd, Bristol

McLeod, Judyth A. 1989, *Our Heritage of Old Roses*, Kangaroo Press, Sydney

McLeod, Judyth A. 1994, *Heritage Gardening*, Simon & Schuster Australia, Sydney

McLeod, Judyth A. 2000, *Lavender Sweet Lavender*, 2nd edn, Simon & Schuster Australia, Sydney

Markham, Gervase 1616, *The Country Farm*, London

Markham, Gervase 1637, *The English Housewife*, new edn 1992, McGill-Queens University Press, Canada

Meiss, Millars 1995, *Les Très Riches Heures du Duc de Berry: The Medieval Seasons*, George Braziller, New York

Nicolle, David 2005, *Crusader Castles in the Holy Land, 1192–1302*, Osprey, Oxford

Nicolle, David 2005, *The First Crusade 1096–99: Conquest of the Holy Land*, Osprey, Oxford

Nicolle, David 2005, *The Third Crusade: Richard the Lionheart, Saladin and the Struggle for Jerusalem*, Osprey, Oxford

Parkinson, John 1629, *A Garden of Pleasant Flowers: Paradisi in Sole Paradisus Terrestris*, Reprinted 1991, Dover Publications Inc., New York (Reprint edition)

Sweeneey, Del (ed.) 1995, *Agriculture in the Middle Ages: Technology, Practice, and Representation*, University of Pennsylvania Press, Philadelphia

Taylor, Patrick 1998, *Gardens of France*, Mitchell Beazley, London

Tusser, Thomas 1572, *Five Hundred Points of Good Husbandry*, new edn 1984, Oxford Paperbacks

Williamson, Craig 1977, *The Old English Riddles of the Exeter Book*, University of North Carolina Press, Chapel Hill

Gardens and places to visit

Many of the gardens listed here are closed from mid-autumn to spring, or are open for limited periods in the colder months. It is advisable to inquire about opening times.

United Kingdom

Acorn Bank Garden and Watermill
Temple Sowerby
Nr Penrith
Cumbria CA10 1SP
Tel.: 01 768 361893
Website: http://www.nationaltrust. org.uk
This garden is notable for its herb garden, which contains the largest collection of medicinal and culinary herbs in the North of England. It is a National Trust site.

Alfriston Old Clergy House
The Tye
Alfriston
Polegate
East Sussex BN26 5TL
Tel.: 01 323 870001
Fax: 01 323 871443
Website: http://www.nationaltrust. org.uk
This was the first property acquired by the National Trust and is a thatched and half-timbered manor house dating to the 14th century. The medieval hall has a crown post roof. The floor was made from rammed chalk sealed with sour milk. There is a delightful small formal garden and beyond that a potager

filled with heritage vegetables. The garden has views over the gentle and lovely Cuckmere River, which is associated with tales of smugglers.

Battle Abbey (St Martin's)
Battle
East Sussex TN33 0AD
Tel.: 01 424 773792
Fax: 01 424 775059
Site of the Battle of Hastings, this was once a very influential 11th century Benedictine Abbey built by William the Conqueror. There is a superb Great Gatehouse, displays and interactive exhibit. The Battle Bonfire, complete with Norman knights from twinned town St Valerie-sur-Somme, takes place on the Saturday closest to 5 November. An annual reconstruction of the battle takes place in October.

Bede's World
Church Bank
Jarrow
Tyne & Wear NE32 3DY
Tel.: 01 914 892106
Email: visitor.info@bedesworld.co.uk
Website: http://www.bedesworld. co.uk
This Museum of Early Medieval Northumbria features the 7th century life and times of the Venerable Bede. It is a living museum, including a rare breeds collection and reconstructed early Anglo-Saxon farm 'Gwyre', medieval herb garden and the twin monasteries of St Paul's and

St Peter's, currently under World Heritage List consideration.

Bodiam Castle
Bodiam
Nr Robertsbridge
East Sussex TN32 5UA
Tel.: 01 580 830436
Fax: 01 580 830398
Email: bodiamcastle@nationaltrust. org.uk
Website: http://www.nationaltrust. org.uk
This is a superb and romantic example of a 14th century castle, heavily fortified with strong towers linked by an ashlar curtain wall and situated within a wide moat. Most unusually, it has three drawbridges.

Bolingbroke Castle
Spilsby
Old Bolingbroke
Lincolnshire
Tel.: 02 076 544900
Fax: 02 076 544894
The castle was built c. 1220 and in the 14th century came into the possession to the earls of Lancaster. After the death of Henry, 1st Duke of Lancaster, it passed to John of Gaunt, who had married Henry's daughter Blanche and became Duke of Lancaster in 1362. Blanche died tragically young at 24 of the plague. Their son Henry, born at the castle, was destined to become Henry IV and the first king of the House of Lancaster. The castle is largely ruined (it was 'slighted' in 1652),

but the site is deeply evocative. A garden filled with bushes of the Red Rose of Lancaster gifted by the ancient town of Provins in France, famous for the culture of this rose, marks the turnoff.

Bolton Castle
Nr Leyburn
North Yorkshire DL8 4ET
Tel.: 01 969 623981
Fax: 01 969 623332
Email: info@boltoncastle.co.uk
Website: http://www.boltoncastle. co.uk
This medieval fortress in the Yorkshire Dales dates to 1399. It features medieval gardens, including a walled herb garden, a vineyard, a rose garden with lavender and arbours, and a bowling green surrounded by edible and useful plants.

Buckland Abbey
Yelverton
Devon PL20 6EY
Tel.: 01 822 853607
Fax: 01 822 855448
Email: bucklandabbey@ nationaltrust.org.uk
Website: http://www.nationaltrust. org.uk
This 13th century Cistercian Abbey, later the home of Sir Francis Drake, has a very fine tithe barn built in 1300, a herb garden and an equally fine 16th century Great Hall. The abbey is said to be haunted by Sir Francis accompanied by hell hounds.

Caerphilly Castle
Caerphilly
Mid-Glamorgan
Wales

Tel.: 01 222 883143
One of the largest surviving medieval castles in Western Europe, it demonstrates in its 23 hectare (50 acre) site the awe-inspiring qualities of medieval military architecture. The 13th century castle design is based on massive concentric rings of defence. The structure is surrounded by vast lake moats created by dams to the north and south. The 14th century Great Hall is exceptional.

Cathedral Church of the Blessed Virgin Mary
Lincoln
Lincolnshire LN2 1PZ
The Cloister Gardens are planted with flowers and herbs associated with the Blessed Virgin Mary.

Chapter House, Pyx Chamber and Abbey Museum
Westminster Abbey
London SW1P 3PA
Tel.: 02 076 544900
Fax: 02 076 544894
Email: info@westminster-abbey.org
Website: http://www.westminster-abbey.org
These areas, built from the 11th to the 13th centuries, house the abbey's treasures. The cathedral was founded by Edward the Confessor but little of the original church remains apart from the Chamber of the Pyx and the undercroft. Rebuilding commenced in 1245 under Henry III.

Cholderton Rare Breeds Farm Park
Amesbury Road
Cholderton

Salisbury
Wiltshire SP4 0EW
Tel.: 01 980 629438
Fax: 01 980 629594
Website: http://www.rabbitworld. co.uk
This much featured attraction is a living museum of Britain's heritage of farm animal breeds.

Corfe Castle
Wareham
Dorset BH20 5EZ
Tel.: 01 929 481294
Fax: 01 929 477067
Email: corfecastle@nationaltrust.org. uk
Website: http://www.nationaltrust. org.uk
This early Norman castle was severely damaged by Parliamentary troops after the Civil War but nevertheless remains impressive.

Cotehele House
St Dominick
Saltash
Cornwall PL12 6TA
Tel.: 01 579 351346
Website: http://www.nationaltrust. org.uk
Located 9.5 kilometres (6 miles) south-west of Tavistock and situated on the estuary of the Tamar River, this is a grand and remarkably complete manor house from the late medieval period. The original manor house was built in 1353 and has been incorporated into the later building. The second manor house was built over the period 1490 to 1520 and a tower was added in 1627. Most of the original furnishings and tapestries remain in

the house, including a 15th century clock in original condition in the chapel. The gardens descend down the hillside to the river, where there is an exhibit by the National Maritime Museum.

Fountains Abbey & Studley Royal
Ripon
North Yorkshire HG4 3DY
Tel.: 01 765 608888
This World Heritage listed site has the ruins of a great and beautiful 12th century Cistercian monastery.

Framlingham Castle
Framlingham
Suffolk IP13 9SP
Tel.: 01 728 724189
This superb example of a 12th century castle is complete with thirteen towers linked by a curtain wall. The externals are fully intact. This is where Mary Tudor awaited the news of Edward VI's death. It is now an English Heritage property.

Glamis Castle
Glamis by Forfar
Angus DD8 1RJ
Scotland
Tel: 01 307 840393
Fax: 01 307 840733
Website: http://www.glamis-castle.co.uk
One of the most haunted castles in Britain but with a fairytale beauty, this is the traditional home of the Earls of Strathmore and Kinghorne and was the birthplace of the late Queen Mother. A holy place in the 8th century, it became a hunting lodge for the Scottish kings and then a fortressed castle, which was the site

of Shakespeare's play *Macbeth*. King Malcolm II died at Glamis Castle in 1034.

Harlech Castle
Harlech
Gwynedd
Wales LL46 2YH
Tel.: 01 766 780552
A superb 13th century castle and a UNESCO World Heritage Site, this is a very well-preserved concentric castle on a rocky hill. It was captured by Owain Glyndwr, and later taken by the Parliamentary forces in the Civil War.

Hever Castle
Edenbridge
Hever
Kent TN8 7NG
Tel.: 01 732 865224
Fax: 01 732 866796
Email: mail@hevercastle.co.uk
This is a double moated fortified manor house. The original castle was built in 1270 and has a wooden drawbridge, outer fortified wall and massive gatehouse. It was the childhood home of Anne Boleyn and was later given to Anne of Cleves by Henry VIII. A grim museum of medieval torture is balanced by superb gardens, including wonderful topiary.

Holyroodhouse Palace and Abbey
Edinburgh
Tel.: 01 315 561096
Standing at the eastern end of the Royal Mile, this Augustinian abbey was founded by King David I (whose mother was Saint Margaret) in 1128. It now lies in ruins. The late

medieval palace was added to and repaired on many occasions, being completed in the early 16th century by James V. The gardens and courtyards are noteworthy. It continues as a royal residence.

Kenilworth Castle
Kenilworth
Warwickshire CV8 1NE
Email: Stephen.spinks@english-heritage.org.uk
Tel.: 01 926 852 078
Fax: 01 926 851 514
Website: http://www.english-heritage.org.uk/kenilworthcastle/
This was once the home of Robert Dudley, Earl of Leicester, a favourite of Queen Elizabeth I. He received both his title and the castle from Elizabeth early in her reign. She was entertained there right royally on many occasions, once being given nineteen days of 'princely pleasure' at an extraordinary cost of one thousand pounds a day. Dudley's treatment of his wife was apparently far from 'princely'. It is said that a young William Shakespeare witnessed the remarkable and magical events arranged for Elizabeth (as did a crowd of local people) and drew on the experience to later write *A Midsummer- Night's Dream*. The 16th century Pleasance gardens created for Elizabeth are now being restored to their original form. The existing Norman castle was built on the site of a previous Saxon castle and additional fortifications were added in the mid-13th century. Kenilworth was associated with Simon de Montfort and the 'Baron's War' to curb the

power of Henry III, leading to the Great Siege of Kenilworth in 1266. It is also associated with John of Gaunt, who transformed the fortified castle into a palace c. 1364.

Kentwell's Traditional Farm
Kentwell Hall
Long Melford
Suffolk CO10 9BA
Tel.: 01 787 310207
Fax: 01 787 379318
Email: info@kentwell.co.uk
Website: http://www.kentwell.co.uk
Kentwell, approached via an exceptional and ancient avenue of lime trees, is a very fine, double moated gentleman's residence, which dates c. 1500. The original Manor of Kentwell Hall was built in 1385. The gardens feature a maze and remnants of the 16th and 17th centuries in its walled gardens, style of layout and use of espaliered fruit trees. There is a large herb garden. The Rare Breeds Animal Farm is a working farm with an excellent array of rare and ancient breeds, including the medieval Norfolk Horn Sheep, Gloucester Old Spot and Tamworth pigs, Longhorn cattle and Suffolk heavy horses.

Leeds Castle
Maidstone
Kent ME17 1PL
Tel.: 01 622 765400
Built in the 12th century and maintained to demonstrate the greatest comforts that were afforded kings of the period, this was the home for a time of both of the wives of Edward I, the wife of Edward III, Katherine de Valois (wife of Henry V), and later Katherine of Aragon and

Elizabeth I, earning Leeds the alternative name of Lady's Castle.

Lindisfarne Priory
Holy Island
Berwick-upon-Tweed
Northumberland
Tel.: 01 289 389200
The island is reached by a causeway, at low tide only. Lindisfarne was founded by St Aidan in the 7th century, and the beautifully illuminated *Lindisfarne Gospels* was created there c. 698. St Cuthbert was a bishop here, although he was buried at Old Melrose Abbey. The priory was sacked by the Vikings and was not re-established until the 12th century.

Little Moreton Hall
Congleton
Cheshire CW12 4SD
Tel.: 01 260 272018
Email: littlemoretonhall@nationaltrust.org.uk
Website: http://www.nationaltrust.org.uk
A moated manor house, this is considered one of England's finest timber-framed manor houses. The earliest part dates c. 1450, the adjacent kitchen c. 1480 and the remaining extensions are from the 16th century. There is a spectacular Long Gallery and a charming knot garden.

Lyddington Bede House
Blue Coat Lane
Lyddington
Leicestershire LE15 9LZ
Tel.: 01 572 822438
Email: customer@english-heritage.org.au

Website: http://www.english-heritage.org.uk
The site of a bishop's palace, this building is considered to be of late 12th or early 13th century date. Permission was given to crenellate in 1336.

Melrose Abbey
Melrose
Scotland
Tel.: 01 896 822562
Website: http://www.historic-scotland.gov.uk
Melrose was founded in 1136 by monks of the Cistercian Abbey of Rievaulx in Yorkshire, and partly rebuilt in the late 14th century following damage by English pillaging. It is considered the finest of the Scottish Border abbeys. An orchard planted with ancient apple varieties, and Priorwood garden, are adjacent. There is also an abbey museum. The original monastery of Old Melrose, founded by St Aidan c. 650 and referred to by the Venerable Bede in 731, is located 3 kilometres (2 miles) away. St Cuthbert was a prior of Old Melrose and was later buried there. The heart of Robert the Bruce, which was taken to the Crusades by the Black Douglas and then returned to Scotland, is buried in Melrose Abbey. It is a Scottish Monuments site.

Michelham Priory
Upper Dicker
Hailsham
East Sussex BN27 3QS
Tel.: 01 323 844224
Email: adminmich@sussexpast.co.uk
An Augustinian priory founded in

1229 with a 14th century moat and defensive gatehouse, this was a resting place for pilgrims on their way from Lewes, Battle, Rye and Canterbury. Later it was the first monastic site granted to Thomas Cromwell and then was granted in part to Anne of Cleves. The churches of Alfriston and Fletching were attached to the priory. It has a delightful medieval-style herb garden.

Mottisfont Abbey
Nr Romsey
Hampshire SO51 0LP
Tel.: 01 794 340757
Fax: 01 794 341492
Email: mottisfontabbey@ nationaltrust.org.uk
Website: http://www.nationaltrust. org.uk
This 12th century Augustinian priory includes the National Collection of old and ancient roses. They are at their height in June, housed in a very large walled garden.

Mount Grace Priory
Osmotherley
Northallerton
North Yorkshire DL6 3JG
Tel.: 01 609 883494
These atmospheric remains of a 14th century priory form the most important Carthusian ruin in England and include an authentically restored monk's herb garden.

Old Sarum
Nr Salisbury
Wiltshire
Situated 3 kilometres (2 miles) from Salisbury, this was originally an Iron Age hill fort dating to 3000 ( ). It was subsequently occupied by Romans and Saxons, and was the place where William the Conqueror disbanded his conquering army. Subsequently, it was the site of William I's royal castle and the original Salisbury Cathedral. The second Salisbury Cathedral dates to 1220. This is an English Heritage site and is close to the Avebury and Silbury Hill sites.

Powis Castle
Welshpool
Powys SY21 8RF
Tel.: 01 938 551929
Website: http://www.nationaltrust. org.uk
Unlike most famous Welsh castles, such as Caernarvon and Harlech, all built by the English to control the people of Wales, Powis Castle was the fortressed home of the Welsh princes of Powys and dates from the 9th century. The castle is now home to the Earls of Powis. The estates of Powis and Clive of India were linked from 1784. There are extensive world famous gardens and the Welsh dragon emblem can be seen on the gates.

Queen Eleanor's Garden
Great Hall
The Castle
Winchester
Hampshire
Tel.: 01 962 846476
Email: info.centre@hants.gov.uk
Website: http://www.hants.gov.uk
This charming and authentic 13th century style garden is located behind the Great Hall. It is named for Eleanor of Provence, wife of Henry III and an enthusiastic gardener.

Rievaulx Abbey
Rievaulx
Helmsley
Yorkshire YO62 5LB
Tel.: 01 439 798228
This was at one time the most important and largest abbey in England. It was created by the Cistercian Order under the instruction of St Bernard of Clairvaux. The church is well preserved and has excellent examples of Early English flying buttresses.

St Augustine's Abbey
Canterbury
Kent
Tel.: 01 227 767345
Founded in 597 by St Augustine and one of the earliest monastic sites in southern England, this is an English Heritage site and a World Heritage site. Nearby is the Church of St Martin, considered the oldest Christian church in England, and Christ Church Cathedral, where Thomas à Becket was murdered in 1170. Christ Church Priory still retains its cloister garth, as well as the infirmary cloister garth.

St Bees Priory
Cumbria
Website: http://www.stbees.org.uk
The mysterious preserved knight known as St Bees Man was excavated here in 1981. He is thought to have died in the Crusades, and although over six centuries old was preserved in near perfect condition within a wooden box secured with iron and protected within a layer of clay, a body wrap of lead sheeting and a beeswax-covered shroud. Also in the

priory are a number of well-carved
grave slabs depicting medieval
knights. They may have belonged to
Knights Templars. This is the site of
a wealthy 11th century Benedictine
Priory, and before that was the home
of an anchoress, St Bega (an Irish
princess who fled marriage with a
Viking prince), and a 9th century
church. The magnificent Dragon
Stone, depicting St George and the
Dragon, is worthy of note.

Scone Palace
Scone
Perth
Perthshire PH2 6BD
Scotland
Tel.: 01 738 552300
Fax: 01 738 552588
Email: visits@scone-palace.co.uk
Website: http://www.scone-palace.
co.uk
This medieval palace has an
outstanding collection of *objets d'art*.

Scotney Castle
Lamberhurst
Tunbridge Wells
Kent TN3 8JN
Tel.: 01 892 893868
Fax: 01 892 890110
Email: scotneycastle@nationaltrust.
org.uk
Website: http://www.nationaltrust.
org.uk
This is arguably the most romantic
and fairytale castle in England with
its wide moat, flagged herb garden
and position at the meeting of the
waters of the rivers Bewl and
Sweetburne. A 12th century manor
preceded the moated castle and one
surviving circular tower dates to the

1370s. Much of the medieval manor
was recycled into a new manor house
in the 17th century. There are very
fine surrounding gardens. The ghost
of a murdered revenue officer is said
to emerge from the moat.

Stockwood Park Gardens
Stockwood Park Craft Museum
Farley Hill
Luton
Bedfordshire LUI 4BH
Tel.: 01582 546739
Email: museumgallery2luton.gov.uk
Website: http://www.lutonline.gov.uk
The series of period gardens are
located in the original walled garden.

Stokesay Castle
Nr Craven Arms
Shropshire
Tel.: 01 588 672544
This quite remarkable and charming
example of a 13th century fortified
manor house is generally considered
the finest of its kind and miraculously
preserved. The castle has two towers
linked by a buttressed Great Hall.
The castle is notable for its large
windows. The quaint but very livable
home is perched high, like a
mushroom cap. Gardens surround
the castle. The timber framed
gatehouse is 16th century. The
curtain wall was slighted after the
Civil War, but for unknown reasons
the destruction was halted.

Sudeley Castle
Winchcombe
Cheltenham
Gloucestershire GL 54 5JD
Tel.: 01 242 604357
Fax: 01 242 602959

Website: http://www.sudeleycastle.
co.uk
Once the property of Ethelred the
Unready, Sudeley remained in royal
hands during the Tudor period and
was the palace of Katherine Parr,
who is buried in the chapel (St
Mary's Church). It was also visited
or lived in by Lady Jane Grey,
Anne Boleyn, Henry VIII, Elizabeth
I and Charles I. It was savagely
attacked during the Civil War and
lay in ruins, neglected for two
centuries before being sensitively,
if partially, restored. The castle was
the inspiration for Blandings Castle
in P. G. Wodehouse's novels
revolving around Jeeves and Bertie
Wooster. Magnificent and extensive
restored Tudor gardens include the
formal Queen's Garden. Ancient
crafts are revived here, and events
such as medieval tournaments are
often staged.

The Canterbury Tales
St Margaret Street
Canterbury
Kent CT1 2TG
Tel.: 01 227 454888
This is an evocative and accurate
re-creation of medieval England,
retracing the steps of a 14th century
pilgrimage to the tomb of St Thomas
à Becket in Canterbury Cathedral,
accompanied by retellings of
Chaucer's famous stories.

The Prebendal Manor House
Nassington
Nr Peterborough
Northamptonshire PE8 6QG
Tel.: 01 780 782575
Email: info@prebendal-manor.co.uk

Website: http://www.prebendal-manor.co.uk
The earliest surviving dwelling in Northamptonshire, it dates to the early 13th century. Also present is evidence of one of the royal timber halls of King Cnut, as well as two medieval fishponds, a 15th century lodging and a 16th century dovecote. There is an excellent re-creation of a garden of a 13th to 15th century person of wealth and position.

The Tradescant Garden and Museum of Garden History

St Mary at Lambeth
Lambeth Palace Road
London SE1 7LB
Tel.: 02 074 018865
Fax: 02 074 018969
Email: info@museumgardenhistory.org
Scheduled for demolition, the ancient church with its rediscovered graves of the great 17th century plant hunters John Tradescant the Elder and Younger was saved by voluntary effort to become a museum of gardens and gardening. The garden located at the back of the church was created in the neglected graveyard and designed by Lady Salisbury in the style of the early 17th century.

The Tudor Walled Garden

Crossing Temple
Witham Road
Braintree
Essex
Tel.: 01 376 584903
Situated on the B1018 between Braintree and Witham, this was originally a Roman settlement. It was occupied by the Knights Templars

c. 1137, then by the Knights Hospitallers c. 1310. After the Reformation it became a private estate. The Walled Garden contains several gardens devoted to the late medieval and Tudor periods.

Tintagel Castle

Tintagel
Cornwall PL34 0DB
Tel.: 01 840 770328
Superbly and precariously situated on the edge of high Cornish sea cliffs, these extensive ruins of a Norman castle are said to have been built on the site of the earlier seat of the ancient kings of Cornwall. The site is associated with Merlin, King Arthur, and Tristan and Isolt. The Tintagel Post Office, with its swayback roofline, is 14th century and well worth a visit. The mysterious wall labyrinth is on the wall of a sea cave below.

Tintern Abbey

Nr Chepstow
Gwent NP6 6SE
Wales
Tel.: 01 291 689251
Website: http://www.cadw.wales.gov.uk
These beautiful and evocative ruins of a Cistercian Abbey in the valley of the River Wye were founded in 1131 by the 'white monks' from the Norman Abbaye de L'Aumone. It was once the richest monastery in Wales. The church, built from the late 13th to early 14th centuries, is a masterpiece. Painted by William Turner and the subject of William Wordsworth's poem 'Lines Written a Few Miles Above Tintern Abbey', it

is said to be haunted by 'Longbow' (Gilbert Fitz Gilbert de Clare, Earl of Pembroke) and also by Cistercian monks.

Tretower Court and Castle

Tretower
Crickhowell
Powys NP8 2RF
Tel.: 01 874 730279
Email: cadw@wales.gsi.gov.uk
Website: http://www.cadw.wales.gov.uk
This group of exceptional medieval buildings includes a 13th century round keep and a superb late medieval house with spacious rooms, a projecting timber gallery and the evocative atmosphere of noble life in the period. Outside there is a cobbled courtyard with recreated medieval gardens, including a herber, an orchard and a flowery mead. Constructed beside Tretower Court and Castle is Sir Roger Vaughan's Garden, a beautiful and accurate reconstruction of a late medieval garden featuring a flowery mead, turf seats, trellised and railed enclosures, and flowers of the period.

Warwick Castle

Warwick
Warwickshire CV34 4QU
Tel.: 01 870 442 2000
Fax: 01 870 442 2394
Email: customer.information@warwick-castle.com
Website: http://www.nationaltrust.org.uk
One of the finest examples of a medieval castle, it was built by Simon de Montfort in 1264. The first castle on the site was erected

by William the Conqueror, although only the mound remains. This gives an introduction to the grimness of castle life with its intact curtain walls, a portcullis, dungeon and haunted room.

Weald and Downland Open Air Museum

Singleton
Chichester
West Sussex PO18 0EU
Tel.: 01 243 811363
Email: office@wealddown.co.uk
Website: http://www.wealddown.
co.uk
The site contains the leading museum of buildings in the UK, the collection spanning the 13th to the 19th centuries and featuring period gardens as well as rare breeds of farm animals.

Winchester Cathedral

Winchester
Hampshire SO23 9LS
Tel.: 01 962 857200
Fax: 01 962 857201
Winchester was the ancient capital of Wessex and the seat of government of King Alfred the Great. The first Saxon cathedral was built there in AD 648 and St Swithun was its bishop from 852 to 862, and later its patron saint. Winchester Cathedral was begun in 1079 and completed in the 14th century. Nearby is St Cross Hospital, a charitable house established in 1126, and the Great Hall, all that remains of the Norman Castle, which houses 'King Arthur's Round Table' and the original stained glass coats of arms of England's medieval monarchs and nobles.

France

Abbaye de Sénanque

84220 Gordes
Tel.: 04 90 72 05 72
Email: visites@senanque.fr
Website: http://www.senanque.fr
This Cistercian abbey founded in the 12th century had a chequered career, being for some time extremely rich and powerful until a rebellion in the mid-16th century by local people resulted in all the monks being hanged. The abbey struggled for three centuries but became an active monastery again in 1989. In July the abbey is surrounded by a sea of lavender in full flower.

Abbaye Royale de Fontevraud

49590 Fontevraud-l'Abbaye
Tel.: 02 41 51 73 52
Fax: 02 41 38 15 44
Founded in 1101 by Robert d'Arbrissel, the Abbey of Fontevraud was a double monastery richly endowed by the Plantagenets (and their predecessors the Angevins) and is one of the largest and best preserved abbeys in France. Henry II of England and his consort Eleanor of Aquitaine, their son Richard the Lionheart and daughter-in-law Isabella of Angoulême are all buried in the church. A medieval potager of herbs and vegetables and a flowery mead are just two of the the attractions in the extensive grounds.

Capitulare de Charlemagne

Porte-de-Soissons
02380 Coucy-Le Chateau
Picardie

Tel.: 03 23 52 67 30
Fax: 03 23 52 67 31
Email: ucpecoucy@tiscali.fr
This is an authentic medieval potager garden planted with recommendations for plantings made in the *Capitulare de Villis* issued in 800 by Charlemagne. It is at the foot of the medieval fortress of the Sires de Coucy.

Chapelle Saint-Blaise-des-Simples

Rue Jean-Moulin
91490 Milly-la-Forêt
Tel.: 01 64 98 83 77
The 12th century chapel of Saint-Blaise-des-Simples, which is the burial place of Jean Cocteau, also contains in its grounds the Conservatoire National des Plantes à Parfum, Médicinales et Aromatiques (National Conservatory of Perfume, Medicinal and Aromatic Plants), a living museum and important National Collection of 1200 species. The town also contains a huge and still very active marketplace built in 1479. Constructed from forty-eight massive oak pillars, the chapel is classified as a national monument.

Château Val Joanis

84120 Pertuis
Tel.: 04 90 79 20 77
Fax: 04 90 09 69 52
Email: info.visites@val-joanis.com
Website: http://www.val-joanis.com/
Deserving of wide acclaim, this magnificent large potager garden, abundantly and elegantly planted in the spirit of the 17th century with authentic vegetables, fruits and herbs, is associated with a large winery.

Jardin Botanique des Cordaliers
College Maria Bourrelly
Place des Cordaliers
04000 Digne-les-Bains
Tel.: 04 92 31 59
This is a charming smaller garden set out in a simple medieval style and brimming with fragrant herbs and flowers.

Jardin d'Herbes
La Mairie
26700 La Garde Adhémar
Tel.: 04 75 04 41 09
This remarkable garden spread down several terraces lies behind an ancient church. It was designed by Danielle Arcussi. Every plant is creatively and informatively labelled. There are over 200 medicinal species alone, all arranged in boxwood edged parterres. This is unquestionably one of the most beautiful, and peaceful, herb gardens to be found.

L'Abbaye de Fontfroide
RD 613
11100 Narbonne
Tel.: 04 68 45 11 08
Fax: 04 68 45 18 31
Email: info@fontfroide.com
Website: http://www.fontfroide.com
Fontfroide, 15 kilometres (9 miles) south-west of Narbonne, was founded in 1093 and followed the Rule of St Benedict. In 1144 it adopted strict Cistercian Rule. Fontfroide was at the forefront of the battle against Catharism after the murder of a Fontfroide monk and legate of Pope Innocent III precipitated the Albigensian Crusade. Three-quarters of the

monks died during the Black Death. The abbey was dissolved in 1791 but was undamaged by the revolution. It was reoccupied from 1858 to 1901. This magnificent abbey remains in excellent condition, with beautiful gardens, including a famous rose garden containing 2500 bushes. More than 2000 monks have been interred in this monastery since medieval times.

L'Abbaye de Valsaintes
04150 Simiane la Rotonde
Haute Provence
Tel.: 04 92 75 94 19
This exceptional site with a strongly mystical feel is located a short distance outside the medieval fortification of Simiane. The intimate, peaceful gardens are associated with a medieval abbey, which dates in part to the 12th century (the shell of St James in the small church marks it as a place visited by pilgrims en route to northern Spain). In the clear Provençal light, olives and masses of organically managed roses (over 600 kinds) tumble down shallow terraces that provide commanding views of Haute-Provence. There is evidence of Druidic use of the site.

L'Abbaye de Vauclair
02860 Bouconville-Vauclair
Aisne
Picardie
Tel.: 03 23 22 40 87
The great Cistercian Abbey was founded in 1134 and lies close to Laon, a medieval hilltop city, and to the medieval Château Thierry, the Gothic cathedral of Senlis and other

important medieval sites. Close to the ruins of Vauclair lies an extensive garden of medieval medicinal plants set out in authentic style, and an orchard of rare heritage fruit trees. For those interested in World War I history, the Chemin des Dames, with its terrible story, lies close by.

L'Abbaye Royale de Chaalis
60300 Fontaine-Chaalis
60305 Senlis
Picardie
Tel.: 03 44 54 04 02
Fax: 03 44 54 07 90
Email: chaalis@aol.com
Located 40 kilometres (25 miles) north of Paris, this large and important abbey, which was built in the 13th century, was later converted into a chateau with a 29 hectare (72 acre) park and a domain of 300 hectares (750 acres). It is now a museum. The very extensive park-gardens were originally designed by Cardinal d'Este, who also designed the Tivoli gardens near Rome, and include a magnificent 3.5 hectare (9 acre) walled garden now filled with roses at their peak in June and celebrated in a weekend event *Journées de la Rose* (Days of the Rose). The ruins of the abbey church and chapel survive, along with the 18th century orangery, library and stables.

La Ferme Seigneuriale de Bois-Richeux
28130 Maintenon-Pierres
Eure-et-Loire
Tel.: 06 11 88 20 20
Email: contact@boisricheux.com
Website: http://www.boisricheux.com

This superb recreated medieval garden is situated in a large courtyard beside the 12th century fortified manor of Bois Richeux, with its farm, chapel and tithe barn, together with a dovecote dating to 1364. In 1674, it became the property of Madame de Maintenon, mistress of Louis XIV. The farm, within the Carnutes forest, is one of the oldest in France and dates to the Celtic period. The gardens are set out with great elegance in medieval chequerboard fashion, filled with aromatic, medicinal and culinary plants and courtly flowers of the medieval period. A hornbeam cloister links the Room of Love and the Room of Meditation.

Le Château d'Yvoire

Le Jardin de Cinq Sens
Rue du Lac
74140 Yvoire
Tel.: 04 50 72 88 80
The castle of Yvoire was founded in 1308 and is strategically situated on the shores of Lake Geneva. Most of it was destroyed c. 1591 in conflicts with Bern and only the keep remains. It has been in the D'Yvoire family since 1665. Walled gardens recreate the world of courtly love and the garden of Déduit described in the *Roman de la Rose*. The theme of the Garden of the Five Senses was inspired by the series of medieval unicorn tapestries known as *La Dame à la Licorne*. Within the walled gardens is the Labyrinth of the Five Senses, a medicinal herb garden and an array of medieval vegetables, fruits and flowers.

Le Donjon de Loches

37600 Loches
Indre-et-Loire
Tel.: 02 47 59 07 86
An inspirational medieval garden has been built around the austere 33 metre (100 feet) high keep built in 1040. The 'anteroom' garden, with its turfed seats arranged in the shade of trees, grape vines and honeysuckle, opens through an ornamental living willow screen into a delightful medieval garden of herbs and ancient vegetables. A memorable major medieval festival takes place in July, including re-enactment of a knights' tournament.

Le Jardin Carolingian

Service des Espaces Verts
79500 Melle
Deux-Sevres
This 9th century garden features the plants listed for inclusion in all his gardens by Charlemagne the Great.

Le Jardin de l'Abbaye de Saint-Arnoult

60430 Warhuis
Picardie
Tel: 03 44 89 24 95
This is an interesting medieval garden, particularly the terraced kitchen garden, situated in the grounds of a former Cistercian abbey. The current interest in medieval gardens in France is partly attributable to the influence of Saint-Arnoult.

Le Jardin de l'Alchimiste

Mas de la Brune
13810 Eygalières-en-Provence
Tel.: 04 90 90 67 67
Email: infos@jardin-alchimiste.com
Website: http://www.jardin-alchimiste.com
Described within this book, this is a very sophisticated, elegant and magical garden that takes its inspiration from medieval designs and plants. It is also an outstanding demonstration of gardening in hot climates. Open from mid-May to mid-October, Tuesday to Sunday, 10 am to 1.00 pm and 3 pm to 6.30 pm.

Le Jardin de Plantes Médicinales de l'Abbaye de Daoulas

21 Rue d'Eglise
BP 34
29460 Daoulas
Tel.: 02 98 25 84 39
This beautiful and extensive recreated monastic garden includes a garden of simples, with more than 300 plant varieties. It is centred on the ruins of the abbey, which was founded in 1167.

Le Jardin des Plantes Médicinales de Dignac

Dignac
Charente
Tel.: 05 45 24 50 12
A truly charming and beautifully maintained garden, located behind the church of Saint-Cybard, it is designed in the style of a monastic garden with a central well head. It is filled with rare medieval plants and includes a shady arbour walk trained with grapes and roses. The abbey dates to AD 775.

Le Jardin Médiéval du Musée National du Moyen Age à Paris

Hotel de Cluny

6 Place Paul-Painlevé
5th arrondisement
75005 Paris
Tel.: 01 53 73 78 00
Fax: 01 53 73 78 16
Email: lettreinfo.musee-moyenage@
cult
Website: http://www.musee-
moyenage.fr
The museum houses a superb
collection of medieval art, including
tapestries (the very early 16th
century *Lady and the Unicorn* series
of tapestries is housed in the
Rotunda), jewellery and sculptures.
The site was originally occupied
by a Roman bath and later had a
15th century residence for monks
of the great Benedictine Abbey of
Cluny in Burgundy when visiting
the capital. Extensive medieval-style
gardens have been created around
the museum.

Le Jardin Monastique de Tusson
Maison du Patrimonie
16140 Tusson
Charente
Tel.: 05 45 31 17 47
The monastery was founded in 1115
by Robert d'Arbrissel, who also
founded Fontevraud, and was
originally a double monastery. It was
largely destroyed in the Hundred
Years War. The beautiful garden of
simples is arranged around an
octagonal fountain, and the design
and plantings draw on Carolingian
concepts and also the plans for
the Abbey of St Gall.

Le Prieuré de Salagon
04300 Mane
Tel.: 04 92 75 70 50

Fax: 04 92 75 70 58
Email: info@musee-de-salagon.com
Website: http://www.musee-de-
salagon.com
The 15th century Romanesque
abbey standing in fields now houses
the Ethnological Conservatory
Museum of Haute-Provence. The
impressive buildings are surrounded
by authentic re-creations of medieval
gardens, as well as very extensive
ethno-botanical gardens, including
rare plants of Haute-Provence
that were historically used for
medicinal purposes.

Le Prieuré Notre-Dame d'Orsan
18170 Maisonnais
Cher
Tel.: 02 48 56 27 50
Fax: 02 48 56 39 64
Email: prieuredorsan@wanadoo.fr
Website: http://www.prieuredorsan.
com
Described elsewhere in this book,
these are medieval inspired gardens
of the greatest elegance and beauty
in the grounds of a priory founded
by Robert d'Arbrissel, who also
founded Fontevraud Abbey. The
gardens are deservedly acquiring a
high profile internationally.

Roseraie de Berty
07110 Largentiere
Ardeche
Tel.: 04 75 88 30 56
Fax: 04 75 88 36 93
This is a celebrated garden of over
500 ancient and species roses, grown
organically, and also a much in-
demand mail order nursery. There is
also a great variety of perennials, and
the prolific use of fragrant wild

strawberries as a groundcover to
roses. Opens 20th May to 20th June.

Italy

Padua Botanic Garden (Orto Botanico)
University of Padova
Via Orto Botanico 15
Tel.: 049 656614
Fax: 049 656614
This was the first botanic garden to
be founded as a place of study, in
1545. It contains many collections of
rare plants, including medieval plants,
and was devoted from the beginning
to 'simples'. Approximately 6000
species are maintained.

The Vatican Gardens
Vatican City
Tel.: 39 06 69884866
The gardens were established in the
medieval period and show
considerable Renaissance influence.

United States

St Clare Garden
Santa Clara University
500 El Camino Real
Santa Clara
CA 95053
Website: http://www.scu.edu/mrs/
Created as a typical medieval garden
of southern Europe, this garden is a
generalised interpretation based on
the research carried out by various
garden historians. Relatively little is
known of the gardens at the church
and convent of San Damiano where
Clare of Assisi spent most of her long

life, and the gardens are not intended as a reconstruction. They are arranged into areas that represent Clare's childhood (a garden containing the wildflowers of Central Italy), girlhood (with medicinal and household herbs), conversion (a lavender garden), monastic life (symbolised by a medieval kitchen garden) and spiritual life (symbolised by a Mary garden).

The Cloisters
(Metropolitan Museum)
Fort Tryon Park
NY 10040
Tel.: 212 923 3700
Website: http://www.metmuseum.org
Overlooking the Hudson River is this series of delightful medieval cloister gardens designed by Susan Moody and situated within a monastic setting created from the seamless joining of elements from five medieval monasteries, originally from southern France. The site occupies approximately 1.8 hectares (4 acres) and the buildings contain the Metropolitan Museum's priceless medieval collections, including *The Hunt of the Unicorn* tapestries and some five thousand works of medieval art from the 8th century onwards, with particular emphasis on the 12th to 15th centuries.

The Medieval Garden
Penn State Horticulture Trial Gardens
University Park
PA 16802
Tel.: 814 863 7595 (Professor Martin McGann, designer)
Email: mrm19@psu.edu

These very successful educational gardens are in three parts: a medieval kitchen garden; a pleasure garden, including a flowery mead and decorative wattle fencing; and a garden of contemplation. An exhibition of medieval field crops has been planted outside the main gardens.

Australia

Red Cow Farm
Illawarra Highway
Sutton Forest
NSW 2577
Tel.: 02 4868 1842
This quite exceptional and extensive private garden is open seasonally. The garden opens through a series of beautifully scaled garden rooms of sophistication and simplicity and features a monastery garden, an abbess's garden, a sanctuary, an orchard and a kitchen garden, together with other features such as a beech walk, bog garden and exceptional collections of rare shrubs, perennials and heritage roses.

Resources

United Kingdom

Bernwode Nursery
Kingswood Lane
Ludgershall
Buckinghamshire HP18 9RB
Tel.: 01 844 237415
Fax: 01 844 238920
Email: ask@bernwodeplants.co.uk
A leading supplier and conservator of heritage fruit trees, the nursery also has large collections of perennials, many of which are old and rare. An excellent and extensive catalogue of fruit trees is available and they can be obtained by mail order.

C. W. Groves and Sons
Groves Dorset Violets
The Nurseries
West Bay Road
Bridport
Dorset DT6 4BA
This nursery specialises in rare and old violets.

Chiltern Seeds
Borstree Stile
Ulverston
Cumbria LA12 7PB
Tel.: 01 229 581137
Fax: 01 229 584549
Email: info@chilternseeds.co.uk
Website: http://www.chilternseedss.co.uk
Exceptional collections of heirloom vegetable seeds, English wildflowers and rare plants are available.

David Austin Roses Ltd
Bowling Green Lane
Albrighton
Wolverhampton
Staffordshire WV7 3HB
Tel.: 01 902 376300

Fax: 01 902 372142
Email: retail@davidaustinroses.com
Website: http://www.davidaustinroses.com
David Austin's English roses are now famous worldwide. They resemble (and were bred from) heritage roses but have repeat flowering qualities and an emphasis on fragrance. They are ideal for garden restorations where long-term flower displays are required. The company also stocks selected heritage roses and perennials.

Hollington Nurseries Ltd
Hollington Lane
Woolton Hill
Newbury
Berkshire RG20 9XT
Tel.: 01 635 253908
There is an outstanding herb collection and a sophisticated display within a very large walled garden.

Iden Croft Herbs
Frittenden Road
Staplehurst
Kent TN12 ODH
Tel.: 01 580 891432
Fax: 01 580 892416
Email: idencroftherbs@yahoo.co.uk
Website: http://www.herbs-uk.com
Located within the once derelict, large walled garden of Staplehurst Manor, this is an important herb nursery housing National Collections. It has a very large offering of herbs and native wild flowers, many rare. There are also extensive thematic display gardens.

Keepers Nursery
Gallants Court
East Farleigh

Maidstone
Kent ME15 OLE
Tel.: 01 622 726465
Fax: 08 707 052145
Website: http://www.keepers-nursery.co.uk
An outstanding collection of rare and antique fruit varieties are available.

Peter Beales Roses
London Road
Attleborough
Norfolk NR17 1AY
Tel.: 01 953 454707
Fax: 01 953 456845
Email: support@classicroses.co.uk
Website: http://www.classicroses.co.uk
An outstanding collection of heritage and classic roses is held here, and also a collection of perennials. There are display gardens and a mail order catalogue is available.

United States and Canada

Antique Rose Emporium
9300 Lueckemeyer Road
Brenham
TX 77833-6453
Tel.: 800 441 0002
Fax: 979 836 0928
A wonderful and very extensive collection of heritage roses is available from this long-established nursery. Mail order is available.

Monticello Garden Shop
Within the grounds of Monticello
931 Thomas Jefferson Parkway
PO Box 316
Charlottesville
VA 22902
Tel.: 434 984 9821

Fax: 434 977 6140
Website: http://www.monticello.org/
shop
The Centre for Historic Plants offers
historic seeds, bulbs and plants. The
annual journal *Twinleaf* and a
catalogue are available.

Old House Gardens
536 Third Street
Ann Arbor
MI 48103-4957
Tel.: 734 995 1486
Fax: 734 995 1687
Email: charlie@oldhousegardens.
com
Website: http://www.
oldhousegardens.com
The gardens are devoted entirely to
antique and heirloom bulbs,
including medieval daffodils.

Roses of Yesterday and Today
802 Brown's Valley Road
Watsonville
CA 95076-0398
This long-established specialist
nursery has a large range of heritage
roses. A catalogue is available.

Sandy Mush Herb Nursery
Rt. 2 Surret Cove Road
Leicester
NC 28748
The nursery has a large range of old
and rare herbs. It aslo has an
exceptional catalogue.

Seed Savers Exchange
PO Box 70
Decorah
IA 52101
Huge collections of heirloom seeds
are held here and members trade
through annual catalogues.

Wellsweep Herb Farm
317 Mt Bethal Road
Port Murray

NJ 07865
This long-established nursery has a
very large range of rare and old herb
varieties, including violets, lavenders,
sages and thymes. Catalogue and
mail order are available.

Australia

Badger's Keep Nursery
1 Fairbairn St
Chewton
Vic. 3451
Tel./Fax: 03 5472 3338
This is considered the largest nursery
range of heritage apples, including
cider apples, in Australia.

Bob Magnus' Fruit Tree Nursery
c/- PO Woodbridge
Tas. 7162
Tel.: 03 6267 4430
Approximately eighty heritage apple
varieties are available, plus old
varieties of quinces, plums, hazelnuts
and pears. Catalogue is available
each March/April.

Diggers Plants Co.
105 La Trobe Parade
Dromana
Vic. 3936
Website: http://www.diggers.com.au
Heirloom vegetable and herb seeds,
together with a wide range of
perennial plants, are held. Seasonal
catalogues are available. The
company maintains extensive
gardens at Heronswood on the
Mornington Peninsula and the
Garden of St Erth.

Honeysuckle Cottage Nursery
Magnolia Farm
30 Bowen Mountain Rd
Grosevale
NSW 2753
Tel./Fax: 02 4572 1345
Email: kamcleod@zeta.org.au

Website: http://www.honeysuckle-
cottage.com.au
The nursery has Australia's largest
nursery listing of heritage plants,
including very extensive listings of
medieval roses, herbs, clove pinks,
sweet violets, lavenders, perennials,
English wildflowers and fruits, within
extensive display gardens. Two mail
order catalogues are available. The
nursery issues a newsletter bimonthly
and provides highly qualified advice,
and a landscape design service and
consultancy.

**Huon Valley Apple and Heritage
Museum**
2064 Main Rd
Grove
Tas. 7109
Tel.: 03 6266 4345
Fax: 03 6266 4109
Website: http://newnorfolk.org/
apple_museum
The excellent display orchard
contains around 500 apple varieties
and is open year round.

Petty's and Yarra Valley Orchards
Jason and Margaret Alexandra
Monckton Rd
Templestowe
Vic. 3106
Approximately 200 organically
managed varieties of heritage apples
are on display and there is an
education centre.

**The Heritage Fruits Group
(Melbourne)**
Website: http://www.heritagefruits.
org
This special interests group of
Permaculture Melbourne is
cataloguing and conserving many
different types of fruits.

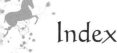

Index